P9-BZT-224

# PARADOX 5 FOR WINDOWS FOR DUMMIES™

# PARADOX 5 FOR WINDOWS FOR DUMMIES™

**by John Kaufeld**

**IDG BOOKS**

IDG Books Worldwide, Inc.
An International Data Group Company

San Mateo, California ♦ Indianapolis, Indiana ♦ Boston, Massachusetts

# Paradox 5 For Windows For Dummies

Published by
**IDG Books Worldwide, Inc.**
An International Data Group Company
155 Bovet Road, Suite 310
San Mateo, CA 94402

Library of Congress Catalog Card No.: 94-77744

ISBN  1-56884-185-X

Printed in the United States of America

10 9 8 7 6 5 4 3 2 1

1D/QZ/QS/ZU

Distributed in the United States by IDG Books Worldwide, Inc.

Distributed in Canada by Macmillan of Canada, a Division of Canada Publishing Corporation; by Computer and Technical Books in Miami, Florida, for South America and the Caribbean; by Longman Singapore in Singapore, Malaysia, Thailand, and Korea; by Toppan Co. Ltd. in Japan; by Asia Computerworld in Hong Kong; by Woodslane Pty. Ltd. in Australia and New Zealand; and by Transworld Publishers Ltd. in the U.K. and Europe.

For general information on IDG Books in the U.S., including information on discounts and premiums, contact IDG Books at 800-434-3422 or 415-312-0650.

For information on where to purchase IDG Books outside the U.S., contact Christina Turner at 415-312-0633.

For information on translations, contact Marc Jeffrey Mikulich, Director of Rights and Licensing, at IDG Books Worldwide; FAX NUMBER 415-286-2747.

For sales inquiries and special prices for bulk quantities, write to the address above or call IDG Books Worldwide at 415-312-0650.

For information on using IDG Books in the classroom, or for ordering examination copies, contact Jim Kelly at 800-434-2086.

 is a registered trademark of IDG Books Worldwide, Inc.

# About the Author

## John Kaufeld

John Kaufeld got hooked on computers a long time ago. Somewhere along the way, he found out that he enjoyed helping people resolve computer problems (a trait his Computer Science friends generally considered a character flaw, but that everyone else seemed to appreciate). John finally graduated with a B.S. degree in Management Information Systems from Ball State University, and he became the first PC Support Technician for what was then Westinghouse, outside Cincinnati, Ohio.

Since that time, he's logged thousands of hours working with normal people who, for one reason or another, were stuck using a "friendly" personal computer. He's also trained more than 1000 people in many different PC and Macintosh applications. The vast majority of these students survived the experience.

Today, John is the president of Access Systems, a computer consulting firm. He does troubleshooting, conducts technical and interpersonal skills seminars for up-and-coming computer support gurus, and writes in his free moments.

He's called by a lot of different names, ranging from Hey, It's The Computer Guy to Red (although this last one is a mystery because he was born, and remains, a blond). His favorite name of all is Daddy, except when the toddlers are particularly grimy. He lives with his wife and two children in Indianapolis, Indiana.

Welcome to the world of IDG Books Worldwide.

IDG Books Worldwide, Inc., is a subsidiary of International Data Group, the world's largest publisher of business and computer-related information and the leading global provider of information services on information technology. IDG was founded more than 25 years ago and now employs more than 5,700 people worldwide. IDG publishes more than 200 computer publications in 63 countries (see listing below). Forty million people read one or more IDG publications each month.

Launched in 1990, IDG Books is today the fastest-growing publisher of computer and business books in the United States. We are proud to have received 3 awards from the Computer Press Association in recognition of editorial excellence, and our best-selling ...For Dummies series has more than 10 million copies in print with translations in more than 20 languages. IDG Books, through a recent joint venture with IDG's Hi-Tech Beijing, became the first U.S. publisher to publish a computer book in the People's Republic of China. In record time, IDG Books has become the first choice for millions of readers around the world who want to learn how to better manage their businesses.

Our mission is simple: Every IDG book is designed to bring extra value and skill-building instructions to the reader. Our books are written by experts who understand and care about our readers. The knowledge base of our editorial staff comes from years of experience in publishing, education, and journalism — experience which we use to produce books for the '90s. In short, we care about books, so we attract the best people. We devote special attention to details such as audience, interior design, use of icons, and illustrations. And because we use an efficient process of authoring, editing, and desktop publishing our books electronically, we can spend more time ensuring superior content and spend less time on the technicalities of making books.

You can count on our commitment to deliver high-quality books at competitive prices on topics customers want to read about. At IDG, we value quality, and we have been delivering quality for more than 25 years. You'll find no better book on a subject than an IDG book.

*John J. Kilcullen*

John Kilcullen
President and CEO
IDG Books Worldwide, Inc.

IDG Books Worldwide, Inc., is a subsidiary of International Data Group. The officers are Patrick J. McGovern, Founder and Board Chairman; Walter Boyd, President. International Data Group's publications include: **ARGENTINA'S** Computerworld Argentina, Infoworld Argentina; **AUSTRALIA'S** Computerworld Australia, Australian PC World, Australian Macworld, Network World, Mobile Business Australia, Reseller, IDG Sources; **AUSTRIA'S** Computerwelt Oesterreich, PC Test; **BRAZIL'S** Computerworld, Gamepro, Game Power, Mundo IBM, Mundo Unix, PC World, Super Game; **BELGIUM'S** Data News (CW) **BULGARIA'S** Computerworld Bulgaria, Ediworld, PC & Mac World Bulgaria, Network World Bulgaria; **CANADA'S** CIO Canada, Computerworld Canada, Graduate Computerworld, InfoCanada, Network World Canada; **CHILE'S** Computerworld Chile, Informatica; **COLOMBIA'S** Computerworld Colombia, PC World; **CZECH REPUBLIC'S** Computerworld, Elektronika, PC World; **DENMARK'S** Communications World, Computerworld Danmark, Macintosh Produktkatalog, Macworld Danmark, PC World Danmark, PC World Produktguide, Tech World, Windows World; **ECUADOR'S** PC World Ecuador; **EGYPT'S** Computerworld (CW) Middle East, PC World Middle East; **FINLAND'S** MikroPC, Tietoviikko, Tietoverkko; **FRANCE'S** Distributique, GOLDEN MAC, InfoPC, Languages & Systems, Le Guide du Monde Informatique, Le Monde Informatique, Telecoms & Reseaux; **GERMANY'S** Computerwoche, Computerwoche Focus, Computerwoche Extra, Computerwoche Karriere, Information Management, Macwelt, Netzwelt, PC Welt, PC Woche, Publish, Unit; **GREECE'S** Infoworld, PC Games; **HUNGARY'S** Computerworld SZT, PC World; **HONG KONG'S** Computerworld Hong Kong, PC World Hong Kong; **INDIA'S** Computers & Communications; **IRELAND'S** ComputerScope; **ISRAEL'S** Computerworld Israel, PC World Israel; **ITALY'S** Computerworld Italia, Lotus Magazine, Macworld Italia, Networking Italia, PC Shopping, PC World Italia; **JAPAN'S** Computerworld Today, Information Systems World, Macworld Japan, Nikkei Personal Computing, SunWorld Japan, Windows World; **KENYA'S** East African Computer News; **KOREA'S** Computerworld Korea, Macworld Korea, PC World Korea; **MEXICO'S** Compu Edicion, Compu Manufactura, Computacion/Punto de Venta, Computerworld Mexico, MacWorld, Mundo Unix, PC World, Windows; **THE NETHERLANDS'** Computer! Totaal, Computable (CW), LAN Magazine, MacWorld, Totaal "Windows"; **NEW ZEALAND'S** Computer Listings, Computerworld New Zealand, New Zealand PC World, Network World; **NIGERIA'S** PC World Africa; **NORWAY'S** Computerworld Norge, C/World, Lotusworld Norge, Macworld Norge, Networld, PC World Ekspress, PC World Norge, PC World's Produktguide, Publish& Multimedia World, Student Data, Unix World, Windowsworld; IDG Direct Response; **PAKISTAN'S** PC World Pakistan; **PANAMA'S** PC World Panama; **PERU'S** Computerworld Peru, PC World; **PEOPLE'S REPUBLIC OF CHINA'S** China Computerworld, China Infoworld, Electronics Today/Multimedia World, Electronics International, Electronic Product World, China Network World, PC and Communications Magazine, PC World China, Software World Magazine, Telecom Product World; IDG HIGH TECH BEIJING'S New Product World; IDG SHENZHEN'S Computer News Digest; **PHILIPPINES'** Computerworld Philippines, PC Digest (PCW); **POLAND'S** Computerworld Poland, PC World/Komputer; **PORTUGAL'S** Cerebro/PC World, Correio Informatico/Computerworld, Informatica & Comunicacoes Catalogo, MacIn, Nacional de Produtos; **ROMANIA'S** Computerworld, PC World; **RUSSIA'S** Computerworld-Moscow, Mir - PC, Sety; **SINGAPORE'S** Computerworld Southeast Asia, PC World Singapore; **SLOVENIA'S** Monitor Magazine; **SOUTH AFRICA'S** Computer Mail (CIO),Computing S.A.,Network World S.A., Software World; **SPAIN'S** Advanced Systems, Amiga World, Computerworld Espana, Communicaciones World, Macworld Espana, NeXTWORLD, Super Juegos Espana (GamePro), PC World Espana, Publish; **SWEDEN'S** Attack, ComputerSweden, Corporate Computing, Natverk & Kommunikation, Macworld, Mikrodatorn, PC World, Publishing & Design (CAP), Datalngenjoren, Maxi Data,Windows World; **SWITZERLAND'S** Computerworld Schweiz, Macworld Schweiz, PC Tip; **TAIWAN'S** Computerworld Taiwan, PC World Taiwan; **THAILAND'S** Thai Computerworld; **TURKEY'S** Computerworld Monitor, Macworld Turkiye, PC World Turkiye; **UKRAINE'S** Computerworld; **UNITED KINGDOM'S** Computing /Computerworld, Connexion/Network World, Lotus Magazine, Macworld, Open Computing/Sunworld/; **UNITED STATES'** Advanced Systems, AmigaWorld, Cable in the Classroom, CD Review, CIO, Computerworld, Digital Video, DOS Resource Guide, Electronic Entertainment Magazine, Federal Computer Week, Federal Integrator, GamePro, IDG Books, Infoworld, Infoworld Direct, Laser Event, Macworld, Multimedia World, Network World, PC Letter, PC World, PlayRight, Power PC World, Publish, SWATPro, Video Event; **VENEZUELA'S** Computerworld Venezuela, PC World; **VIETNAM'S** PC World Vietnam

# Dedication (s)

To Jenny for patience, love, and a constant supply of home-cooked goodies.

To J.B. and the Pooz for all the treasures you bring me and the patience to explain what they are when I don't understand the first time.

To my friends at IDG Books Worldwide for the opportunity of a lifetime.

Thank you, one and all.

# Credits

**Publisher**
David Solomon

**Managing Editor**
Mary Bednarek

**Acquisitions Editor**
Janna Custer

**Production Director**
Beth Jenkins

**Senior Editors**
Tracy L. Barr
Sandra Blackthorn
Diane Graves Steele

**Production Coordinator**
Cindy L. Phipps

**Acquisitions Assistant**
Megg Bonar

**Production Quality Control**
Steve Peake

**Editorial Assistant**
Laura Schaible

**Project Editor**
Colleen Rainsberger

**Technical Reviewer**
Scott Palmer

**Production Staff**
Paul Belcastro
Valery Bourke
Linda M. Boyer
J. Tyler Connor
Angela F. Hunckler
Drew R. Moore
Patricia R. Reynolds
Gina Scott

**Proofreader**
Betty Kish

**Indexer**
Nancy Anderman Guenther

# Acknowledgements

Wow — another one's done.

Thanks to Janna Custer, Megg Bonar, and Suki Gear in Acquisitions for, well, *being* Acquisitions. You three are a joy to work with. (Please send more money.)

On the other end of the country, supreme thanks to my project editor, Colleen Rainsberger (now maybe we'll have the time to get together for videos and carry-out Chinese). Thanks also to Scott Palmer for a great technical edit, ensuring that the book's actually right. Further up the food chain, special thanks to Tracy Barr for keeping the whole book thing going in one direction. As always, the Production group gets a great big *you're wonderful* for everything they do (and that's a lot). Finally, a grateful tip of the hat to John Kilcullen and David Solomon for the unique vision you instill in those around you.

Outside the walls of IDG, I want to thank Tamara Samuels of Borland for her help when I was getting this whole sordid process started. Also, my vote for *Phone Rep of the Year* goes to Danielle in the Borland Sales group for helping me double-check all the Borland phone numbers.

(The publisher would like to give special thanks to Patrick J. McGovern, without whom this book would not have been possible.)

# Contents at a Glance

# Cartoons at a Glance

## By Rich Tennant

page 6

page 7

page 145

page 193

page 61

page 279

page 228

page 289

page 245

page 312

# Table of Contents

# Introduction

· · · · · · · · · · · · · · · · · · · · · · · · · · · · · · · · · · · · · · · · · · · · · · · · · · · · · · · · ·

*W*elcome to *Paradox For Windows For Dummies,* a book that's not afraid to ask the tough questions like "When's lunch?" and "Who finished the cookie dough ice cream?" If you're more interested in food (or Australian Wombats, for that matter) than you are in Paradox for Windows, this book is for you. If you're more interested in Paradox for Windows, please get some professional help before going out into society again.

My goal is to help you get things done despite the fact that you're using Paradox. Whether you're at home, in your office, or at home in your office (or even if you just *feel* like you live at work), *Paradox For Windows For Dummies* is your all-in-one guidebook through the treacherous, frustrating, and appallingly technical world of the relational database.

## A Few Thoughts about You

Because this is a book *for* you, it only makes sense that I've been thinking *about* you. (Were your ears burning?)

No one book can be all things to all readers, so I made the following assumptions about you and your knowledge of computers:

- ✔ You're using the latest, greatest copy of Paradox for Windows, version 5. If you're still using Paradox for DOS or an older Paradox for Windows, you have my deepest sympathy.

- ✔ You may or may not be familiar with Paradox for DOS or any previous incarnation of Paradox for Windows. If you *do* have some previous Paradox experience, so much the better. If not, you just have that much more hair.

- ✔ You know the basics of Windows — the easy stuff, such as choosing things from a menu, moving and resizing windows, and using Cut, Copy, and Paste.

- ✔ You're comfortable with a mouse (or other pointing device of your choice) and know the basic mouse moves: click, double-click, and click and drag.

- ✔ You're not a DOS expert, but you understand files and DOS subdirectories.

If the topics seem out of focus, check your eyeglasses. If they're just plain unfamiliar, find a copy of *DOS For Dummies* or *Windows For Dummies,* both from IDG Books Worldwide. These books will help—I promise.

# Making Sense of the Scratchings

This book isn't necessarily meant to be read straight through. You *can* read it that way, but if you don't, the Dummies Cops won't burst through the wall. This book wants to give you fast answers that put you back to work. This is no literary treatise on the inherent beauty of a Paradox table; it's a work-a-day manual for getting stuff done.

The material in this book is organized. (Isn't that a good thing?) It's split into six parts and an appendix. Each part focuses on a particular aspect of doing things with Paradox; the appendix does whatever such anatomical appendages do. Each part contains a bunch of chapters that keep all the details from bothering each other.

The chapters also contain sidebars and icons to point out particularly important, dangerous, trivial, or bothersome text. There's more about icons later in the introduction.

On special occasions (such as Phillippe Kahn's birthday), I need you to type things into Paradox. Such things are marked as follows:

**This is stuff you type.**

Because you spend a lot of time telling Paradox what to do, it feels obliged to talk back every now and then. Pearls of wisdom from the Scott's Valley Soothsayer look like the following:

```
This is Paradox for Windows humbly offering its comments.
```

Often, you need to pick things from the menus that are part and parcel of life with Paradox for Windows. When your target is a menu item, the book describes it as follows:

Select File⇨Working Directory.

The underlined letters are *shortcut keys* for the mouse-phobics of the world. To use the shortcuts, hold down the Alt key on your keyboard, press the underlined letters one after another, and then release Alt. The shortcut for the preceding example is Alt+F,W. You don't type the comma—it's just there to make things more understandable (and because I'm a little long on commas right now). Any time there are underlined letters in a menu, there's a keyboard shortcut just waiting for you.

If you're a true mouse fiddler, Paradox gives you plenty of opportunities for mousing around. Here are the rodent gymnastics you'll find in Paradox:

Click                Position your mouse pointer somewhere, and then quickly press and release the left mouse button.

Double-click         Position the pointer, and then click twice, one click right after the other.

Click and drag       Position the pointer, press and *hold* the left mouse button, and then move the mouse across the screen. Release the button when you're done highlighting. Usually, you click and drag to mark text when you're editing, deleting, or otherwise wreaking havoc on your files.

Right-click          This move is peculiar to Paradox, so it may be new to you. Position the mouse pointer and click the right mouse button. Paradox calls this the *Object Inspector*. It's reasonably important, so it's mentioned several times in the book.

You probably know this already, but the mouse pointer is the on-screen arrow that moves with your mouse.

# The Executive Overview

As I mentioned before, the book is divided into parts. Each part delves into a facet of Paradox for Windows through text discussions, figures, and icons. To give you a sneak preview of the good stuff to come (and either reassure you of the wisdom in your purchase or push you over the edge into buying this tome), here's a brief description of the book's six parts.

## Part 1 — The Paradox Starts Here

This part gets you out of the starting gate and off into the race. It walks through a typical day of using Paradox and helps you figure out what's what in Paradox's new and improved on-screen look. Finally, it gives you some insight on where to find help for perplexing problems that require a personal touch.

## Part 2 — Table Talk

Most of the time, working with Paradox means working with databases (which Paradox calls *tables*). Part 2 covers almost everything you could ever think about wanting to know on the subject of tables. It covers everything from designing the table to sharing your successful database with other programs. Whether you're building, changing, filling, or finding, you can find the how-to's in here.

## Part 3 — A Good Question Is Half the Answer

Sometimes, a simple "where is it?" isn't enough answer for your question. What you need is the power of a Paradox for Windows query — and Part 3 is where you'll find it. This part starts by building a simple query. Each chapter explores different tools to expand the query into an informational powerhouse. You find out how to create queries, use calculations, and even edit your tables right from a query.

## Part 4 — Truth Is Beauty (and These Reports Look Great)

It's great to have your stuff all neatly stored in a table, but you need something more presentable when management wants answers. Paradox for Windows has a great report system, capable of doing most anything you need and doing it well. That's the focus of Part 4 — hauling your data out of a table and making it look great on paper. It covers all the aspects of creating a Paradox report, including summaries and calculated fields. It also includes walk-throughs with the new Report Expert and Coaches.

## Part 5 — Leftovers from the Fridge

Part 5 has little bit of everything — kind of like the refrigerator on Saturday night. It's a potpourri of interesting topics ranging from on-screen forms to capturing your data in the perfect graph. There's neat stuff in here, so make time to visit.

## Part 6 — The Part of Tens

*Paradox For Windows For Dummies* closes with the classic and much-antici-
pated final part of any good *...For Dummies* book: The Part of Tens. These lists
provide some final ideas, insight, and perhaps a few laughs about the whole
Paradox thing. The last chapter brings up issues of future interest, foreshadow-
ing a time when you're ready to move deeper into Paradox (but not further
from normalcy).

## Appendix: Installing Paradox for Windows

Using the program is one thing, but you can't use it until it's installed. This
appendix helps you get Paradox from the diskettes to your hard disk and keep
all (or at least most) of your hair.

# Icons for Fun and Informational Profit

Dotting the book — like things that dot other things — is a group of clever
icons. They're designed to draw your attention to things that, for one reason or
another, are important to your sanity and your data's continued well-being.
They're scattered hither and thither, depending on the chapter. Each icon
carries a special meaning, as described in the following list:

Among Paradox for Windows' new features are the Coaches. These are
interactive teachers that explain various Paradox concepts and walk you
through some common techniques. This icon lets you know when a Coach can
help you understand the concept covered in that section of text.

The Object Inspector plays an active, although esoteric, role in Paradox's daily
life. This icon indicates instances where you can use the Object Inspector to
gain a better look at something or to accomplish a peculiar but highly
important task.

There's nothing like a friendly, sincere, and genuine reminder to, uh, do
something. Yeah, that's it — *do something*. That's what this icon does: reminds
you to do something.

Things under a technical icon are at best mind numbing and at worst technical
(*eeew!*). I included them to give you something interesting to say to your local
tech-weenie. Avoid these sections whenever possible.

Probably the most common icon, this is a shortcut, tip, or generally cool thought to help you on your way. *Always* check out the tips. They'll make your life easier.

This marks traps, pitfalls, problems, and other snares to avoid. Read carefully, tread lightly, and eat your greens — everything turns out okay in the end.

## Time to Attack the Smorgasbord

You heard the menu; now it's time to dig in. If the software is still safely shrink-wrapped under the desk (not an entirely bad thing), flip to Appendix A and start installing. If you're new to Paradox for Windows, check out Chapter 1. If you're somewhere beyond that, flip to a random page and look for something of interest. Whatever your particular circumstance, jump in and get moving. Paradox *can* be conquered — by you. Carry on!

## The 5th Wave          By Rich Tennant

"I TOLD HIM WE WERE LOOKING FOR SOFTWARE THAT WOULD GIVE US GREATER PRODUCTIVITY, SO HE SOLD ME A DATABASE THAT CAME WITH THESE SIGNS."

# Part I
## The Paradox Starts Here

"WHAT DO YOU MEAN IT SORT OF IS AND ISN'T COMPATIBLE?"

# In This Part...

*How quaint the ways of Paradox!*
*At common sense she gaily mocks!*

Act II, Gilbert and Sullivan's *The Pirates of Penzance*

Here you are, poised on the edge of the Great Paradox
Adventure. Take a deep breath, crack all your knuckles,
howl in pain, then wonder why in the world you did that just
because it said to in the book.

When you're suitably recovered, press forward into the
world of Paradox. Carry on!

# Chapter 1
# Enough to Get You Started

● ● ● ● ● ● ● ● ● ● ● ● ● ● ● ● ● ● ● ● ● ● ● ● ● ● ● ● ● ● ● ● ● ● ● ● ● ● ●

## In This Chapter

▶ Starting Paradox for Windows

▶ WYSIWYB (What You See Is What You Bought)

▶ Opening a table someone else created

▶ Cruising through your stuff

▶ Searching for data

▶ Making changes

▶ Printing tables

▶ Not losing your work

▶ Quitting while you're ahead

● ● ● ● ● ● ● ● ● ● ● ● ● ● ● ● ● ● ● ● ● ● ● ● ● ● ● ● ● ● ● ● ● ● ● ● ● ● ●

*T*here's no start like a quick start, so this chapter gets right to the important business of Paradox for Windows. It's the basics of the basics, giving you that little push out of the plane and yelling comforting instructions on the way down (*just remember the rip-cord thing and you'll be fine!*). Grab your mouse and yell "Geronimo!" as we fly into the wild Borland yonder.

## Making It Go

I said this was a quick start and I'm serious. To run Paradox for Windows, follow these steps:

1. **Turn on your computer, the monitor, and anything else that moves you.**

   If your equipment is attached to a power strip or surge protector, remember to turn that on; otherwise, nothing works.

2. **If Windows doesn't start automatically, type** WIN **and press Enter to get it going.**

   Window appears, in one of its many configurations. Be sure that Program Manager and the Paradox for Windows program group are open.

If you want Windows to start every time you turn on the computer (or have some other burning questions about Windows), consult *Windows For Dummies,* by Andy Rathbone (IDG Books Worldwide).

3. **Look around for the Paradox for Windows icon (the one with the big yellow check mark) and double-click it.**

   Paradox for Windows should rear its pretty head in just a couple of moments (longer if you're on a network). Congratulations on a job well done! Continue on to the next section to find out precisely what you've gotten yourself into.

   - If you don't see a Paradox icon anywhere, look for a program group icon named something clever like *Paradox for Windows.* Don't worry — if you have Paradox for Windows, the odds are the program group is there somewhere. When you find it, double-click it and watch a new window open. The Paradox icon shoud be in there.

   - If nothing happens when you double-click the Paradox icon, try double-clicking it again. Sometimes Windows gets difficult and pretends it doesn't hear you.

   - If a box pops up complaining about a File Error or an Application Execution Error, call your computer guru — all's not well with your copy of Paradox. If you're on your own, try reinstalling the program (see Appendix A for detailed instructions).

To make Paradox take up the whole screen, click the little up arrow in the upper right corner of Paradox's window (called the *Maximize button*).

# *WYSIWYB (What You See Is What You Bought)*

If everything worked right up to this point, you should see the Paradox for Windows desktop on you screen looking a whole lot like Figure 1-1. Yours isn't *exactly* like mine, but it's pretty obvious they're from the same genetic pool. Here are the highlights:

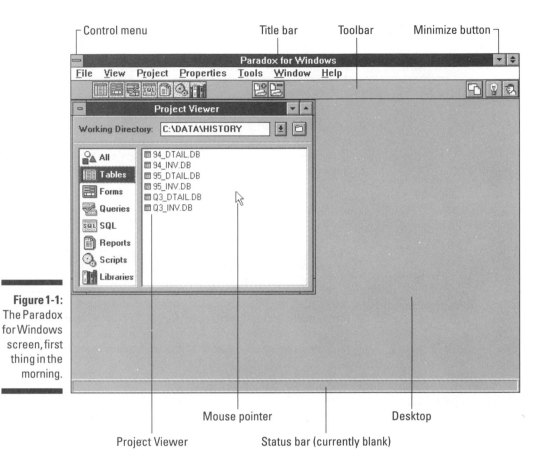

Control menu · Title bar · Toolbar · Minimize button

**Figure 1-1:**
The Paradox
for Windows
screen, first
thing in the
morning.

Project Viewer · Mouse pointer · Status bar (currently blank) · Desktop

## Seeing Stuff with the Project Viewer

When you first fire up the new version of Paradox for Windows, you're greeted with all the menus, buttons, and pretty pictures you expected, plus something new: the Project Viewer window. This is Borland's latest tool to help the terminally disorganized (like me) get a grip on their stuff.

It's your window on the disk—your catalog of what's available wherever you are. By simply

clicking an icon, you can list the main Paradox objects — *Ha! I got it right!* — in the current (or *working*) directory. It's a slick piece of work.

Check out Chapter 3 for everything you want to know about objects, directories, and keeping everything organized with the Project Viewer.

Table 1-1 describes each screen element in detail.

| Table 1-1 | Paradox for Windows Screen Elements |
|---|---|
| *Element* | *Description* |
| Desktop | Your tables, queries, and reports (don't worry about these terms yet — just smile and nod for now) appear on the desktop when you're working with them. Like your real desk, it gets cluttered from time to time, but it's a lot easier to clean. From time to time, the desktop is also called the *workspace*. |
| ToolBar | You'll learn to love this feature. In an amazing stroke of usability, your most common commands appear here as buttons, easily available for your use — no more slogging through five layers of menus just to find out you have six more to go. The ToolBar buttons change depending on what you're doing, so don't panic if a button you're looking for is temporarily gone. It will come back — I promise. |
| Project Viewer | This is a brand new feature in Version 5. It's a quick way to see all the tables, reports, queries, and associated stuff in the current directory. In the old days, you had to walk uphill to the office, jump-start your mouse, and spend hours clicking here and there to even come *close* to what this dialog box tells you. Best of all, it's pretty easy to use. |
| Status bar | Paradox for Windows uses this space to chat with you, often about whatever ToolBar tool you're currently pointing at. To see what I mean, place the mouse pointer on one of the ToolBar icons and look at the status bar (you don't have to click on anything). Paradox displays a brief description of what the tool does. Is this slick or what? Other comments appear here from time to time, depending on what naughtiness you're up to. |
| Other controls | Elements such as the Control menu, title bar, mouse pointer, and Minimize and Maximize buttons are regular features of Windows. For more information about them, refer to *Windows for Dummies*. |

If Paradox for Windows is *totally* new to you and you're feeling a little queasy about the whole thing, take a few minutes and check in with one of Paradox's Coaches. I recommend the first two under Paradox Basics: A Quick Look at Paradox and Getting around in Paradox.

# Opening a Table Someone Else Created

When Paradox refers to tables, it's talking about your database files. Because Paradox is a database management program, a good portion of the time, you'll be working with tables. To pull a table up on the desktop (ostensibly so that you can work with it), follow these quick steps:

1. **From the ToolBar, click the Open Table button, or select File⇨Open⇨ Table from the menu bar.**

   Either way, the Open Table dialog box appears.

2. **Click the name of the table you want to see and then click the OK button.**

   Without a moment's delay, the table comes up in a window on the workspace. Almost too easy, isn't it?

If the table you want isn't listed in the Open Table dialog box, Paradox couldn't find it in your current directory (the working directory). See Chapter 3 for more information about changing the working directory and using directories in general.

When you have a table open, the ToolBar changes. Paradox displays any of several different ToolBars depending on what you're up to at the moment. In this particular case, you get the Table View ToolBar—an assortment of buttons and gizmos for keeping your table completely under control.

✔ Creating a table is a slightly more involved process than opening one that already exists. See Chapter 6 to become a table architect.

✔ The Project Manager makes dealing with tables much easier. Meander over to Chapter 3 for the whole scoop.

# *Cruising through Your Stuff*

Moving through a table isn't hard at all. In fact, it's almost frighteningly intuitive. Paradox has options for both keyboard people and mousers, but this section discusses only the keyboard methods. For information on effortlessly mousing through your tables, see Chapter 7.

You can use the arrow keys to move one field at a time in whatever direction you want. The arrow keys are great when "there" isn't too far from "here." When you press these keys, a highlight indicates where you currently are in the table.

Pressing Ctrl+arrow keys takes you as far as possible in the direction you indicate. Press Ctrl+Up arrow to move to the top of the table; press Ctrl+Right arrow to move to the far right side. You can use Ctrl+Down arrow and Ctrl+Left arrow to move in the directions appropriate for those arrow keys.

The PageUp and PageDn Keys let you run up and down through the table by sets of records. In the world of Paradox, a *set of records* is however many records fit into one window on you workspace. With Ctrl+PgUp and PgDn, you can move one screen at a time, only side-to-side instead of up and down. These guys are tricky, aren't they?

Not to be outdone, the Home and End keys do tricks, too. Home takes you to the first field in a record; End moves you to the last field in that same record. Using the Ctrl Key turns these two keys into supercharged powerhouses. Ctrl+Home immediately sends you to the first field in the first record. Ctrl+End does the opposite, going to the last field in the last record.

To change the number of records you see at once, resize the window by using the mouse.

# A Brief, Frantic Search

Browsing through tables is fine, but if you're looking for a particular piece of data, browsing won't help you find the data. What you need is a good search. Luckily, Paradox for Windows is ready for you. Follow these steps, and you'll find that piece of data in record time:

1. **Using the arrow keys, move the cursor to the field you want to search. Mouse lovers can click the desired field instead of using the keyboard.**

   The highlight appears in the field you choose. Paradox always starts searching from the top of the table; it doesn't matter how far up or down you are in the table — Paradox always goes through the whole table.

 2. **From the ToolBar, click the Locate Field Value button, or press Ctrl+Z.**

   The Locate Value dialog box appears.

3. **In the box marked Value:, type the value you want to find (see Figure 1-2). Press Enter when you're finished typing.**

   The Locate Value dialog box closes, and the mouse pointer changes to an hourglass.

   The hourglass is something you'll see quite a bit in your travels through Paradox for Windows — you might as well get used to it now. Paradox is busy conducting the search. You have to hang loose and wait for the results.

   If you're working with an exceedingly small table or just have a really fast machine (lucky you!), the Locate will be so incredibly fast you may not even see the hourglass. Don't fee deprived, though—there are plenty of other times awaiting you where it won't be so shy.

   If the search is a success, Paradox shows you whatever it found. Well, it actually shows you the first thing it came across that matched your specifications. There may be others out there that Paradox hasn't found yet, but that's what makes working with a computer so much fun, isn't it? If the search failed, the highlight stays where you originally put it and Paradox laments its lack of success with a brief message in the status bar.

Locate button

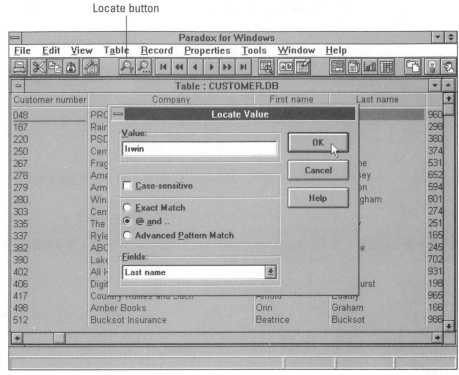

If you don't know the whole name (or whatever it is) you're looking for, you need a special character, called a *wildcard,* to create your search. See Chapter 8 for information about searching on the wild side.

Chapter 7 contains many more details on conducting quick and easy searches. Part 2 guides you through more complex searches (called *Queries).*

# Making Changes

One of the joys of working with a computer (few though they sometimes seem) is how easily you can change things. Paradox thankfully carries on this tradition. Fixing errant data is as easy as click, click, type, click — and that's pretty easy. For more information on adding new entries, see Chapter 7.

Be very, very careful when you're editing. Paradox will let you maul and mutilate the table to your heart's content, all without asking whether you're sure or whether you meant to do what you did. Before you start making big-league changes to your data, make a backup copy of the table. Please. If this backup thing is new to you, refer to the "Keep It Backed Up" section of Chapter 5 for some further works of wisdom (and more stuff from me, too).

1. **Notice the blemish on your otherwise magnificent table. Click it.**

   The part I didn't mention is that you usually find the error immediately *after* printing a report or giving a copy of the table to your boss. Sorry, but it's just another law of databases.

2. **Press F9.**

   You're now in Edit mode. You may not have noticed (goodness knows I didn't for a long time), but the Edit Mode button on the ToolBar clicked in when you pressed F9. That's normal and expected behavior.

3. **Type the new entry.**

   Paradox erases the old entry as soon as you start typing, so think before you type.

   If you find you're working on the wrong record or want to cancel your work for some other reason, press Esc before you touch any other key. If you leave the field, press F9, or even sneeze wrong, Paradox will think you're happy with what you typed and save it forever.

4. **Press F9 again when you're done.**

   This tells Paradox to end the edit and permanently save your changes.

   If you get to this step and want your old entry back, *immediately* press Alt+Backspace (or select EditÍUndo). This "undoes" your last action. It's not a total safety net, but it's better than a lead parachute.

# Killing Trees Ream by Ream

People often aren't satisfied with merely looking at their work on-screen. They must commit it to paper; it's like a compulsion. But just because it's easy to print a 2000-record database doesn't mean you have to print it. There are many ways to see and work with your information without printing it (see Part 4 for the details). Print only what you must and use your on-screen tools to view your database the rest of the time.

1. **Make sure that the table you want to print is open and active.**

   If the table is open but not the active table, click somewhere on it. The title bar changes color, cleverly informing you that it's now active.

2. **Select File⇨Print and click OK.**

   It's all over — you printed again.

# Not Losing Your Work

Paradox for Windows takes great pains to make sure that you don't lose your work. In fact, it goes so far to save what you've done that it can be obnoxious. Instead of fighting to protect what you've accomplished, as is more commonly the case, it's you and Paradox locked in a battle to keep from destroying your data.

Paradox, you see, has a strong desire to save your work. Say you're changing a field (someone's name, for example). You do everything just right, but at the last minute, you notice that you changed the wrong record — you wanted to change the one above it. If you press F9 before you notice the mistake, it's too late. Paradox has already saved what you typed. There's no command to undo your change — you must manually retype the entry. See what I mean about Paradox's burning need to save your stuff?

For the most part, if you're careful when editing your data and pay attention to what you're doing, everything will be fine. Keeping a current backup is important as well; that's the ultimate "undo." Chapters 5 and 29 have plenty of tips for backing up your tables. And you'll hear more about backups throughout the book. Lots more.

You should be aware of one important pitfall: if you're editing a record and accidentally delete it, you can't undo your little boo-boo. You must retype the record from scratch.

# Quitting While You're Ahead

Having skirted the traps and avoided the pitfalls, it's time for some rest. Luckily, getting out of Paradox for Windows is easier than getting in — just select File⇨Exit, and you're back in Windows. If a table is on your desktop, however, you may not be ready to leave quite yet.

Remember that Paradox wants to help in every way it can, so if you quit the program and there is still a table on-screen, Paradox assumes that you're not done working with it. The next time you start the program, it loads the table automatically. What a surprise! Although this feature is nice, you need to be aware of how it works.

Take a moment and close all the tables you have open before exiting Paradox. If you'd like to use a particular table immediately next time you use Paradox, leave it on the workspace and select File⇨Exit. Paradox will have it ready and waiting the next time you begin.

# Chapter 2
# Putting Names with Faces

• • • • • • • • • • • • • • • • • • • • • • • • • • • • • • • • • • • • • • • • • • • • • • •

## In This Chapter
▶ Objects for your affection
▶ The Object Inspector
▶ The Electronic Cavalry

• • • • • • • • • • • • • • • • • • • • • • • • • • • • • • • • • • • • • • • • • • • • • • •

*R*unning a new program is like walking into a reunion: some of the faces look familiar, but overall everything's a little out of kilter. If Paradox for Windows is your *first* database program, forget the reunion metaphor — you're stranded on another planet (or further out than that — like California).

There is hope, though. The key is to learn the language and know whom to ask advice. This chapter gets you on your linguistic feet by explaining some of Paradox's peculiar vocabulary. And once you get the hang of objects and Inspectors, it introduces you to the Experts and Coaches, your native guides to the best that Paradox has to offer.

This is better than the automobile club!

## Objects for Your Affection

Paradox is chock full of *objects*. Normal programs have tools, files, and other stuff, but Paradox has objects. I think it's a marketing thing, but that's the lingo Borland uses, so it's up to me to make it understandable for you.

Table 2.1 provides a breakdown of the most common things — uh, objects — in Paradox for Windows. Think of it as a Paradox to Human translation.

| Table 2-1 | Paradox for Windows Objects |
|-----------|------------------------------|
| *Object* | *Description* |
| Tables | This is Paradox's official name for a database. Most everything you do with Paradox involves at least one table. |
| Forms | You can't escape them in the real world and you can't in Paradox, either. Paradox forms are more fun than paper forms, though — if *any* form can really be fun. Forms give you an incredibly flexible way to work with your data on-screen. Unfortunately, power has a price: Forms aren't the easiest thing in Paradox's world. To protect your brain, forms are covered in a single chapter way back in a dim corner of the book. Don't go there unless you're ready for a fight. |
| Queries | When you need answers from your data, you ask with a *query*. Queries provide an almost endless variety of information, depending on how you frame your question. Paradox people sometimes refer to this as QBE (for *query by example),* so be prepared to hear it both ways. Part 3 tells you everything you ever wanted to know about this powerful part of the program. |
| SQL | Don't worry about SQL (pronounced "sequel") unless you're working at a big company that forces innocent employees to deal with things such as Structured Query Language. If that's you, I wish you well and suggest you start shopping for some good psychiatric help. |
| Reports | Seeing your stuff on paper can bring tears to your eyes. Sometimes just getting it there brings tears to your eyes. Paradox's reports organize, summarize, and terrorize your data onto the printed (or on-screen) page. There's a lot of ground to cover in Reports, so check out Part 4 for more info. |
| Scripts | Paradox for Windows is a full-featured developer's dream tool. That means it has an utterly incomprehensible programming language lurking beneath its pretty, friendly facade. Unless you're feeling pretty adventuresome — as in one-person kayaking through an alligator-infested swamp just to drop off your luggage before the trip — you won't have to work with scripts. Be glad. |
| Libraries | Libraries are storage points for scripts you use all the time. As such, they're nothing you or I care about. |

| Object | Description |
|--------|-------------|
| Design object | When you get into reports or forms, you suddenly open a whole new can of objects. Granted, you're working inside an object, but the whole object thing doesn't stop there. The boxes, fields, lines, and text you create are called *design objects*—because you use them to design your report or form. Don't get too hung up on design objects yet—there's plenty of time later in the book to get strung out about them. |
| Files | It's really not a Paradox-specific term, but you still run across it all the time. A *file* is anything stored on a disk. Tables, reports, and everything else in Paradox (or any other program) exist as files on your disk. |

If that brief overview didn't turn your brain into goop, try the Coach called A Quick Look at Paradox. This is the electronic version of *Europe in a Day for $14*. Look for it in the Paradox Basics section. Really, try it — you might pick up something. Skip ahead and call the Electronic Cavalry for help getting the coach to come out and play.

Keep in mind that throughout the book, *object* and *file* are interchangeable terms. *Tables* are objects (according to the Paradox purists), but they're also files. This confusion-reducing information is brought to you by someone who once was more hopelessly confused about the whole object-versus-file thing than you'd ever believe.

## Table terms you simply *must* know

I can't totally shield you from the brain-jelloing jargon of databases, but if you get it in small doses, you shouldn't suffer any permanent mental damage. Since this chapter's already knee-deep in the whole *what Paradox calls it* thing, prepare yourself for another terminology treatment.

*Data* is the stuff you organize with Paradox. It might be a mailing list, baseball card inventory, or car maintenance records. The data must have a common thread (such as a name, card number, or service date) and must be organized the same way (each mailing list entry has a name, address, city, state, and postal code).

A *record* is all the data referring to one particular item (Jane Stewart's address, Timmy Tuthill's rookie card, or the car's Big *Merry Christmas to You* Breakdown during last year's holiday season).

A *database* is a collection of records. Paradox for Windows refers to these as *tables* (but you knew that already).

# It is I, Inspector Mouseau!

So you have all these objects running around loose on your computer. How do you interrogate them? Or change them? You use the *Object Inspector* — the right mouse button. You know, the button that never did *anything* before.

Yes, they dressed up that little laggard, gave it a name, and put it to work. Whenever you want to look at the properties or settings of some innocent object, point to it and click the right mouse button. Up pops an inspection menu, right where you clicked. From this point, you can change almost anything about the object, like its color, font, or other very personal attribute.

Figure 2-1 shows the Object Inspector doing its thing to a Customer Number field. The box that appears contains different menu items depending on the object you're working with. Because I'm examining a field, the available options include alignment, font, color, and some others that can wait until later.

You can't change *everything* with the Object Inspector, but you really don't know until you try. It doesn't hurt to right-click something that doesn't respond. It just doesn't respond (kind of like my calling my cat).

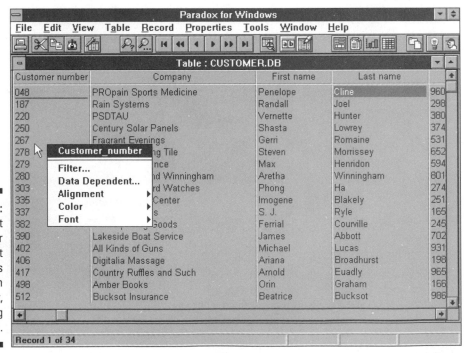

**Figure 2-1:**
The Object Inspector caught doing its thing with an honest, law-abiding field.

Although you can do the same thing with menus, using the Object Inspector is quicker and easier. Get in the habit of using it — it keeps your frustration level low. The Inspector icon, shown in the margin, lets you know when it's time to go inspecting.

# The Electronic Cavalry

Don't get the idea you're alone in a strange software world — there are lots of people lost right along with you. Luckily, this version of Paradox includes some built-in help to lead you out of the wilderness (for the times when your officemate borrows this book and leaves you wandering in circles).

Riding to your rescue are the Experts and Coaches. Regardless of where you are in Paradox, they're available on the ToolBar under the "light bulb" and "ugly little guy" icons. Figure 2-2 shows them hanging out with the other buttons, waiting for a chance to help.

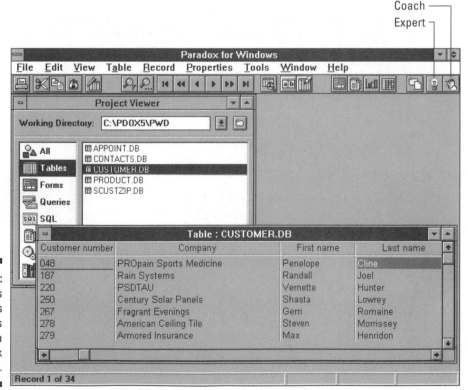

**Figure 2-2:**
Paradox's new Experts and Coaches are only a mouse click away.

The Experts (the light bulb button) help you do things. They ask questions and use your answers to create tables, queries, reports, and other fun things. When you need something fancy in a hurry, an Expert can help.

Details on the Experts are scattered throughout the book in sections titled "Expert Advice on ...." Because all the Experts act about the same way (they're notoriously friendly and patient), you'll be an *Expert* expert after the first time you work with one.

The Coaches (the grim little guy in the baseball cap) walk you step-by-step through various tasks, taking you by the hand and telling you which button to click or which menu to use. It's nice if you're lost on a particular task because the Coach walks through the steps *while you're doing the job*. When the Coach is done, you're done too. Coaches are available on everything from designing a new table to creating a report.

The Coach icon appears in the margins of this book next to tasks that have a Coach available to help you. Chapter 4 tells you more about which Coaches are available and gives you a taste of dealing with one. Really, they're pretty friendly little guys, once you get past the fact that they know everything.

Using Experts and Coaches is easy—just click the ToolBar button for whichever one you want and then pick the specific Expert or Coach from the ensuing dialog box. The helper of your choice appears and immediately begins making your life easier.

# Chapter 3

# Places for Your Stuff

. . . . . . . . . . . . . . . . . . . . . . . . . . . . . . . . . . . . . . . . . . . . . . . .

. . . . . . . . . . . . . . . . . . . . . . . . . . . . . . . . . . . . . . . . . . . . . . . .

*T*here isn't any way around it. You can't escape. Sooner or later, you must come to grips with *directories.* It may or may not be a pretty sight.

When Paradox for Windows thinks *directories,* it's thinking about several things. This chapter gives you some insight into Paradox's twisted thought process, explains the terms at hand, and introduces the tools at your disposal to conquer the whole directory thing once and for all.

## Directories for Every Season

In the beginning, there was a disk and it was empty. Gradually, you created this and that, these and those, and saved the collective *them* on your nice, previously empty disk. This worked fine until the day you noticed *these* with *those* and that the collective *they* were doing unspeakable things in the corner. *This* (collectively) had to stop!

To put those unruly files in order, your disk needs a healthy dose of *directories.* Directories organize your disk space like folders arranged in a filing cabinet. Instead of lumping your stuff into one huge pile, things are parceled out by customer, project, or whatever other way works for you (and your stuff).

Making and maintaining directories is really a DOS thing. Windows, being the caring program it is, provides the friendly File Manager to keep you well insulated from the cold, heartless world of DOS. If all this directory and File Manager stuff is news to you, pick up a copy of IDG Books' *Windows For Dummies.*

When Paradox thinks about directories, it thinks of several things. Below are some explanations of what's on its mind and what you should do about it.

## The Working Directory

The Working Directory is more of a job title than a specific place. Whatever directory you're currently in is your *Working Directory*. Your Working Directory changes when you move from project to project through an average day (if anyone's days are really average any more).

Changing the Working Directory is a snap. Here's how to do it:

1. **From the main Paradox menu, select File⇨Working Directory.**

   The Set Working Directory dialog box opens. It shows the directory you're currently using in the Working Directory box.

2. **Click the Browse button (or press Alt+B).**

   Paradox's new Directory Browser dialog box appears. It lists the first level of directories on your current disk drive. Figure 3-1 shows the Browser checking out the subdirectories within the DATA directory.

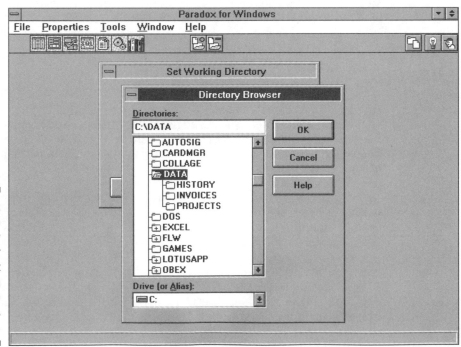

**Figure 3-1:**
The Directory Browser caught thumbing through the DATA directory.

You can also choose the Working Directory by using an alias. An alias is nothing more than a fancy electronic nickname for a directory, but it sure sounds cool, doesn't it? Anyway, look in the "It's Good to Have an Alias (or Two)" section later in this chapter for the whole story about how aliases make life with directories a little easier.

If you know the exact DOS path of the directory you want (complete with appropriate backslashes and colons), type it directly into the Working Directory box and then click OK to finish the job. You're done!

3. **Click the name of directory you want to use, and then click OK.**

The Directory Browser closes and places the directory name you chose in the Working Directory box. When you click the directory, its official DOS path name appears in the Directories box. I agree — who cares?

A plus sign in the file folder icon next to the directory name indicates that other directories are below that one. Double-click the directory name to see what's there. Double-click the name again to close the list.

To change disk drives or use an alias, click in the Drive or Alias box. Click the disk drive or alias you want to use.

4. **Click OK once more to officially set the new Working Directory.**

The Set Working Directory dialog box closes, the disk drive flutters for a moment or two, and then all is quiet in Paradox land.

If you choose the wrong directory, click Browse and try again. To completely throw in the towel and stay in your current Working Directory, click Cancel.

You can also change directories by using the Project Viewer. See the "Using Project Viewer to Find Your Stuff" section later in the chapter for all the details.

## *The Private Directory*

Private Directories just want to be left alone. You don't usually mess with your Private Directory. It just hangs out and does its Private Directory thing behind the scenes (it's happiest *out* of the limelight).

So what does it do in the murky shadows of Paradox? A lot of grunt work, that's what. The Private Directory stores all of Paradox's temporary files, which is quite a job — be thankful *you* don't have to deal with them. If Paradox runs out of space in the Private Directory, it complains to you and says that it can't finish whatever it's doing. Usually, this happens when you're running a query and don't have time to be mucking around with a whiney software package that feels confined. Such is life in the Paradox lane.

If your Private Directory overflows and you're on a network, you can change the Private Directory to an area on the network and continue your work at hand. Get help from your network guru to choose a good landing spot.

Those of you who *aren't* on a network and run out of Private Directory space are, I'm sorry to say, out of luck. The only thing you can do is recover some disk space by erasing old files or programs and try your query again. Remember to exit Paradox *before* erasing anything (that makes sure all your files are closed safely). Erase carefully so you don't nuke part of Paradox or (eek!) some of your data.

To change the Private Directory (if it ever comes to that), follow these steps:

1. **Select File⇨Private Directory from the main menu.**

   The Private Directory dialog box steps up front and center. The DOS path of your current Private Directory appears in, appropriately enough, the Private Directory dialog box.

2. **Click Browse (or do the Alt+B keyboard shortcut thing).**

   In a move that's strikingly similar to setting the Working Directory, the Directory Browser appears.

   If you know the exact name of the new Private Directory (complete with all the funky slashes and colons), go ahead and type it directly into the Private Directory box and then click OK. That's it — you're through. Now *that's* a serious shortcut.

3. **Click the name of the new Private Directory, and then click OK.**

   The Directory Browser flees, leaving you alone with the Private Directory dialog box. The name of the directory you chose appears in the Private Directory box.

   If you need help navigating the Directory Browser dialog box, refer to step 3 in "The Working Directory" section of this chapter.

4. **Click OK to finish the process.**

   Your Private Directory is *permanently* changed to the new location.

   At this point, you have a couple of options:

   • To forget that you were ever here, click Cancel.

   • For reflection on the Meaning of Life, turn off all the lights, meditate in the closet, and see whether anyone notices that you're gone.

If you accidentally choose the wrong directory (you can tell because your network guru is frantically jumping up and down — an altogether entertaining sight, I might add), click Browse and then pick again.

## The Data Directories

This is it. *This* is where the rubber chicken meets the traveling novelty salesman. Data directories are the heart and soul of your organizational strategy. They're where your stuff lives.

Don't get the idea that data directories *have* to be named DATA — they don't. You can call them anything you want (even SWEETUMS). Provided the names make sense to you and are legal with DOS, they're okay with Paradox. Is this ultimate flexibility or what?

If you're on a network, your data directories may be in the computer on your desk or somewhere in the electronic ether of your company's Information Super Side Street (that's ISSS for the acronymophiles out there). It's not a big deal, though, because Paradox doesn't see any difference between a table that's right next to it on the disk drive and one that's miles away down some wire. Paradox just sees disk drives and data directories and is happier because of it.

Making directories isn't too complicated, but it does require an extra understanding of DOS (*ewww!*). Use Windows' File Manager to add any data directories you need. For a great step-by-step explanation of that process, refer to *Windows for Dummies*.

## The Phone Directory

This directory is published annually by your local phone company. It lists your name (possibly misspelled), address (often a year behind if you move a lot), and phone number (that used to belong to a deadbeat drug dealer). Depending on the size of your metropolitan area, it may be just one book or a small library complete with a short, gray-haired woman who perpetually says "shhh!"

Aside from all that, the phone book is a great example of a database:

- ✔ It's a collection of one type of information.
- ✔ Each record contains the same things (name, address, and phone number).
- ✔ The whole book is organized in a particular way (alphabetically by name).

## Some specific thoughts about data directories

Most people make the same errors with directories: they either use *one* and stuff everything they own into it, or they create *thousands* and spend all their time looking for things instead of working. Against this background, allow me to present three simple rules for building a successful data directory system.

Rule 1: *Start with two or three directories.* Very few people need more than five directories for their Paradox tables and associated accouterments; two or three will likely be enough for a long time.

Rule 2: *Name the directories appropriately.* Just because *QFS2ICPX* makes sense today doesn't mean you'll have the faintest idea what's in there a few months down the road. Simple and straightforward names *always* work the best.

Rule 3: *It's better to have too few directories than too many.* After you use your initial two or three directories for a while (like a year), consider adding some new ones. Don't get carried away, though. Too much organization is as bad as too little — both reduce your productivity.

# Using Project Viewer to Find Your Stuff

When you first start the newest version of Paradox for Windows, a new friendly face greets you from the corner of the screen. It's the Project Viewer, here to make your life easier. Figure 3-2 shows the Project Viewer waving hello from its home at the upper left edge of the workspace.

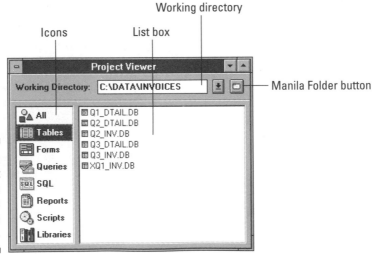

**Figure 3-2:** The Project Viewer says "hi" (it's okay to wave back).

The Project Viewer is like an interactive access panel for all your Paradox files, er, objects (I'll get that straight yet). With a quick mouse click, you can see just your tables, reports, or queries, or all the files in your working directory. It even gives you a quick way to change the Working Directory. This thing is *great*.

If the Project Viewer isn't on-screen, click the button emblazoned with a file folder and piece of paper. It's on the right side of the ToolBar, next to the Expert and Coach buttons.

It's time to zoom in for a closeup. Refer to Figure 3-2 while I take you on a quick tour with Table 3-1.

| Table 3-1 | Elements of the Project Viewer |
|-----------|-------------------------------|
| **Element** | **Description** |
| Working Directory | The appropriately labeled box at the top of the window displays the full, technical DOS name of the current working directory. If you click in the down arrow next to this box, Paradox displays a drop-down list of the most recent Working Directories you used. If the directory you want to change to is listed there, just click it and *poof!* Paradox is there. This is a *really* fast way to flip back and forth between directories. |
| Manila Folder button | Opens the Directory Browser dialog box for an easy Working Directory change. |
| Pretty, pretty icons | The eight icons on the left side of the Project Viewer are your instant access buttons for Paradox for Windows' objects. Click one of these to list any particular kind of object (see "Oooh — Look at the Objects!" for details). |
| The list box | When things list, they list here. There you have it. |

If you want some on-screen discussion about the Project Viewer, check out the Getting Around in Paradox Coach. He's a kinda general guy, but bear with him and you can pick up some things about the Project Viewer. He's in the Paradox Basics section of the Coaches dialog box.

## *A quick (Working Directory) change artist*

Changing the Working Directory is a snap with the Project Viewer. It's almost too easy to explain in numbered steps, but for consistency's sake, I'll do it that way.

1. **Click the Manila Folder button (located on the upper right of the Project Viewer).**

   The good ol' Directory Browser appears. It's the same one you've seen many times before (if you're working through everything in this chapter, that is).

2. **Double-click the new Working Directory in the Directories list.**

   That's it — you're through. Was that easy or what?

   This task is covered to exhaustion in step 3 of "The Working Directory" previously in the chapter.

## *Oooh — Look at the Objects!*

The neatest thing about the Project Viewer is how it enables you to easily browse through your tables and such. It doesn't get much easier than a mouse click, and that's about all there is to it.

To view the tables, queries, reports, or what-have-you in the Working Directory, decide what you want to see, click the associated icon (refer to Figure 3-2), and *poof!* they're listed for your (project) viewing pleasure.

## *You're not from these parts, are you?*

At first glance, the Project Viewer only shows objects in the Working Directory. That's nice, but to do your real life work, you usually need this stuff *and* one or two tables from some other place, plus the report hiding behind that potted plant. Can Project Viewer help? (Nervous organ music builds to a crescendo here.)

Yes, it can. (Organ plays the gallant hero theme.) You can include files — darn it, *objects* — from any data directory, not just the Working Directory. Here's how:

1. **Get into your favorite Working Directory.**

   There are several ways at your disposal and they're covered in this chapter. Use your favorite method and make things happen.

 2. **Click the Add Reference button or choose Project⇨Add Reference from the main menu.**

   The Select File dialog box appears, looking bright-eyed and ready to help, as shown in Figure 3-3. Despite the fact that I chose the Reports icon in the Project Viewer (you can see it peeking out in the back), the Select File dialog currently lists tables. It's just how the Select File dialog box works — it *always* starts out displaying tables. Call it a feature, I guess.

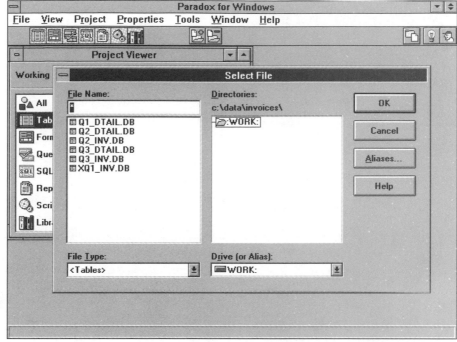

**Figure 3-3:**
The Select
Files dialog
always lists
tables at first.
I guess it's
particularly
proud of
tables for
some reason.

3. **Click the File Type pull-down list near the bottom of the dialog box, and then click the type of file you want to include in the list.**

   When you do this, the list area displays all files of that type from the current directory.

   The Files entry in the File Type list is the same as the All icon in the Project Viewer — it lists absolutely everything in the directory. Odds are, you won't ever need to use it.

4. **Because the whole point is to include things that aren't in the current directory, click the Drive (or Alias) pull-down list, and then scroll through the list until you find disk drive that's home to the file in question. Click the drive letter.**

   Rest assured that this part is much easier to do than explain. When you scroll through the list, you may encounter some entries that are *aliases*, such as PRIV: or WORK:. They're covered at the end of this chapter. For now, just ignore them (but they won't go away).

5. **The Directories area lists all the available — you guessed it — directories on the disk drive you choose. Wander through the list and click your target.**

   When you click that fateful directory, the big list box on the left side of the dialog box fills with file names. It lists all the files of the type you're looking for.

This list works just as the Directory Browser, which you used to change the working directory. You can use the same techniques to choose your directory here: click to choose a directory, and double-click to expand a directory that contains other directories (they're marked with a plus sign in the little manila folder).

6. **Double-click the file you want in the File Name list, as shown in Figure 3-4.**

   The Select File dialog box closes and — surprise! — nothing happens. Well, it *looks* like nothing happened.

7. **Go back to the Project Viewer and click the icon for the type of file you just added.**

   Hey — there it is! As shown in Figure 3-5, your new object takes its place alongside the old residents of the working directory.

   You haven't *moved* the file to a new location. Instead, you created a *pointer* to the file so that you could use it quickly.

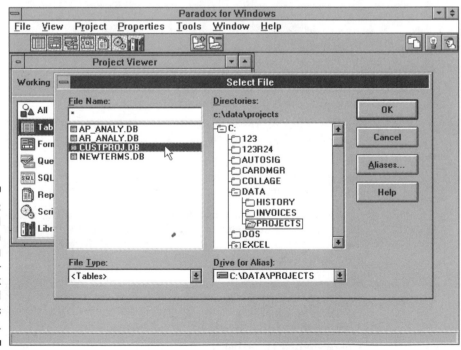

**Figure 3-4:** The final step in a long process— double-click that file and the job's done.

**Figure 3-5:**
There's the
table I told
Paradox to
include.
Now it
appears
every time I
use this
Working
Directory.

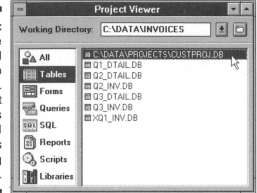

 8. **To trash a foreign reference you don't use any more, click the Remove Reference button on the ToolBar or select Project⇨Remove Reference. In the Remove Item From Folder dialog box that pops up, click the reference to remove, and then click OK.**

It's gone (the reference, not the table).

 There's another secret in the Project Viewer: If you right-click a file name in the big list box, one of those instant-menus appears and lets you do all kinds of amazing things. Folks, it's another usability breakthrough. Can I get a round of applause for Paradox for Windows? Chapter 10 has the full story.

# It's Good to Have an Alias (or Two)

A good alias certainly keeps you out of trouble. No, not with the *police* — with *directories.* What kind of a book do you think this is?

Beginning in the first version of Paradox for Windows, Borland introduced aliases as an easy way to deal with long-winded directory names. Someone discovered that it's much easier to remember :INVOICES: than C:\DATA\FINANCE\INVOICES (or was that C:\FINANCES\INVOICE\DATA?). Why this discovery was news I leave to your imagination. Just remember that you're talking about programmers here; these people actually *set* the clock on their VCRs.

You can substitute an alias in Paradox anywhere you'd normally use a directory name — calculations, reports, forms, and whatever else you can think of. That's a big help if you're on a network and your system administrator likes to move the data directories for fun.

Paradox creates two aliases automatically: WORK and PRIV. These point to your Working Directory and Private Directory (you can figure out which is which). You can't change these aliases with the Alias Manager. Paradox (and *only* Paradox) takes care of them whenever you change your Working or Private Directory.

Forward-thinking network administrators (yes, there are a few out there) often create aliases for all the Paradox users on the network. If a new alias is important to you, it might be important to others as well — a good reason to let the network people know what you're up to.

If you're on a network, check with your chief techno-weenie before creating a whole bunch of aliases. It's a courtesy thing.

This section tells you how to create and manage your aliases. The details of applying aliases to your on-line existence are scattered throughout the rest of the book, like golf balls in the rough.

## *Establishing Your Alias (es)*

Creating an alias really isn't a big deal. Before you can do that, though, you have to know the precise DOS name of the directory you want. Aliases only work if they point to a real, live directory; otherwise, they don't know where they're going (kinda like me when I'm driving). With that self-depreciating thought clearly in mind, it's time to make an alias.

If you need some personal help with the process, call up the Creating an Alias Coach in the Paradox Basics section.

1. **Decide what directory you're aliasing and write down the whole name, including the disk drive letter and all the silly punctuation.**

   If you don't understand directories, don't try tackling aliases on your own. Seek help from your local guru or directory-wise coworker. You might learn some fascinating terms:

   - *Aliasing,* in this context, is an active verb meaning "to make an alias for." (Leave it to the computer jockeys to twist an innocent noun into a computer-related verb.)

   - *Haleyasing,* on the other hand, means "to sing like Bill Haley and the Comets."

   An easy way to find the exact, correctly-punctuated directory name is to use the Project Viewer's Directory Browser. Click the manila folder icon in the Project Viewer to get the Directory Browser on-screen. Use the mouse to click your way through the directory list until you find the directory you're looking for. The complete DOS name (punctuation, too!) appears in the Directories box at the top of the Directory Browser, as shown in Figure 3-6. Write that name down and you're over this hurdle. Click Cancel to close the Directory Browser and get on with your regularly scheduled alias.

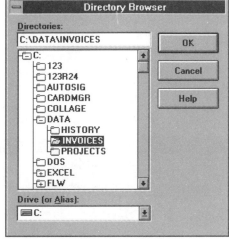

**Figure 3-6:**
Use the
Project
Viewer's
Directory
Browser to
discern the
obscure
DOS name
for your
directory.

2. **From the main menu, select File⇨Aliases.**

   The Alias Manager dialog box appears on the scene.

3. **Click New to start the alias creation process.**

   To prove that it heard you, Paradox clears the Database Alias box and changes the New button to Keep New. To be helpful, it places the blinking toothpick cursor in the Database Alias box, which is your next stop.

4. **Type the alias name into the Database Alias box.**

   The word *flexibility* doesn't even begin to describe your alias-naming options. Alias names can include any combination of letters, numbers, and underscores (_). You can use up to 40 characters (whoa!), but try to contain yourself to 20 characters or less.

   In another masterstroke, Paradox doesn't complain if you try to use a character that's not legal in an alias. Try using a space or some bizarre punctuation mark. When you create the alias, Paradox calmly converts the offending item into an underscore.

Keep your aliases short. Aliases are supposed to make it *easier* to refer to your directories. Replacing a long, obscure directory name with a lengthy, incomprehensible alias is like trading the thumbscrews for a nice new rack — either way, you're still in the dungeon.

5. **Press Tab twice to get into the Path box. Carefully type the DOS directory name you carefully wrote down in Step 1.**

   Figure 3-7 shows a ready-to-finish alias entry. The Path entry includes the disk drive letter (c:) and the *exact* name of the directory (\data\invoices). Capitalization doesn't count, so don't worry about it.

6. **To keep your new alias for ever and ever, click OK. Click Yes when Paradox displays the Public Aliases Have Changed (and I'm *terribly* worried about it) dialog box.**

   Your alias is now ready, willing, and awaiting your command.

   Paradox saves aliases in a file called IDAPI.CFG. I just thought you'd like to know.

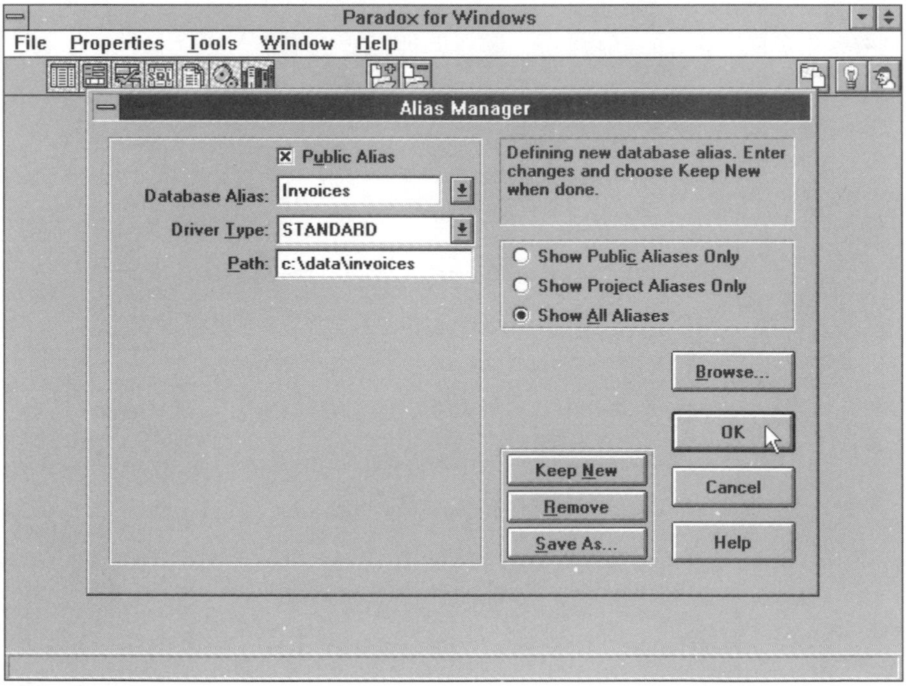

**Figure 3-7:**
An alias is
born.

## Deleting the Pointless Ones

When an alias outlives its usefulness, Paradox helps you send the little guy on to his final resting place. As with all computer things, deleting an alias is faster than creating one:

1. **Decide which alias you want to bid a fond farewell.**

2. **Choose File⇨Aliases from the menu.**

   The Alias Manager appears, looking solemn.

3. **In the Database Alias box, click the down arrow to pull down the alias list. Click the alias that's headed for the pasture.**

   After you choose an alias, the Path box shows where that alias points. This is a good time to double-check your work and make *really sure* you tagged the right alias. If you didn't, just pull the list back down and try again.

4. **Raise your hand, wave good-bye, and click Remove.**

   The dirty deed is almost done. Continue to the next step to finish the job.

5. **Click OK. When Paradox displays the Public Aliases Have Changed dialog box, click Yes to delete the alias forever.**

   The little guy, once so helpful and friendly, is no more. He's an *ex*-alias.

## Pointing Them in a New Direction

Here's something Borland can improve in the next version of Paradox because they *still* don't have it quite right. You can't change an alias. Instead, you delete it and then create a replacement. Quaint, old-fashioned approach, isn't it? Anyway, here's a full breakdown of the task at hand:

1. **Discover that one of your aliases is misguided. Figure out the DOS name for the directory it *should* point to. Write down both the alias and the new directory name.**

2. **Remove the old alias.**

   Follow the steps in the previous section, "Deleting the Pointless Ones."

3. **Create an alias that points to the new directory.**

   Be sure to use *exactly* the same name as the old alias. Otherwise, anything that used the old alias (such as a report or form) won't work right any more.

   Creating an alias is covered earlier in the chapter. Look for the section called "Establishing Your Alias(es)" for all the details.

# Chapter 4

# We're from Borland; We're Here to Help

● ● ● ● ● ● ● ● ● ● ● ● ● ● ● ● ● ● ● ● ● ● ● ● ● ● ● ● ● ● ● ● ● ● ● ● ● ● ● ●

*In This Chapter*

▶ Using on-line Help

▶ Checking your status

▶ Using Coaches

▶ Exploring product support

● ● ● ● ● ● ● ● ● ● ● ● ● ● ● ● ● ● ● ● ● ● ● ● ● ● ● ● ● ● ● ● ● ● ● ● ● ● ● ●

*G*etting help is a melodramatic subject. Maybe it's just my visual nature, but the roles just fit so well. There you are, helplessly chained to some huge crisis as the disastrous deadline approaches. Looming darkly in the corner is dastardly Paradox (in a slightly crushed black top hat and imitation silk cape), chuckling as it considers your fate. Meanwhile, product support (clad entirely in white beach attire with a light floral print pattern) does whatever it is they do, which apparently doesn't involve answering your phone call.

It's a good thing deadlines aren't *deadly* in real life (although sometimes they come close). If they were, untold thousands of computer-using heroines would perish with the assurance that "your call is very important to us, so please stay on the line."

These days, the Heroine's Union motto is *Heroine, help thyself.* Built-in help menus, on-line discussions, fax-back information lines, and software helpers are the order of the day. The arsenal isn't much good if you don't know how to use it, however. This chapter instructs you in the (rarely) gentle art of computer self-defense.

# *Help! It's a Menu!*

The first weapon at hand is arguably the easiest to use and yet most overlooked: the on-line Help system. Help's always there, just a keystroke, menu choice, or button click away, ready to give you advice and assistance. Granted, it takes nearly 7MB of disk space, but that's a testimonial to how exhaustive the system is. Borland went out of their way to make the latest version of the Help system *extra* helpful and easier to use. And in my opinion, they did a pretty good job.

You can start Help in three ways. Two of these ways give you context-sensitive help (help that's arguably about whatever you're doing); the other way just runs the Help system and displays the Contents screen. Here's what you need to know:

✔ **No matter where you are or what you're doing, you can press F1 for context-sensitive help.**

Think of this as the *context-sensitive help key* because that's really what it does. After you press F1, the Help system briefly looks at what you're using in Paradox and displays an appropriate help screen. If you're hanging out with the Project Viewer and press F1, Help comes roaring to life and displays the information shown in Figure 4-1. Because Project Viewer was on-screen, Project Viewer is the help topic.

| Help |

✔ **Use the Help button (if there's one available).**

If you're in a dialog box, a Help button that acts just like the F1 key is usually available. Click it to get context-sensitive assistance about your current crisis.

✔ **Select Help⇨Contents from the main menu.**

The last option yields *generic* help. The Help system starts and displays the Contents screen. From there, you can wander around and explore like crazy.

When you press F1 for context-sensitive help, Paradox kindly offers you a topic on its own, but you still have the whole Help system at your disposal. Often, I just press F1 because it's the easy way to start Help. Once it's running, I use the other buttons and menus to fine-tune my informational search.

Well, now you have Help running. Because this is Paradox for *Windows,* the help screens here look strikingly similar to the help screens in, say, Solitaire or Program Manager. Ah, consistency, sweet consistency — that's what you paid the money for, darn it, and that's what you got.

Help screen buttons

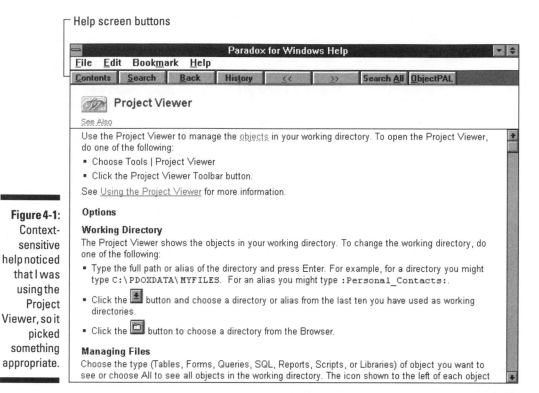

**Figure 4-1:**
Context-
sensitive
help noticed
that I was
using the
Project
Viewer, so it
picked
something
appropriate.

Notice the row of buttons across the top of Paradox's Help screen. These buttons are the navigational tools for your voyage into the Ocean of Information. Table 4.1 provides a quick breakdown of what they do (because everybody assumes you already know and nobody ever bothers to actually tell you):

| Table 4-1 | Help Screen Buttons |
|---|---|
| *Button* | *Description* |
| Contents | Returns you to the Contents screen (like the table of contents for the whole Help system). |
| Search | Displays the Search dialog box to quickly find a specific topic. |
| Back | Returns to the previous Help screen. If the button is gray, this is the first Help screen you viewed this time. |
| History | Shows a list of all the topics you've seen this time in Help. |

*(continued)*

**Table 4-1** *(continued)*

| Button | Description |
|---|---|
| `<<` `>>` | Display the previous (<<) or next (>>) help screen for the current feature. If a certain feature (such as the Project Viewer) has a number of screens that describe it, the Help system groups all those screens together. These buttons let you look at other screens in the same group as the current one. |
| `Search All` | Searches both the general Paradox help file *and* the ObjectPAL help file. The odds are against you ever needing this button. |
| `ObjectPAL` | Switches from the general Paradox help file to the ObjectPAL help file. ObjectPAL Help is chock full of techno-weenie garbage. Even glimpsing it can cost you valuable Humanity Points and being the inexorable process of turning you into (I shudder to say it) a *programmer.* If you accidentally (or purposefully) click this button, it's immediately replaced by one labeled Paradox. Click it hard — that's the electronic equivalent of running away as fast as you can. |
| `Paradox` | Appears on your help screen if you're in the ObjectPAL help system. If this is you, take a deep breath and click it. Slowly let the breath out and be thankful you escaped injury. |

One last thing. To get out of Help, just press Esc — you don't have to dink around with the menus. That's another new feature for your increased convenience and total computing pleasure.

# Checking Your Status

Paradox is a talkative program. Chatter, chatter, chatter — that's Paradox for Windows. If it's not yammering in a dialog box, it's probably muttering in the status bar. Pay attention to those mutterings because often they're quite helpful.

The status bar extends along the bottom of the screen. It's cleverly disguised as a blank gray box. It's so well disguised that I didn't know about it for my first few months with Paradox for Windows — talk about embarrassing.

## Teaching Help a few tricks

There are two secret features in the Help system that almost *nobody* knows about. They work with just about *every* Windows program, too — not just Paradox.

✔ *You can use a bookmark.* If you find yourself referring to the same help screen over and over, you can create an electronic bookmark that takes you there in one step.

When you're looking at a Help screen you want to mark, choose Bookmark⇨Define from the Help menu. The name of the current help screen appears in the Bookmark Name box of the Bookmark Define window. You can change the bookmark name (by typing), but I recommend leaving it as is. Click OK to save the bookmark.

To use your bookmark, select Bookmark. The last nine bookmarks are listed in the menu (if you have more than that, click the More entry at the bottom of the list). Click the one you want and Help immediately displays that screen. Bookmarks are saved when you quit Help, so they'll be there the next time you need them.

If you want to get rid of a bookmark, select Bookmark⇨Define to display the Bookmark Define dialog box. Click the bookmark you want to trash, and then click Delete. It's gone.

Click Cancel — *not* OK — to close the dialog box. Clicking OK adds a new bookmark for whatever help screen you happened to be looking at right then.

✔ *You can write a note.* You can jot down your *own* shortcuts, workarounds, and tips by *annotating* a help topic.

As with bookmarks, first go to the screen you want to annotate. From the Help menu, select Edit⇨Annotate. A window pops up with plenty of space for your musings and other thoughts. When you're done, click Save to store everything. Annotations are saved for ever and ever (until you delete them, that is).

You can easily tell which help screens have annotations. In the upper left corner of the help text (below the screen title), a little green paper clip is displayed. That's the Annotation icon. Click it to view the annotation.

Deleting an annotation is a cinch. First view it by clicking the Paper Clip icon, and then click Delete. *Poof!* The annotation is history.

Now you know the Great Secrets of Help. Feel free to share them with your friends and coworkers (and be a hero) or keep them to yourself (and let people wonder how you know so much).

One of the most useful things about the status bar is the helpful descriptions that Paradox shows there. If you put the mouse pointer on a ToolBar button, for example, Paradox tells you what the button does down in the status bar. Isn't interactive help a great thing?

There's more to watch for in the status bar (such as table information and general system messages and musings), but that's for later in the book.

# Calling Coach-in-a-Box

The *Coaches* represent yet another cool innovation in Paradox for Windows. Paradox has a whole slew of the little know-it-alls. They take you step-by-step through the most common things you do in Paradox, such as designing a table, inserting and deleting records, and creating a simple report.

The Coaches sit in the corner of the screen and pour forth their knowledge. Like a good teacher, they don't do things *for* you; they tell you about the next step and explain how to accomplish it. As you can see in Figure 4-2, the Coaches use good visual aids to make sure that you know what they're talking about.

To start the Tutors, either click the Ugly Coach button on the ToolBar or choose Help⇨Interactive Tutors from the menu.

To start the Coaches, either click the Ugly Coach button on the ToolBar or choose Help⇨Coaches from the menubar.

One drawback (although it was a *nice thing* in the last step) about the Coaches is that they won't let you go wrong. They *do* give you some flexibility (like allowing you to pick field names), but most of the time they're pretty lockstep.

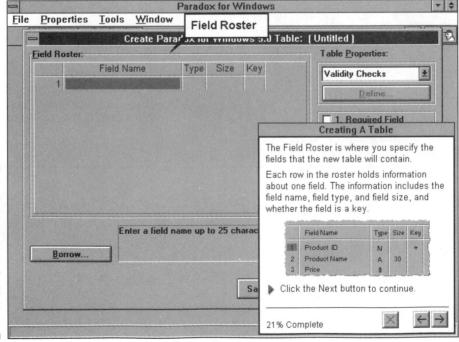

**Figure 4-2:** Like any good presenter, the Coach explains and clearly points out the topic at hand.

Make sure that you read the Coach's instructions *carefully*. Otherwise, the Coach may become annoyed and huffy (and, goodness knows, the *last* thing you want is an annoyed and huffy Coach — you might have to run laps).

# If All Else Fails, Use the Phone

Sometimes you need more information than a book (yes, even this book) can provide. Regardless of the problem, help is available — don't panic yet. (Save it and have a really big scream later.)

Borland provides a variety of live, somewhat live, and faxed support services. Most of them only cost a long-distance phone call; some are even *free*. It doesn't get much better than that.

For the most current and up-to-date information on Borland's product support offerings, look in the Paradox Help system under the topic "Product Support."

## Actually talking to someone

If you have a phone and want to talk to a real human being, you can call the friendly folks at Technical Support. Depending on where you are on the face of the globe, several phone numbers are available:

| | |
|---|---|
| U.S. and Canada | (408) 461-9166 — 6am to 5pm Pacific time |
| U.K. | 0734 320777 |
| Australia | (02) 911-1022 |

For the truly desperate of North America, there's also a 900 number that guarantees to put you through to a technician in one minute. The number is (900) 555-1006. It's open the same hours as the regular support line.

If you're really patient or are too cheap to pay for the 900 service, I suggest trying Borland's 800 Automated Support line. The phone number is (800) 524-8420. It's one of those obnoxious phone menu things, where the system reads you 110 options and expects you to remember the whole list until it's through. If you can successfully use one of these things without going insane, go for it. When it can, the Automated Support service refers you an appropriate TechFax document.

See "Getting the Fax" later in this chapter for more about this useful support option.

## Enlisting your modem

An increasingly popular way to get support is through on-line services such as CompuServe and GEnie. Borland (and many, many other software companies) maintain areas on these services that are like digital clubhouses. Many people gather to swap tips, answer each other's questions, and do the human interaction thing.

To get answers this way, you need an account on the service, a modem, and some kind of communications software. Many computers include a modem at no extra charge these days, so you may already have what you need. Paradox comes with a free trial subscription offer for CompuServe.

I recommend trying out CompuServe. Many vendors no longer provide free phone support. It's just a matter of time before Borland makes the same decision. On-line support service is the wave of the future. Either you can get used to it now (when you still have phone support to fall back on) or later (when it's your only option).

Borland support is waiting for you on three services. Here's a list of services and the commands to get to the Borland area:

| | |
|---|---|
| CompuServe | GO BORLAND |
| GEnie | BORLAND |
| BIX | JOIN BORLAND |

If you don't want to join the on-line world, you have one more option: the Borland File Download Bulletin Board System. You can't write a message and have someone respond to it, but you can find a bunch of technical information, sample files, and other such items. One more thing I'm sure you want to know: it's *free* (but you pay for the phone call).

To contact the Download Bulletin Board, call (408) 431-5096. It supports modems up to 9600 baud, using eight data bits, no parity, and one stop bit. If you need help, call Borland at (408) 439-1236.

If the previous paragraph made little or no sense but you wish it had, pick up a copy of *Modems For Dummies* from IDG Books Worldwide. Read it and everything will be okay.

# Getting the fax

If you have access to a fax machine or fax modem, Borland has a great service for you. It's called TechFax, and it's free. Yes, it's *really* free — you don't even pay for the phone call. Dial 1-800-822-4269 with a Touch Tone phone and follow the menu prompts. You can call from any phone; just make sure you have your fax number handy.

TechFax gives you access to every kind of Paradox technical information you can imagine. I'm talking about common questions and answers, technical updates, compatibility information, general fact sheets, and more. There's even genuine Borland propaganda, like a news release describing Paradox's role in South Africa's first free, multi racial elections. I'm not making this up.

# Chapter 5

# Doing Silly Things Like Solving Problems

● ● ● ● ● ● ● ● ● ● ● ● ● ● ● ● ● ● ● ● ● ● ● ● ● ● ● ● ● ● ● ● ● ● ● ● ● ● ● ● ● ● ●

*In This Chapter*

▶ Turn the computer off

▶ Start with the problem

▶ Use the "Keep It" rules for solutions that work

▶ Find the best solution

▶ Turn on the computer

● ● ● ● ● ● ● ● ● ● ● ● ● ● ● ● ● ● ● ● ● ● ● ● ● ● ● ● ● ● ● ● ● ● ● ● ● ● ● ● ● ● ●

*F*or some people, using a computer is a compulsion. They just *have* to use it — at work, at home, in the car. It's really sick. Most of us, however, are *forced* into using it by some sadistic person at the office (the boss) or at home (the other boss). But it wasn't always like this. A long time ago — way back in the 70s — people often used paper and pencil to solve business problems. And it worked.

This chapter is about combining the childlike simplicity of those days with the particular problems of today. In short, it's about finding the best way to solve problems, with or without your computer. Really radical stuff for a computer book!

## *First, Turn the Computer Off*

What kind of crazy software book tells you to turn *off* the computer just when you're ready to really use it? One that wants you to have hair left when you're done solving the problem — and that's the kind of book this is. (If you're one of those people who brainstorms with a word processor, you're excused from this diatribe. Carry on.)

When you're working on a problem, using your computer can be, well, distracting. You start thinking about Paradox and all the neat things it does, you fiddle with something else, and later you remember a crisis with one of your tables. After a few hours of pointless wandering, you're no further on the original problem than you were to begin with.

I recommend turning *off* the blasted machine and dragging out a pencil and some paper. These quaint, analog tools, reminiscent of another era (or at least another decade), give you a certain flexibility in recording your thoughts. You can write on the lines, jot in the margins, or scribble over everything. They get out of your way and let you think clearly, unimpeded by the wonders of modern electronics.

All I'm saying is this: business survived and arguably flourished in the days before the computer. Yes, it's surprising, but it really did happen that way. Don't get hung up on the idea you *have* to use your computer to solve every problem that comes along. You don't.

# Start with the Problem, Not the Solution

This little tidbit of wisdom may seem obvious, but apparently it's a big secret.

Many people look at a problem and immediately think "How can I solve this horrible crisis with *{insert name of fancy new software package here}*?" That approach has a serious flaw: it's focused on a solution rather than a problem. It leads to some beautiful solutions which, unfortunately, have little or nothing to do with the original problems.

The whole point of a solution is to solve a problem, not to be *primo cool.* I'm not saying that cool solutions are bad, but rather that you shouldn't go looking for the super neat-o whiz bang answer right from the start. Instead, find the answer that does the best job of solving the problem, *and then use it.*

You may often have the general feel of a problem, but that's not enough to start solving it. Break the problem down into progressively smaller pieces until you really understand what you're trying to solve. After you know the issues, start up your solution machine.

If getting sales numbers is a hassle in your business, for example, ask yourself what's really wrong. Is the problem getting the numbers, or do you already have them, but not in a useful form? Do you need more information than you're already getting? Are you getting details when you need broad brush strokes?

After you have the problem cut into bite-sized chunks, brainstorm some solutions. Don't analyze everything you think of, just *think*. When you're in the midst of this process, keep notes of your ramblings. Write as quickly as you can so that you don't lose anything. Above all, never let yourself think "that's a silly answer" — at this stage, anything is possible. Silly thoughts often lead to serious breakthroughs.

Remember to have fun, but stay on track. Serious thinking about one topic quickly leads to another related topic, which in turn sends you off toward something else. On occasion, I've started thinking about lunch and ended up pondering the role of the media in elections. I'm not sure how I got there, but it was one wild ride.

To remember digressions without letting them derail your train of thought, jot them down on a piece of paper. That way, you won't forget them, but you're not stuck on them, either. After you commit the rambling to paper, put the thought out of your mind and get back to the original problem.

When the brainstorm putters out, take a break for a few minutes, and then start back through your notes. Now is the time for analysis. Consider all the ideas you wrote down, regardless of how odd or silly they seem at first. Ask yourself whether the idea would work, how you would implement it, and how easy (or hard) it will be to maintain.

Keep an open mind for the novel solutions that can really make a difference. Just because an answer is different than what you initially thought of doesn't mean that the new one isn't right.

Optimally, one solution stands out head and shoulders above the rest. But even a miracle answer can pick up a few pointers. Pare the list down until you have the two or three that you think are the best. Take those finalists and look at the best and worst of each. Can they be combined into something truly amazing? Should you just leave the best one alone?

I can't give you hard and fast rules for choosing the right solution, but hopefully this chapter led you in the right direction. Following are some highlights — a quick reference for problem solving. Good luck!

- ✔ By starting with the problem and making it the focus of your work, you're constantly reminded of your original goal: to solve the problem.

- ✔ Solve one problem at a time, and solve it completely. A bunch of half-solved problems is much worse than one solid answer and a few scattered, unaddressed enigmas.

- ✔ Look for the second right answer to a problem. Sometimes, a solution is waiting just outside the boundaries of your problem. Just because it's the first one you run across doesn't mean it's the best. Think a little further and see if you come up with anything better.

- ✔ An elegant solution that's a bear to keep running is no solution at all.

- ✔ If you're stuck, ask a creative co worker for some help. A new set of eyes often sees the most amazing things.

# The "Keep It" Rules for Solutions That Work

With your eyes precisely targeted on the problem and a solution (table, report, form, or whatever) in the works, it's time for some tips to make you a problem-solving star. These tips aren't limited to computer stuff — they work for any business process, whether it's computerized or not. Read them, remember them, follow them, and you'll be famous.

Regardless of the success you aspire to and achieve, don't forget your friends. Goodness knows they won't forget you.

## Keep it simple

Too much of anything is a problem in itself. When you're solving a problem, don't create too much solution or use too much technology. Keep it simple for the best results.

Simple solutions usually work as well as their complex counterparts and are much easier to maintain. Usually, a simple answer is smaller and requires less time to build and continue using. It's also easier to train someone on than a complex monster that solves the world's problems while making a most amazing pot of tea.

Consider the following rules:

- ✔ Generally speaking, simple things work better.

- ✔ Use enough technology to solve the problem. Too much becomes a problem unto itself.

- ✔ Avoid flash and glitz for the sake of flash and glitz — just fix the problem and get on with life.

## *Keep it focused*

There's an old adage about how being up to your posterior in sharp-toothed reptiles makes it hard to remember that your original goal involved draining the swamp. When problems crop up like those aforementioned reptiles, it's hard to remember your original goal, whatever it was. And if you lose sight of that goal, your ultimate solution ends up being no solution at all. How depressing.

When you're solving something, just address that one problem and be done with it. Don't try to fix everything that's wrong with the business; just address the current opportunity the best you can, and then move on to the next one. If two problems are inexorably intertwined, well, that's a different matter. Take those as they come.

On a related note, if you're solving a new problem by adjusting an old solution, you might be building an ultimately bigger problem. Every time something is patched, it gets weaker — and more prone to breakdowns. And a patched solution never works quite as well as an actual solution. Use this as a general rule of thumb: after two or more enhancements, it's time to reclassify that poor, patched solution as a new problem.

Here are some more rules:

- ✔ Pick a problem — just one — and solve it.
- ✔ Don't get sidetracked into resolving everything that's currently wrong with your business, life, and corner of the world. Attempting this can cause frustration.
- ✔ Don't enhance old solutions to the point they look like patchwork quilts. After two or three updates to address some new problem, take a long, hard look at the patched-up solution and consider whether or not it's now a problem.

## *Keep it documented*

This tip is simple and straightforward: keep some notes about this marvelous solution you devised. The more complex your solution, the more detailed the explanation needs to be.

It's only a truly great solution if someone else can use it in your place.

I've inherited my share of *legacy systems* (the technical term for "it's been here so long that *nobody* knows how it works"), and it's no fun — at all. When something breaks, you don't know how to put it right. When it works, you can't really explain why. In short, you're in a pickle.

The fact that *you* understand how and why your solution works is great (heck, if you didn't, people might wonder about you). Unfortunately, all that knowledge gets up and leaves the building every time you go home for the night. That's why documentation is so important.

What kind of documentation am I talking about? Anything from plain to fancy, although my personal preference is somewhere between the two. As long as it's current, understandable, thorough, and available, it counts as documentation in my book. For Paradox tables, explain any peculiar fields, where the data comes from, and how you update it. The same goes for electronic reports and forms. Remember to include the location (DOS path or alias) and the names of the files!

And some more rules:

- ✔ Document what do you well enough that someone else can do it.
- ✔ Don't worry about making it beautiful; make it complete and understandable. That's what counts.
- ✔ Have someone who doesn't know what you do read through your documentation. Reword or expand any parts they don't quite comprehend.
- ✔ If you're too busy to create something long and drawn out, write down a page of notes (file names, aliases, and whatever else someone would need) and tape record yourself explaining how things work. Make sure that other people know where the notes and tapes are, in case they ever need them.

## Keep it backed up

Backups go hand in hand with documentation. If there's a catastrophe with your work, safe backups and good documentation make you look like a hero.

A backup is anything from a copy of a paper log sheet to a tape of everything on your computer. Computer backups are particularly important—PCs seem to fail if you *look* at them wrong one day.

Good backups are done regularly and include everything necessary to get things running again. Depending on how important your stuff is, you might make backups every month, week, or day. Critical data may be backed up two or three times each day. The frequency is up to you — do it often enough to capture all the changes, but not so much that it becomes a major hassle (in which case you avoid doing it and end up with a great plan that nobody cares about).

If your business lives and dies by your computer, get some professional help from your local guru or a consultant to plan a backup system. Small businesses (and large ones, too) have completely failed because their computers went down and took the receivables information along for the ride. A good backup is insurance — nothing more, nothing less.

Remember the following:

- Everything fails now and then, so be ready with a good backup.
- Make a plan (getting help, if necessary) and stick to it.
- Test your disaster recovery procedure *before* you actually need it. Making backups is great, but they're little good if you can't use them.
- Ask your computer guru or a local consultant to help plan your backup system and get it rolling. Support people (particularly in a corporate environment) absolutely love it when someone asks for help with backups. (No, I'm not kidding — try it and see for yourself.)
- Train someone else to do your job. (Think of it as a live backup.)

# Driving Nails with Hammerhead Sharks

This section really isn't about things like nails and sharks — it's about choosing the right tool for a given job. The surprising thing is that the tool may or may not be your computer.

As you probably discerned by now, there are some downright heretical things in the next few paragraphs. If you're heavily into Paradox (or computers in general), brace yourself because the worst is yet to come.

Just because you have Paradox doesn't mean it's always the best choice for your solutions. Drum me out of the Computer Nerd's Society, take away my Paradox Whiz Club membership card — it doesn't change the simple truth of the matter. Depending on the situation, there very well might be a better, easier way to solve things than by using Paradox for Windows.

What other tools should you consider? Well, there's the classic standby, the paper and pencil. If you're into legibility, try using a pen instead (and not one of those stinky erasable ones, either). If your needs are a little more complex, consider Windows Cardfile (see "Turn of a Friendly Cardfile" for more about that). Or there might be some commercial software specifically designed to help people in your situation. You always have options — and some are better than others.

My philosophy is simple: do whatever it takes to solve the problem, but don't reinvent the wheel if you don't have to. Translated into non-Kaufeldian terms, this means that if someone else wrote a massive, gonzo-whopper program that does, oh, 75% of what you want, take a look at it. Do you *really* need the other 25%? Can you customize it and get at least part of the way there without having to start over from scratch?

I'm just trying to save you some work. After all, the ultimate goal is to get the job done (except for the corporate folks whose goal is to keep the corporate Computer Department from getting mad at them). Building your own solution from the ground up is certainly challenging, but so is keeping within your monthly budget.

Finding the best solution — whether or not it requires a computer — shows off your creativity, adaptability, and spunk. And that might even get you a raise.

Here are some more things to remember:

- ✔ Don't assume that Paradox is the best choice for every problem. Sometimes it is; sometimes it isn't.

- ✔ If you're not sure how to solve some problem or another, try using a simple paper form. You can always adapt it to work with Paradox.

- ✔ Windows' Cardfile is handy for phone lists and anything else you might use a stack of index cards for. Cardfiles are great to share, too, because everyone who has Windows also has Cardfile.

- ✔ There's commercial software out there for almost anything you could ever want to do. There are even developers who create customized systems in Paradox's mysterious programming language. If you have a big need that *must* be done in Paradox, rent these folks and get some spectacular results.

- ✔ If you have a corporate computer guru department, enlist their help and advice. Don't go around them unless you absolutely must because they invariably come back and bite both you and your project.

## Turn of a Friendly Cardfile

Cardfile is the most incredibly useful thing that Microsoft put into Windows. Okay, maybe I'm exaggerating a little, but I really think it's great. If you're tracking phone numbers, contacts, or doing anything else you'd normally do with index cards, Cardfile gives you a quick and useful way to get it done.

Cardfile usually lives in the Accessories group of Windows' Program Manager. Its icon looks just as you would expect: a desktop cardfile. When you double-click the icon, Cardfile shows you a small window containing a blank index card. This is the first card in your stack.

Each card has an index line (the top line) and a body. The cards are automatically sorted by index line. Cardfile even has an autodialer that works with your computer's modem (if you have one), so you don't have to risk a nail dialing the phone by hand. Is this one great piece of software or what?

For more information about the workings of Cardfile, consult *Windows For Dummies* from IDG Books Worldwide.

# It's Finally Time to Turn On the Computer

Now that you have a solution safely in mind, it's okay to start your electronic Bubba. You're far enough along in the solution process that even the computer can't mess it up.

Well, maybe it still can. You never really know about computers.

# Part II
## Table Talk

# In This Part...

*Here's your crowbar and your centrebit,*
*Your life preserver — you may want to hit;*
*Your silent matches, your dark lantern seize,*
*Take your file and your skeletonic keys.*

Act II, Gilbert and Sullivan's *The Pirates of Penzance*

You're through the general stuff; now it's time hit the tables. This part explores the tools and techniques for creating, filling, emptying, and generally abusing your tables. There's even a chapter dedicated to rescuing data from other, less fortunate people who don't have Paradox. From building to tuning, if it's about tables, it's in here.

# Chapter 6
# Table Birthing for the Faint of Heart

- - - - - - - - - - - - - - - - - - - - - - - - - - - - - - - - - - - - - - -

## In This Chapter
▶ What tables are made of

▶ Field types

▶ The best in ready-to-use fields

▶ When a number not a number (when it's text)

▶ Creating a table

- - - - - - - - - - - - - - - - - - - - - - - - - - - - - - - - - - - - - - -

*B*efore the nice folks at the hospital let you take home that bouncing bundle of burps, spit-ups, and other sundry excretions, the staff members teach you all sorts of useful things. For example, you learn how Baby is assembled, which parts currently work (usually limited to the vocal chords and the Other End), and which subsystems will be activated after you pay off the bill. The goal is to build your understanding of the baby thing and conclusively prove that the whole affair is not the hospital's fault.

Computers imitate life. There's a great deal of planning before that fateful day a new table comes kicking and screaming into your life. In Chapter 5, you figured out what the new table would do. Now the gestation period is over and it's time to say *Hi!* to your electronic progeny.

This chapter gets down to the nuts and bolts of table building. It looks at basic anatomy (relax — I'm talking about *table* anatomy here), introduces the various pieces and parts, and summarily wanders through the whole birthing process. Best of all, you don't get a bill at the end.

## That's What Little Tables Are Made of

You have to start somewhere, and what better place than table anatomy. Because you spend most of your time with Paradox for Windows using tables, you might as well find out what makes the little buggers tick right off the bat.

The whole database thing begins with stuff — lots of stuff. Stuff in piles, stuff in stacks, stuff jammed into nooks and crammed into crannies. This is one *grim* quantity of stuff I'm talking about. And your job is to organize all of it. (Thanks for volunteering.)

Your first task is simple: put the stuff that's alike into groups. Baseball cards go in the card stack, holiday recipes belong in recipe box, and tomatoes go with, um, either fruits or vegetables, depending on whether you're a biologist or the Food and Drug Administration. Each group can ultimately be a database.

In Paradox lingo, a database is a *table;* stuff is *data.* When the data gets more organized, you can describe it with the terms *records* and *fields*, but (alas!) you're not quite there yet.

***Key concept #1:*** One database holds one kind of stuff. There will be no mixing of the stuff — Paradox only makes respectable databases.

Now that the stuff has some semblance of organization, it's time to organize it even more. Yes, the process does resemble your last attempt to clean out the garage, but don't let your track record there deter you in your newfound electronic career.

The goal of this second organizational pass is to look at a single pile of stuff and decide what you want to remember about each thing therein. If you're dealing with customer stuff, for example, you might choose account number, company name, contact person, address, phone number, and electronic mail address. Movie stuff would include things such as title, production company, director, release date, and whether it flopped at the box office. Presidential campaign stuff requires candidate name, party, running year, tax cuts promised, and a small field for campaign promises kept.

All these things (Account Number, Movie Title, Year Impeached, and the rest) are the *fields* for your new table. The group of fields describing one thing in the table is collectively called a *record.* A bunch of records working together make up a table. There is no official name for a bunch of tables that hang around in a group, so feel free to make one up and confuse everybody.

***Key concept #2:*** A record is composed entirely of fields. Each field records one piece of data, one little tidbit of pointless trivia.

***Key concept #3:*** A table is made up of records. Each thing in the table (movie, rookie card, or political hack) takes up one record in the table.

Yes, those last two points are a little redundant with the regular text, but this is the most confusing part of the whole database thing. Once you get the *field begets record begets table* thing straight, the rest is child's play.

All the records in a table contain the same fields. You can't have an extra field for just *one* record — either everybody gets it or nobody gets it. This is data democracy, darn it.

Usually, a record has between 5 and 20 fields, but that's just a rule of thumb. Paradox has a theoretical limit to the number of fields you can put into a table, but it's so incredibly high that it doesn't even matter.

Sometimes, geeks or gurus say "that table has 12 fields in it." Translated to the common tongue, this means "each *record* in that table contain 12 fields." Don't let the different usages bother you — they both mean basically the same thing.

# What's What with Field Types

Before you can get on with the fun and frolic of creating the table, you need to know a couple more things about the fields you're using. Specifically, you need to choose a *type* for each one. This section explores what a field type is, what types Paradox for Windows has to offer, and why in the world you even hope to care about such things.

Although it may sound like rocket science, figuring out the details of your fields really isn't terribly technical. I'd go so far as to say it's kinda fun, but then you'd think I'm some kind of weird, twisted techno-weenie — and I'm not weird.

A field's type determines what kind of information the field can hold (numbers, letters, letters and numbers, dates, times, and so on). This decision is very important, but it's not set in stone. Even after the table has data in it, you can change field types pretty easily.

Paradox for Windows comes with 17 (whoa!) different field types. Don't panic — you don't care about all of them. From the normal person's perspective, there are four basic and six special field types (the remaining ones are reserved for people who don't have real lives outside Paradox). Table 6-1 explains the 10 types you're interested in.

| Table 6-1 | Paradox Field Types | |
|---|---|---|
| *Field Type* | *Type* | *Description* |
| Alpha | Basic | This one is your buddy. Alpha fields hold letters or numbers masquerading as letters (see "When Is a Number *Not* a Number?" later in this chapter for more about that peculiar twist). Alpha is the most common field type — they're everywhere. |
| Number | Basic | Here's another brain teaser. Number fields hold, well, numbers — any kind of numbers. Like Alpha fields, they're terribly common. |
| Date | Basic | Third in the field type popularity contest is the Date type. As you guessed by now, it stores dates. At first, the programmers tried to fit an entire evening (dinner *and* a show) into it, but they finally settled for just storing the *calendar* date — silly programmers. |
| Memo | Basic | When you need space to pontificate, to hold forth, or to ramble at great length on some topic of mind-boggling importance to future generations, you need a Memo field. Memo types let you type and type and type and type. There's an upper limit to how much you can type, but it's really, *really* big, so don't worry about it. |
| Money | Special | This is a specialized relative of the Number type. As the name implies, fields with this type store data about Dollars, Pounds, Marks, and Pesos. All other kinds of currency are accepted as well. Unfortunately, Paradox does not accept personal checks. For those of you migrating up from older versions of Paradox, this type used to be Currency. No, I don't know why they changed the name either. |
| Short Integer | Special | Everybody who remembers what an integer is raise your hand. Anybody? An integer is a whole number — one that doesn't have any decimal places. Occasionally, you come across a need for this specialized type, but not too often. Most of the time, the regular Number type is just fine. |
| Logical | Special | Sometimes, a simple *yes* or *no* is good enough. That's precisely what the Logical field type is for. It holds things like *yes* and *true*. It also holds negative replies (*no* and *false*), but because this is an upbeat book, I won't depress you by mentioning them. |

| Field Type | Type | Description |
|---|---|---|
| Time | Special | Time is another self-explanatory type. It can store either 12-hour (with a.m. or p.m.) or 24-hour format times, depending on what you tell it to do. |
| Timestamp | Special | This is a new feature in Paradox for Windows 5. It's great if you need to store both the date and time in one easy step. The standard format is date first, time second. |
| AutoIncrement | Special | The final special field type is new in this version of Paradox. AutoIncrement fields fill themselves in with a sequential number every time you add a new record to the table. If you're creating an invoice table, for example, AutoIncrement would be perfect for the invoice number field. Every time you enter a new invoice, Paradox for Windows would automatically put in the next available invoice number. |

Unlike other, less friendly database products (which shall remain nameless because Borland makes one of them), Paradox for Windows only makes you enter a size for Alpha and Memo field types, but the setting is only important for Alpha fields.

The size of an Alpha field is the number of characters the field can hold. If you have a size 5 field and want to put *Indianapolis* into it, you're in trouble — the field can only hold *India* and that's a far cry from the home of the 500-Mile Race.

Memo fields have a size option, but it means something completely different (and vastly less important) than the size setting for Alpha fields. For now, for later, and forever, just enter 10 as the size for all your Memo fields.

To figure out how big your Alpha fields need to be, think of the largest thing you'd ever put in it. Write it down and count the number of letters it contains. Congratulations, you have your field size.

It's easy (and safe) to make a field larger. It's just as easy to make it smaller, but it's also a potentially dangerous maneuver. If you make the field too small, the longest entries in it are *trimmed* to fit the new size (that's a fancy way to say "brutally hacked off"). Anything that's chopped off — uh, rather, *trimmed* off — is lost forever.

If you aren't sure exactly how large to make an Alpha field, come up with an estimate and add two or three to it. You can always change the size later.

## Naming names in Paradox

This may surprise you, but Paradox has a whole set of rules about how to name fields. This couldn't be a simple, anything's okay kind of thing — there have to be rules and *you* have to follow them. (So much for electronic anarchy this year.)

To be valid in Paradox for Windows, a field name must pass these incredibly complicated tests:

- It has to start with a letter or number (so there!).

- It can contain any combination of letters (upper- or lowercase), numbers, spaces, and the pound sign (#).

- It can be up to 25 characters long (but shorter is better).

- It must be unique — you can't have two fields in the same table with the same names.

Here's a very important note: field names in Paradox are *not* case-sensitive. Paradox only recognizes the letters themselves, not their case. This means that *Phone Number, Phone number*, and *phone number* are all the same to Paradox.

If you want to have some similarly named fields, just change one character of the field name. To use three phone number fields in one table, for example, add a number to each one (Phone number 1, Phone number 2, and Phone number 3). The number makes each one unique, so Paradox is happy.

If you're a visual learner, let your eyes wander through these examples to get the hang of the whole field naming thing:

| | |
|---|---|
| Invoice number | You're off to a good start — it's a perfectly valid name. |
| Phone number (2) | Buzz — nobody said anything about putting parentheses in a field name. |
| Zip_Code | Buzz — underscores are out of the question. Use spaces instead. |
| YALAFN | Yet another law abiding field name. |
| Picture # | Pound signs are okay, so this field name passes muster. |
| # of Attendees | Buzz — although a field can *contain* a pound sign, it can't start with one. |
| 1994 Sales | It's okay to start with a number — this field is fine. |

# When Is a Number Not a Number? When It's Text!

At first blush, this section seems like it needs some serious mental help. *When is a number not a number?* Oh, for goodness sake.

You're dealing with a computer here, so anything is possible — even entries that look like numbers aren't numbers.

To Paradox, a number is something you can add, subtract, or find the square root of. It never starts with zero, but it can have a decimal (although it's not required). Invoice amounts, salaries, the number of pies thrown during Blake Edward's movie *The Great Race* — these are all numbers. They live in Number, Money, or Integer type fields.

Turn those rules around and you have numbers that aren't numbers — they're text. You can't do math with text numbers. They can start with zero. Heck, they can even have a decimal, but it's only for looks. Things like postal codes, customer ID's, and account numbers all fall into this category. They're numbers, but they live in Alpha fields along with the letters.

If you're doing math with a field, it needs to be a Number, Money, or Integer type field. If you never need to add, subtract, or total the field, or if the values in it need to start with zero, make it an Alpha type.

# Presenting the Best in Ready-to-Use Fields

This section is designed to save you time, energy, and frustration. Table 6-2 describes a slew of common fields, complete with name, type, size, and any other information I could think to include. Instead of trying to figure out what fields you need, what to call them, and all that other stuff, pick and choose from this list. It's not all-encompassing, but it's pretty good.

| Table 6-2 | Fields for (Almost) All Seasons | | |
|---|---|---|---|
| **Name** | **Type** | **Size** | **Notes** |
| Title | Alpha | 4 | Mr., Ms., Mrs., Miss |
| First name | Alpha | 15 | first name |
| MI | Alpha | 4 | middle initial; allows for two initials, complete with periods |
| Last name | Alpha | 20 | last name |
| Job | Alpha | 25 | job title |
| Company | Alpha | 25 | company name |
| Address 1 | Alpha | 30 | first of two address lines |
| Address 2 | Alpha | 30 | second of two address lines (to handle extra-long addresses) |
| City | Alpha | 20 | city name |
| State | Alpha | 4 | state or province |

*(continued)*

## Table 6-2 *(continued)*

| *Name* | *Type* | *Size* | *Notes* |
|--------|--------|--------|---------|
| Zip code | Alpha | 10 | zip or postal code; stored as text, not numbers |
| Country | Alpha | 15 | country; necessary if you deal with other lands |
| Voice phone | Alpha | 12 | voice phone number; use size 17 to include extension |
| Fax phone | Alpha | 12 | fax phone number |
| Home phone | Alpha | 12 | home phone number |
| Cellular phone | Alpha | 12 | cellular or car phone number |
| Other phone | Alpha | 12 | any other phone the person happens to have |
| CompuServe ID | Alpha | 12 | ID number from CompuServe |
| AOL ID | Alpha | 10 | America Online ID's are called screen names; they can't be more than 10 characters long |
| E-mail address | Alpha | 30 | General e-mail address; long enough for most complex addresses |
| Internet address | Alpha | 40 | their Internet address; often longer than most rational e-mail addresses |
| Telex | Alpha | 12 | telex number; use size 22 to include answerback |
| Assistant | Alpha | 25 | name of assistant or secretary |
| SSN | Alpha | 11 | Social Security number |
| Referred by | Alpha | 25 | who referred this person to you |
| Notes | Memo | 10 | free-form notes; size entry is automatic; can be any length |
| Description | Memo | 10 | long text description of something or other |
| Terms | Alpha | 12 | Net 10, Net 30, 2/10 Net 30 |
| Check number | Number | n/a | check number |
| Card number | Alpha | 18 | standard credit card number; handles Visa, Master Card, and Whatever Card |

# Paradox 5 For Windows For Dummies

**Cheat Sheet**

## Field Types

These are all the field types available in Paradox for Windows. The ones marked *TW* are for techno-weenies only, so if they don't make sense to you, that's probably a good sign.

See Chapter 6 for more information about choosing the right type for your field.

| Field Type | Symbol | Description |
|---|---|---|
| Alpha | A | For all kinds of text, and numbers that aren't *really* numbers |
| Number | N | Decimal numbers you can use in mathematical calculations |
| Money | $ | Just like a Number field, but it's predisposed toward currency |
| Short | S | Little whole numbers between -32,767 and 32,767. |
| Long integer | L | *TW* — *Much bigger* whole numbers between -2,147,483,648 and 2,147,483,648 |
| BCD | # | *TW* — A special number field for people who use dBASE files with Paradox |
| Date | D | No guessing here — it's a date. |
| Time | T | Does anybody *really* know what time it is? |
| Timestamp | @ | Stores the date *and* the time — it doesn't get better than this |
| Memo | M | An Alpha field on steroids |
| Formatted memo | F | It's a Memo field with a built-in word processor — type whatever you want, and then change the font, size, and style |
| Graphic | G | *TW* — Holds a picture in BMP, PCX, TIF, GIF, or EPS format |
| OLE | O | *TW* — Stuff connected to other Windows programs through Object Linking and Embedding |
| Logical | L | Simple comparisons such as true or false, yes or no, and male or female. |
| Autoincrement | + | Makes a read-only (you can look but not touch) serial number that goes up by 1 every time you add a record to the table |
| Binary | B | *TW* — Stores sound, movies, and anything else Paradox doesn't really understand |
| Bytes | Y | *TW* — A smaller version of the Binary field type |

## Coaches

| Section | Topic | Description |
|---|---|---|
| Paradox Basics | A Quick Look at Paradox | The nickel tour |
| | Getting around in Paradox | Mousing, keying, and buttoning around in the program |
| | Creating an Alias | Give your directories a new identity |
| Building a Database | Database and Table Basics | Basic table anatomy |
| | Planning a Database | Table design Boot camp |
| | Creating a Table | Doing the dirty deed |
| | Adding a Key | Gain lots of benefits by adding a key field |
| Working with a Table | Viewing a Table | How to peep at your data |
| | Editing Records | Changing what's there |
| | Inserting and Deleting Records | Out with the old and in with the new |
| Queries, Forms, and Reports | Creating a Query | Making a query from the ground up |
| | Creating a Standard Form | Basic how-to's for forms |
| | Creating a Standard Report | Doing your average report |

## Out Standing in a Ready-Made Field

Here are my favorite fields, all ready and waiting to help you. Consider this an appetizer because there are more waiting for you in Chapter 6.

| Name | Type | Size | Notes |
|---|---|---|---|
| Title | Alpha | 4 | Mr., Ms., Mrs., Miss |
| First name | Alpha | 15 | First name |
| MI | Alpha | 4 | Middle initial; allows for two initials, complete with periods |
| Last name | Alpha | 20 | Last name |
| Job | Alpha | 25 | Job title |
| Company | Alpha | 25 | Company name |
| Address 1 | Alpha | 30 | First of two address lines |
| Address 2 | Alpha | 30 | Second of two address lines (to handle extra-long addresses) |
| City | Alpha | 20 | City name |
| State | Alpha | 4 | State or province |
| Zip code | Alpha | 10 | Zip or postal code; stored as text, not numbers |
| Country | Alpha | 15 | Country; necessary if you deal with other lands |
| Voice phone | Alpha | 12 | Voice phone number; use size 17 to include extension |
| Notes | Memo | n/a | Free-form notes; size entry is automatic; can be any length |
| Description | Memo | n/a | Long text description of something or other |
| Terms | Alpha | 12 | Net 10, Net 30, 2/10 Net 30 |
| Card number | Alpha | 18 | Standard credit card number; handles Visa, Master Card, and Whatever Card |

### ...For Dummies: #1 Computer Book Series for Beginners

# Paradox 5 For Windows For Dummies

Cheat Sheet

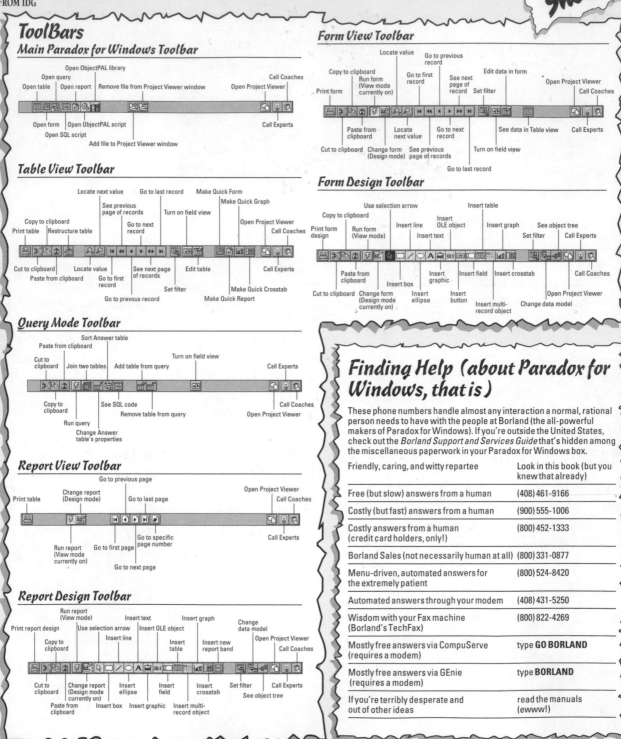

## ToolBars

### Main Paradox for Windows Toolbar

- Open table
- Open query
- Open report
- Open ObjectPAL library
- Remove file from Project Viewer window
- Open Project Viewer
- Call Coaches
- Open form
- Open SQL script
- Open ObjectPAL script
- Add file to Project Viewer window
- Call Experts

### Table View Toolbar

- Print table
- Copy to clipboard
- Restructure table
- Locate next value
- See previous page of records
- Go to next record
- Go to last record
- Turn on field view
- Make Quick Form
- Make Quick Graph
- Open Project Viewer
- Call Coaches
- Cut to clipboard
- Paste from clipboard
- Locate value
- Go to first record
- Go to previous record
- See next page of records
- Set filter
- Edit table
- Make Quick Report
- Make Quick Crosstab
- Call Experts

### Query Mode Toolbar

- Cut to clipboard
- Paste from clipboard
- Sort Answer table
- Join two tables
- Add table from query
- Turn on field view
- Call Experts
- Copy to clipboard
- Run query
- Change Answer table's properties
- See SQL code
- Remove table from query
- Open Project Viewer
- Call Coaches

### Report View Toolbar

- Print table
- Change report (Design mode)
- Go to previous page
- Go to last page
- Open Project Viewer
- Call Coaches
- Run report (View mode currently on)
- Go to first page
- Go to next page
- Go to specific page number
- Call Experts

### Report Design Toolbar

- Print report design
- Run report (View mode)
- Copy to clipboard
- Use selection arrow
- Insert line
- Insert text
- Insert OLE object
- Insert graph
- Insert table
- Insert new report band
- Change data model
- Open Project Viewer
- Call Coaches
- Cut to clipboard
- Change report (Design mode currently on)
- Paste from clipboard
- Insert ellipse
- Insert box
- Insert field
- Insert graphic
- Insert crosstab
- Insert multi-record object
- Set filter
- See object tree
- Call Experts

### Form View Toolbar

- Print form
- Copy to clipboard
- Run form (View mode currently on)
- Locate value
- Go to first record
- Go to previous record
- See next page of record
- Set filter
- Edit data in form
- Open Project Viewer
- Call Coaches
- Paste from clipboard
- Cut to clipboard
- Change form (Design mode)
- Locate next value
- See previous page of records
- Go to next record
- Go to last record
- Turn on field view
- See data in Table view
- Call Experts

### Form Design Toolbar

- Print form design
- Copy to clipboard
- Run form (View mode)
- Use selection arrow
- Insert line
- Insert OLE object
- Insert text
- Insert table
- Insert graph
- See object tree
- Set filter
- Call Experts
- Cut to clipboard
- Paste from clipboard
- Change form (Design mode currently on)
- Insert box
- Insert ellipse
- Insert graphic
- Insert field
- Insert button
- Insert crosstab
- Insert multi-record object
- Change data model
- Open Project Viewer
- Call Coaches

## Finding Help (about Paradox for Windows, that is)

These phone numbers handle almost any interaction a normal, rational person needs to have with the people at Borland (the all-powerful makers of Paradox for Windows). If you're outside the United States, check out the *Borland Support and Services Guide* that's hidden among the miscellaneous paperwork in your Paradox for Windows box.

| | |
|---|---|
| Friendly, caring, and witty repartee | Look in this book (but you knew that already) |
| Free (but slow) answers from a human | (408) 461-9166 |
| Costly (but fast) answers from a human | (900) 555-1006 |
| Costly answers from a human (credit card holders, only!) | (800) 452-1333 |
| Borland Sales (not necessarily human at all) | (800) 331-0877 |
| Menu-driven, automated answers for the extremely patient | (800) 524-8420 |
| Automated answers through your modem | (408) 431-5250 |
| Wisdom with your Fax machine (Borland's TechFax) | (800) 822-4269 |
| Mostly free answers via CompuServe (requires a modem) | type **GO BORLAND** |
| Mostly free answers via GEnie (requires a modem) | type **BORLAND** |
| If you're terribly desperate and out of other ideas | read the manuals (ewww!) |

# It's (Finally) Time to Build the Table

The big day is finally here — it's time to build that table. Gather your notes, scribblings, musings, and miscellaneous thoughts (I'd hate it if you forgot anything), and then follow the steps below. Before you know it, the cyberstork will be at your door carrying a little bundle of digital joy.

1. **Make sure that you're in the right Working Directory.**

   This isn't a must, but it makes life a little easier for you.

   If you don't know what a Working Directory is or how often to change it to prevent a nasty rash, see Chapter 3.

2. **To start the creation process, right-click the Table button on the ToolBar and choose New from the menu that unexpectedly appears.**

   Figure 6-1 shows the little goblin in question. I'm sorry if the picture is a little fuzzy, but I wasn't expecting it to pop out there either.

   If you're a mouse-eschewing menu hound, choose File⇨New⇨Table.

3. **When the Table Type dialog box pops up, make sure that it says** *Paradox for Windows 5.0* **in the Table Type box. If it does, everything's groovy. If it doesn't, click the down arrow next to Table Type and pick Paradox for Windows 5.0 from the ensuing list. Either way, click OK to continue the process.**

   If you want to create a table that works with another database package, this is where you do it. Click the down arrow next to Table Type and choose whatever foreign table format strikes your fancy from the drop-down list.

**Figure 6-1:**
Unexpected
pop-up
menus are
handy, but
often a little
alarming.

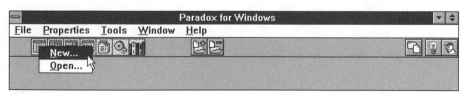

If you didn't know Paradox could (or even *would*) speak to other database packages, check out Chapter 11.

4. **Type the field name into the Field Name area, just as shown in Figure 6-2. When you're done, press Tab.**

   Double-check your spelling before you press Tab — Paradox for Windows isn't particularly good at discerning what you *mean;* it's pretty focused on what you actually *type*.

   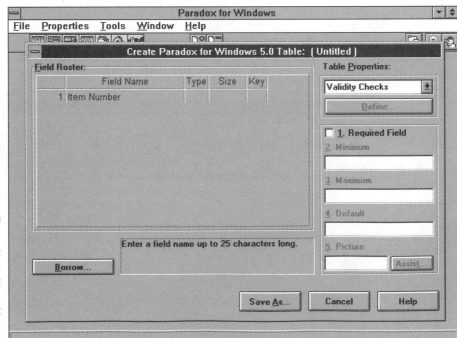

   If you're planning to use a key with the table, Paradox asks — no, *demands* — that the key field is the *first* one in the table.

   If the phrase keyfield makes you think of a field that Paradox uses to sort and generally organize the data in you table, you're on the right track. On the other hand, if you get a mental picture of a place that old keys go to die, mark your place here and then check out Chapter 9 for the "key" information.

5. **Now select the Type for this field. Right-click or press the spacebar to see a list of the available types (shown in Figure 6-3), and then click your choice. Press Tab when you're done.**

   Depending on the Type you chose, the cursor may jump to either the Size or Key areas, or even all the way down to the next line. Don't let the seemingly random movement surprise you — the cursor knows what it's doing.

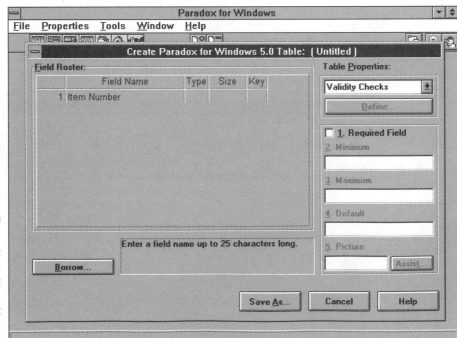

**Figure 6-2:**
The first field name is in — but there's more where that came from.

If you don't like the drop-down list, choose a Type the techno-weenie way: press the first letter of the Type you want (use a $ for the Money type). This trick works for all the basic types (and many of the special ones, too).

If you must, you can change a field's type at any time — even if the field already has data in it. But, like many things in life, just because you *can* change the field type doesn't mean it's a completely *safe* thing to do. Depending on the field types involved in the switcheroo, the process can be simple or complicated, and can even cause data (and hair) loss. The moral of the story: to maximize your hair retention and minimize data loss, take some extra time now to pick the *right* type for your new field.

6. **If the Size area is highlighted, enter a size for the field. Press Tab when you're done. If Key is highlighted, skip to the next step.**

   You only end up here if Paradox needs a size for the field you're creating. Not all fields have a size setting, so don't worry if Paradox doesn't ask for one.

7. **If the Key area is highlighted, double-click in it or press the space bar to designate this field as the table's *key*. Press Tab when you've made up your mind.**

   Figure 6-4 show a freshly made key field. The asterisk in the Field area means "yo — *this* is a key field."

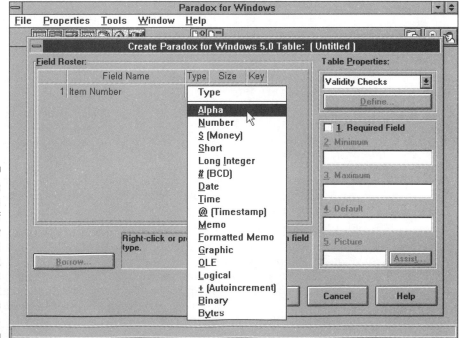

**Figure 6-3:**
Don't let the number of Types blow your mind — just pick what you want and the list goes away.

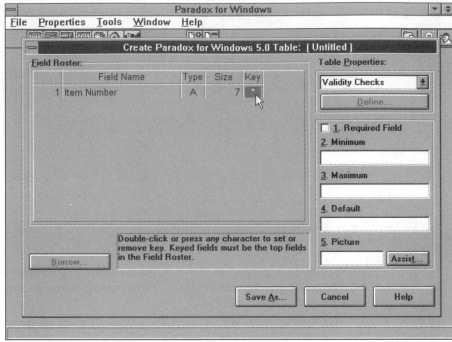

**Figure 6-4:**
Item
Number is
now the key
field for this
table.

As I mentioned earlier, if you're new to the whole key field thing, read up on it in Chapter 9 before keying around in your tables. And in case you're wondering, *keying* is not a new technical term you need to remember. It's just something I made up.

**8. Repeat Steps 4 through 7 for each field in your new table. When you're done, continue to Step 8.**

If you need to add a field somewhere in the table, click where you want the field (or move there with the arrows), then press Insert. A blank line appears for your new field, much like Figure 6-5. Pick up at Step 4 to finish the field.

What if you included a field during a moment of mental vacation and want to get rid of it? No problem. Click the field name (or use the arrow keys to move there) and press Ctrl+Del. *Poof!* The field is gone.

To move a field, press and hold the mouse button on the number of the field to move. Dark bars appear around the field, as Figure 6-6 shows. While still holding down the mouse button, move the mouse up or down (depending on where you want to move the field). Release the mouse button when the dark bar is right where you want the field to be. Figure 6-7 shows the Memorabilia type field ready for landing in its new position between Description and Movie Title.

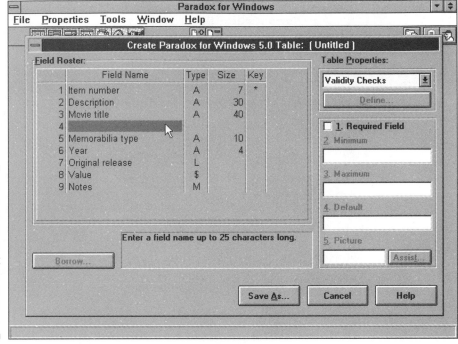

**Figure 6-5:**
Inserting a field you overlooked is easy with the Insert key (and hard with anything else).

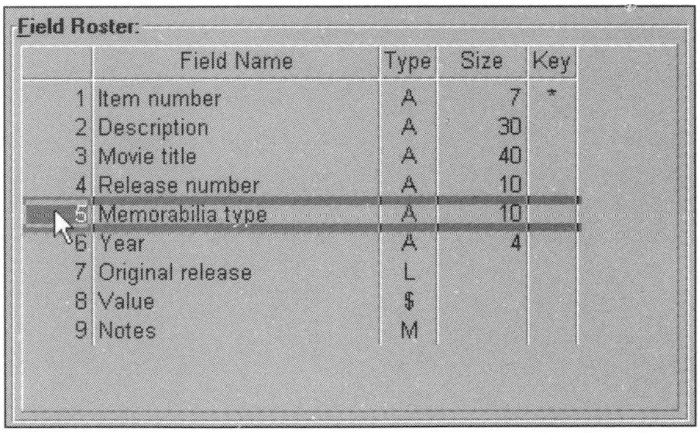

**Figure 6-6:**
Field #5 is on its way ...

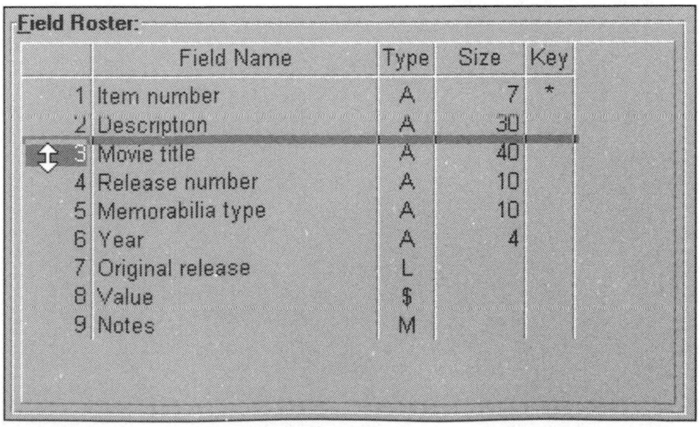

**Figure 6-7:**
... and ready to land.

There's a whole slew of interesting-looking boxes, buttons, and associated things on the right side of this crazy *Create Your Table Here* dialog box. Don't worry about them right now. They're given their due in Chapter 9, "Making the Table Work for You."

9. **Before anything *else* happens, click Save As to bring forth the Save Table As dialog box. Type a name for your table in the New File Name box, and then click OK to save the little sucker on your disk drive.**

If the directory Paradox list under Directories isn't the one you want this table to go into, you need to change directories (don't you wish you'd taken my advice in Step 1 and done it then?).

To use an Alias or completely change disk drives, click in the down arrow next to the Drive (or Alias) box. Choose the appropriate alias or disk drive from the drop-down list. If you want to pick a directory the hard way, click on it in the pretty directory tree box under Directories.

If you know the exact DOS name for your directory, type it into the New File Name box and then type the file name afterwards. Don't worry if the whole thing comes out looking like C:\SOMESTUF\MORESTUF\NEWSTUFF. That's just how DOS paths look sometimes.

If you're seriously stressing out about this whole directory thing, try using Aliases. They *really* make dealing with directories a whole lot easier. Chapter 3 covers aliases in detail.

# Chapter 7

# Adding, Changing, and Deleting with Glee

## In This Chapter

▶ Backing up before you begin

▶ Opening the table (again)

▶ Frolicking in the fields and records

▶ Working in Edit mode

▶ Saving (or salvaging) your hard work

▶ Putting stuff into fields

▶ Inserting and deleting entire records

*W*hether you're filling in a table for the first time or fixing a teeny-tiny little error you just found, it seems like you spend a lot of time fiddling with the data in your tables. Luckily, Paradox makes editing your data pretty easy. Granted, there are some pitfalls to watch out for, but that's just the nature of the beast.

This chapter takes you through everything you need to know about adding records to a table, making changes, and getting rid of the old stuff. It's quite a romp.

## Back Up Before You Begin

Yes, I know you heard it in Chapter 5. Yes, it's discussed *again* later in the book. Yes, it's here, too. Trust me — it's *that* important.

Please, please keep backup copies of your important tables. If you don't know how to make backups, ask your friendly guru or local computer store.

Here is some helpful information regarding backups:

- ✔ If you have MS-DOS 6.2, you already have a nice little backup program at your disposal. It's called MSBACKUP (they are *clever,* aren't they?) and it's already on your computer. Check your copy of *MS-DOS 6.2 for Dummies* for all the details.

- ✔ Older versions of DOS come with a program that's supposed to do backups (in the same way that the Post Office is supposed to deliver mail in a timely fashion). If you value your data, *don't use it.* Go to the computer store and buy a reputable backup program. Your data will thank you.

- ✔ If you're pondering whether backups are a good idea, refer to "Keep It Backed Up" in Chapter 5.

# Opening the Table (Again)

Before you can do *anything* with the records, you have to open the table. There are several ways to do it, depending on your preference for menus, mice, or the keyboard.

The new Project Viewer lets you a open a table in one step. Just double-click a table name and *poof!* it's available on-screen. (To find out more about the other cool tricks Project Viewer has up its sleeve, check out Chapter 3.)

For a truly personal learning experience, call up the Viewing a Table Coach. It's the first option inside the Working with a Table section.

Of course, there are always people who like to do things the tried-and-true way. If that's you, follow these easy steps and get that table open:

1. **If you haven't done it already, change into whatever Working Directory you want to work in.**

   You don't *have* to change the Working Directory when you open a table.

   Chapter 3 explains everything you ever wanted to know about directories (Working and otherwise), including how to move among them. If you're not particularly clear on the directory thing, refer back to that chapter for some help.

 2. **Select File▷Open▷Table from the main menu or click the Table button on the ToolBar.**

   Either way, you end up at the Open Table dialog box (which is where you want to be).

As with all menus, you can use keyboard alternates if you don't want to mouse around. In this case, the keystrokes are Alt+F,O,T.

**3. Double-click the name of the table you want to open.**

In Figure 7-1, the Customer table is being called to action — in fact, you caught it in mid-click.

✔ If the table you want isn't listed, you need to change directories to find it. Click the down arrow next to the Drive box to see a list of aliases and disk drives. If you want use an alias, click the alias name; to manually change your disk drive or directory, click a disk drive, and then choose the new directory from the Directories list. Whichever way you do it, your table name should appear in the File Name list.

✔ If your table *still* isn't listed, something potentially bad is happening. Double-check that you're in the right directory. If all else fails, get out the snackies and call for a guru.

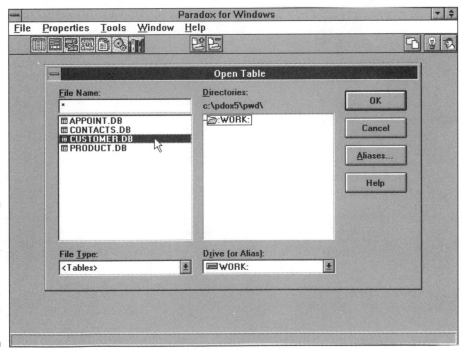

**Figure 7-1:**
The Customer table is roused from its slumber by a rather rude mouse.

# Frolicking in the Fields and Records

When the table appears on-screen, you usually want to have a look around. Once again, Paradox for Windows offers a wealth of options for wandering through your stuff.

Paradox for Windows *is* a Windows application, after all, so there have to be some cute, graphical buttons that move you through the current table. Lo and behold, there are. The buttons in question are smack dab in the middle of the ToolBar and look like a set of renegade VCR controls. They're captured and explained for your viewing pleasure in Figure 7-2.

**Figure 7-2:**
These ToolBar buttons let you pretend you're running a VCR as you wander through a table.

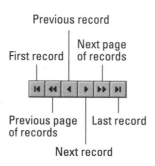

Not everyone is a button fan, though, and Borland certainly knows that. To keep the keyboard people from feeling left out, there's a plethora of keystrokes available to cruise a table. Table 7-1 provides a quick rundown of the list.

| Table 7-1 | Available Keystrokes |
|---|---|
| *Keystroke* | *Movement* |
| *Small movements* | |
| Up ↑ | Move up one record |
| Down ↓ | Move down one record |
| Right → | Move right one field |
| Left ← | Move left one field |
| Tab | Move right one field |
| Shift+Tab | Move left one field |

| Keystroke | Movement |
|---|---|
| *Medium size movements* | |
| Home | Go to the far left side of the table |
| End | Go to the far right side of the table |
| PgUp | See the preceding screen of records |
| PgDn | See the next screen of records |
| Ctrl+PgUp | Scroll the table one window-full to the left |
| Ctrl+PgDn | Scroll the table one window-full to the right |
| *Great big movements* | |
| Ctrl+↑ | Go to the top of the current column |
| Ctrl+↓ | Go to the bottom of the current column |
| Ctrl+← | Go to the far left side of the table (same as Home) |
| Ctrl+ → | Go to the far right side of the table (same as End). |
| Ctrl+Home | Go to the first field of the first record |
| Ctrl+End | Go to the last field of the last record |

To find out what a button on the ToolBar does, put the mouse pointer on it and read the description that magically appears in the status bar.

Hey, menu mavens — you're not forgotten. Check out the Record menu. It gives you all the same functions those button people have with their fancy electronic rodents. Don't bother with the keystroke shortcuts in the menu — who needs a two-key replacement for PgUp?

What's more:

↳ Mouse fans can go directly to a field by clicking it. Now *that's* service.

↳ If you move past the side of the table with an arrow key, Paradox moves the cursor to the next line and lets you continue on your way.

↳ If your table is wider than your screen (a common occurence these days), use the scroll bars along the bottom and right of the window (or Ctrl+PgUp and Ctrl+PgDn) to see everything.

# *In the Edit Mode Mood*

Thus far in your wanderings, all your data was safe. Paradox only lets you make changes if the table is in the right mode — Edit mode, to be precise. It's not something you just wander into, either. You must *want* to edit and successfully inform Paradox of your desires. This section tells you how to get there; the next one explains what to do after you arrive.

When you're in Edit mode, be very, very careful! You can directly change any field in your table — even delete whole records. Paradox's Undo facilities are limited, so read the next section ("Putting Stuff into Your Fields") carefully before attempting any important changes to your valuable information.

The key to Edit mode is F9 (ouch, sorry — that pun was worse than I intended). The keystroke itself is really a throwback to the old days of Paradox for DOS, but so many people already know it that Borland carried it over into the Windows product.

Menu lovers can use <u>V</u>iew⇨<u>E</u>dit Data to get into Edit mode and <u>V</u>iew⇨<u>V</u>iew Data to turn it back off. Like the keystroke and the ToolBar button, this is just another means to an editing end.

 For Windows-centric people, a quick click the Toolbar's Edit Data button does just as good a job as F9. In fact, it does the same thing.

Whatever way you get there, you know for sure that Paradox understood because the Edit Data button appears pushed in. But don't just accept my explanation of how it looks — check out Figure 7-3 and see for yourself. It shows the button in both its normal, *off* position, and the active, *armed* setting.

## Whether 'tis nobler to click, press, or select

There's much discussion in some circles (granted, they're pretty boring circles) about the best way to interact with a Windows program. Should you use a mouse, keyboard shortcuts, or menus? Which one is best?

Personally, I have a do-whatever-works attitude about the whole thing. Granted, that doesn't get me invited back to these parties, but it does make

sense. Please don't get hung up on finding the right way to interact with Paradox. If you use keystrokes for some tasks, menus for others, and mouse manipulations for the rest, that's fine. Whatever gets your job done is cool with me.

And if anyone gives you trouble about it, send them to me.

**Figure 7-3:**
When the Edit Data button is off (left), everything's safe. When it's on (right), watch out.

Edit Data button (off)

Edit Data button (on)

# *Saving (or Salvaging) Your Hard Work*

It may seem strange to shift gears and talk about saving changes before you even make any, but there's a reason: Paradox isn't terribly forgiving about the popular computer command word *oops*.

Saying that Paradox isn't terribly forgiving is really an understatement. It's actually downright sadistic.

There are two kinds of changes you can make in Edit mode: those you can undo, and those you can't. The good news is there are only a few actions you can't undo. The bad news is changes become permanent very quickly, so if you need to undo something you can't find out 15 minutes from now because by then, it's way too late.

Here are some rules to remember:

✔ *When you're editing a field, you can undo any changes before you leave the field.* Once your cursor moves out of the field, any changes to the data (up to and including deleting the stuff that was, until so recently, stored there for posterity) become permanent. The moment you see the error, select Edit⇨Undo or press Alt+Backspace. As long as you haven't left the field yet, the old value pops right back into existence.

✔ *It's easy to un-insert a new record.* Select Edit⇨Undo from the menu — before you leave the new record. As with fields, the changes are recorded when the cursor leaves the newly-inserted record.

✔ *If you accidentally deleted a record, it's gone.* Period. Paradox processes deletions immediately. And once it's done, it's done. That's why you need to make good backups — at this point, your choices are retyping the record from scratch or getting it from a current backup file. Dealing with the backup file is a *lot* more fun.

To limit the number of times your head hits the wall over things like this, carefully check any changes before you move the cursor away. The most common problem — accidentally changing a field's value — is easily fixed if you catch it before leaving the field.

# *Putting Stuff into Your Fields*

It seems like it's taken forever, but you're finally here: it's time to actually put some data into your table (or correct some that's gone awry). Enough talking — let's *do* it!

If you're not clear on the whole editing thing, consider a quick session with the Editing Records Coach. It's in the "Working with a Table" section of the ol' coaching dialog box.

Here is some helpful information:

- *To type stuff into a field,* make sure that the table is in Edit mode, and then move the cursor into the field (through whatever means strikes you at the time) and start typing. Yes, it's *that* simple.

  If nothing happens when you type, make sure that the table is in Edit mode. You can't add or change anything until the table is available for editing.

- *If the field contains text you want to replace,* pretend that you're putting in a brand new entry. Get into Edit mode, move the cursor into that field, and start typing. If you want some visible reassurance that the field really is empty and ready for the new entry, move the cursor to the field and press Ctrl+Backspace. There — the field is empty. Go forth and type.

- *To edit an incorrect entry,* put the table into Edit mode, move the cursor into the field in question, and then get into Field View by pressing F2 or clicking the Field View button on the ToolBar (right next to the Edit Data button). At this point, it's like using your word processor: the arrow keys move the little toothpick cursor; the Del key removes characters to the right of the cursor; the Backspace key trashes the ones to the left; and just typing puts new stuff wherever the cursor is currently hanging out. When you're happy with the results, click the Field View button again — or press F2 — to tell Paradox you're finished.

If you're a menu person (which is perfectly okay, despite what your friends say), select <u>V</u>iew⇨<u>F</u>ield View from the main menu.

Prevent data accidents by taking the table *out* of Edit mode when you're done editing.

# Inserting and Deleting Entire Records

There comes a time in everyone's life when working with a field or two just isn't enough. At that moment, you realize there's something bigger out there calling your name, urging you on to the limits of your endurance. You boldly set forth to conquer a whole record, heeding the call of the wild data frontier.

So it's a little romanticized. Hey, live a little, and then do some more Paradox — that's my motto. Okay, enough living; time to get back to the software at hand.

Working with entire records isn't a big deal at all. There are only two things you need to know: how to insert new records and how to delete old ones. So, here goes.

Seems like there are a lot of Coaches running around loose these days. I'll bet one of them even knows all about Inserting and Deleting Records. Look for him under Working with a Table.

## Inserting new records

To include a new record in your table, put the cursor wherever you want the new record to go, and then press Insert or select Record⇨Insert from the menu. A new, blank record appears in your table, as shown in Figure 7-4. Push bravely onward and enter data into it. When you're done, either turn off Edit mode (press F9 or use any of the other options) or move out of the record by using the up- or down-arrow key. Whatever way you choose, that tells Paradox that the record is done and can be posted.

When you use Ins, the new record pops into being wherever your cursor currently is. All records below it are temporarily moved down a line to make room for the newbie.

To add a record to the *end* of the table, get to the last record (Ctrl+↓ does a fine job) and press ↓ once more. Paradox appends a new record to the bottom of the table.

If your table has a key field, it doesn't matter *where* you insert the new record. As soon as you leave the record, Paradox automatically inserts it into the table according to its key field. It may look like the record simply vanished — trust me, it didn't. It's there in your table, wherever it's supposed to be.

Another key field note: if you attempt to leave the new record but Paradox won't let you out, look at the status bar in the bottom left hand corner of the screen. If it says Key Violation, the record you just entered has the same key field as some other record already in the table. To resolve the problem,

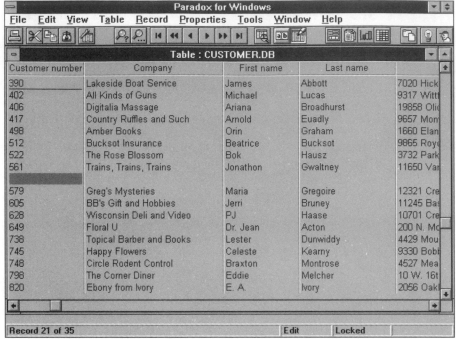

**Figure 7-4:**
A new
record
appears
from the
ether.

either go to the key field and enter a new value or delete the new record and check out the existing one (perhaps you tried to enter the same record twice). Also, make sure that you typed the correct value in the new record's key field.

If you're still a little concerned, confused, or befuddled about this whole *key field* thing, rest assured you're not the only one. Turn to Chapter 9 for what you really *need* to know about key fields.

If you change your mind and decide this was a silly place for a new record, just select Edit⇔Undo from the menu. The new record goes completely away.

## Deleting a record

When a record outlives its usefulness, don't make it hang around and get all depressed — put it out of your misery with a quick, painless delete. Move the cursor onto any field in the record and press Ctrl+Del (or select Record⇔Delete from the menu). The dirty deed is done.

There is *no way* to recover a deleted record. It's truly toasted, gone to the Great Table in the Virtual Sky. Make *really* sure you're deleting the right one before your fingers come down on those fateful keys.

# Chapter 8

# Searching, Sorting, and Spinning All About

. . . . . . . . . . . . . . . . . . . . . . . . . . . . . . . . .

*In This Chapter*

▶ Sorting up and sorting down

▶ Locating individual records fast

▶ Filtering your table for cleaner data

. . . . . . . . . . . . . . . . . . . . . . . . . . . . . . . . .

C ollecting all that data in a table is one thing; finding it when you have a question is something else completely. If you can't track down the data you need, what's the point of keeping it in your computer? You couldn't find it *before* you had the computer, either.

Paradox for Windows gives you quite an assortment of tools for ferreting out answers from your data. This chapter covers the more basic tools: Sort, Locate, and Filter. Part 3 is dedicated to Queries, Paradox's big-time power feature.

Don't assume that the guys in this chapter are lightweights, though. Every craftsman carries a variety of tools; different circumstances require different things. Likewise, the savvy Paradox user reaches for just the right menu or button to solve sticky informational problems. In their own ways, these tools are more powerful than Queries.

## Sorting Up and Sorting Down

Some people are *never* happy. They get a great house, but grouse about the bathroom. They win a new car, but don't like the color. They put their records in one order, but want to see them sorted some other way. It's always *something.*

I don't have any home improvement or car repair tips (I'm a do-it-yourself disaster waiting to happen), but Paradox for Windows can solve the last problem. It *knows* how to sort a table.

First, a brief explanation: *sorting* (according to Paradox) is the fine art of organizing a bunch of records into some semblance of order. It's a once-in-a-while procedure — you don't use sorting to keep a table organized all the time (that's what keys do for you). Sorting really shines when you're analyzing data and looking for similarities or differences (or whatever it is you're looking for).

When you sort a table, you can either create a sorted copy of your data or reorganize the original table itself. The copy is actually *another* table, complete with a name and all of that. If you're working with a keyed table, you can't reorganize the records in the table — you have to make a new table for the sort.

The process itself is pretty simple. You choose the fields to sort with and specify ascending or descending order for each one. Paradox organizes the records according to your instructions.

For example, you can sort a Customer list by zip code in ascending order (smallest to largest), by outstanding bills in descending order (largest to smallest), or by zip code *and* credit limit *and* total purchases last year in whatever amazing combination of sort direction you can think of. As long as you have the fields in your table, Paradox can sort with them. It's very flexible about this stuff.

If your original table is *keyed* (has a key field or two) you can only create a sorted copy of the table. The key field controls the order of the original table and sorting won't override it.

Keep the following tips in mind:

- ✔ Think carefully before you make a bunch of sorted tables. Each one is a full copy of your original table, so if you do several different sorts, you might run out of disk space.

- ✔ Start the name of the sorted table with an S (for *sorted*) and then the first few letters of the original table's name. Fill out the rest of the name with an extremely clever (and short) identifier to remind you what makes that table special. For example, SCustZip would be the Customer table sorted by zip code. This technique makes the file management chores a little easier because you know which tables contain original data and which are sorted duplicates.

- ✔ When you're just playing with ideas and don't want to save your sorted table, name it **X.** This is my Universal Temporary Table Name (or UTTN to confuse my wife). Whenever I'm looking through my files and run across something called X, I know it's a leftover temporary file and that I can safely delete it. For important project files, I come up with a real file name.

- ✔ Each field you choose has its own sort order. Paradox automatically chooses ascending, but you can overrule its decision and pick descending quite easily.

- ✔ If you're sorting one of those mutant text/number fields (such as Customer Number or Account Number), you may get some unexpected results. Say you have Customer Numbers 1, 2, 3, 10, 17, 22, 30, and 35 in your table. Paradox sorts them in a rather unusual way: 1, 10, 17, 2, 22, 3, 30, 35. Because Paradox sees the numbers as *text*, it uses alphabetical sorting rules instead of numeric sorting rules and ends up with a questionable final product. To get around this feature, put a zero in front of the smaller customer numbers so that they're *physically* the same number of digits as the larger ones. In this example, the first three customer numbers should be 01, 02, and 03. Now Paradox for Windows sorts the list correctly.

- ✔ Most of the time, Paradox only needs one field to sort with. If it finds two entries in that field that are identical, it compares the values in the second sort field you specified. If you only chose one sorting field, Paradox doesn't panic (thank goodness) — it looks at the first record in the field and decides which record goes where based on those values. If *they're* the same, it moves to the second field, and so on until it reaches a decision. If it *never* finds a unique field to break the tie, it leaves the records in the order it found them and moves on.

Now on to the meat of the issue. Here's how to sort your Paradox tables:

1. **Figure out what you want to do.**

   Knowing where you're going makes a better trip. Decide *what* you're sorting (the fields involved), *how* you're sorting it (ascending or descending), and *where* it's ending up (new table or the same table).

2. **Make sure that you're in the correct Working Directory.**

   If you aren't, get there *right now*. Chapter 3 has all the details on working with the Working Directory.

3. **One way or another, tell Paradox you want to sort a table.**

   This instruction is deliberately vague because what you do depends on where you are. Following are the specific steps for the two most common *where*'s. Both of the options leave you at the same point: looking at a screen full of Sort Table dialog box.

   From the Project Viewer, right-click the table name to open the pop-up Utilities menu, and then select <u>S</u>ort (see Figure 8-1). If you're into menus, select <u>T</u>ools➪<u>U</u>tilities➪<u>S</u>ort and then double-click the name of the file you want to play with. Either way, you end up with the Sort Table dialog box emblazoned across your screen.

   If you're already browsing through the data, select <u>T</u>able➪<u>S</u>ort from the main menu. This opens the Sort Table dialog box.

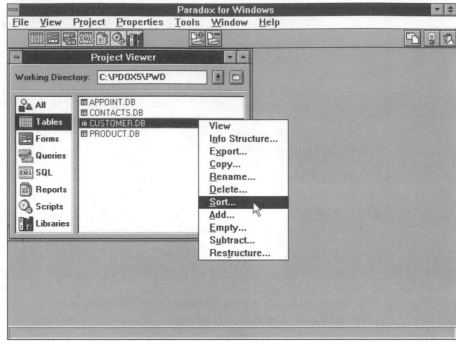

**Figure 8-1:**
Starting a
sort with the
secret pop-
up Utilities
menu in the
Project
Viewer.

**4. If you're sorting a keyed table, type a name for the new sorted table in the New Table box (your cursor is already there).**

With an unsorted table, the dialog box automatically assumes that you *don't* want to make a new table. If you do, click the New Table radio button and then type a file name into the box that magically appears.

**5. To automatically display the newly sorted table as soon as it's ready, click the Display Sorted Table checkbox. Otherwise, leave it blank.**

Don't you wish the steps were *all* this easy?

**6. In the Fields area, double-click the name of the field you want to use to sort the table.**

The field name hops over to the Sort Order box. As you can see in Figure 8-2, the field name is now grayed in the Fields list. It's a reminder that this field is already part of the sort.

If you move the wrong field, click it in the Sort Order area, and then click the left arrow button in the middle of the dialog box. That sends the field back home where it belongs. To completely clear out the Sort Order box (if you're sorting by more than one field), click Clear all. That triggers a mass field exodus.

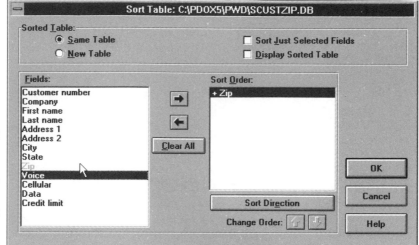

**Figure 8-2:**
Zip is the
first lucky
field in
today's Sort
Order.

7. **By default, Paradox assumes you want to sort in ascending order (that's what the little plus sign next to the field name means). To choose descending order instead, click Sort Direction.**

   If you have more than one field in the Sort Order, first click the field you want to change and then do the Sort Direction button.

8. **To include other fields in the sort, repeat steps 6 and 7.**

   When you sort with multiple fields, choose them in the order of importance. If you want a table showing customer credit limits grouped by zip code, for example, put the zip code field first in the Sort Order, followed by the credit limit field. Paradox sorts the table by zip codes and then organizes the records with duplicate zip codes according to their credit limits.

   If you happen to choose the fields out of order, you can fix that easily. Click the field that's at the wrong place in Sort Order list and then click the up or down arrow buttons labeled Change Order. When you click them, the field moves up or down in the sort order, depending on which button you're clicking. If one of the buttons is gray, the field can't move any further in that direction.

   Paradox only uses the second field if it finds two *identical* values in the first field. Likewise, it only uses a third field if the first two are identical.

9. **Click OK to complete the sort.**

   If you turned on the Display Sorted Table checkbox, the sorted table appears on-screen automatically. Otherwise, you're unceremoniously dumped wherever the Sort command found you.

Figure 8-3 shows the results of a successful two-field sort. In this example, Paradox sorted by zip code (the Zip field) and then by Customer number. Records 6 and 7 have the same zip code (45221), so Paradox put them in order by Customer number. There you have it.

By the way, I moved the Zip field next to the Customer number field to show you how the sorting process worked. The Sort command doesn't reorganize the fields in the sorted table — it just sorts the records and provides you with the results.

# *Locating Individual Records Fast*

Sometimes, you want to find a record *fast* (and I mean *pronto*). Doing a query would take too long (heck, it's not that big of a question) and even a Filter is overkill (you haven't gotten to Filters yet — that's next in this chapter). What are you to do? Try a *locate* on for size.

First, Locate is fast. In the DOS version, it was so quick they called it *Zoom* — seriously, I wouldn't kid you about something like that. Second, it's easy. One

**Figure 8-3:**
The newly sorted table, appropriately named and appearing for the first time.

| | Paradox for Windows |
|---|---|

**File   Edit   View   Table   Record   Properties   Tools   Window   Help**

**Table : SCUSTZIP.DB**

| SCUSTZIP | Zip | Customer number | Company | First name | La |
|---|---|---|---|---|---|
| 1 | 44290 | 335 | The Recycling Center | Imogene | Blakely |
| 2 | 45044 | 605 | BB's Gift and Hobbies | Jerri | Bruney |
| 3 | 45147 | 561 | Trains, Trains, Trains | Jonathon | Gwaltney |
| 4 | 45148 | 856 | The Inner Ewe | Araia | Wildridge |
| 5 | 45220-0481 | 927 | Passion Flower Farms | Cy | Lynch |
| 6 | 45221 | 267 | Fragrant Evenings | Gerri | Romaine |
| 7 | 45271 | 960 | Newe Advertising | Hyun | Roo |
| 8 | 45282 | 872 | Target Bowling Lanes | Byron | Sprague |
| 9 | 45422 | 278 | American Ceiling Tile | Steven | Morrisse |
| 10 | 45971 | 390 | Lakeside Boat Service | James | Abbott |
| 11 | 46118 | 048 | PROpain Sports Medicine | Penelope | Cline |
| 12 | 46147 | 382 | ABC Sporting Goods | Ferrial | Courville |
| 13 | 46219-1550 | 187 | Rain Systems | Randall | Joel |
| 14 | 46225 | 250 | Century Solar Panels | Shasta | Lowrey |
| 15 | 46229 | 498 | Amber Books | Orin | Graham |
| 16 | 46229-4781 | 738 | Topical Barber and Books | Lester | Dunwidd |
| 17 | 46240 | 844 | Voice of the Dunes | Nazario | Mokosak |
| 18 | 46359 | 798 | The Corner Diner | Eddie | Melcher |

Record 6 of 34

quick button click or keystroke is all it takes to start. Third, it only works on one field, but that's not a drawback, it's a feature. Remember, you heard it here first.

Locate is pretty straightforward. You tell it where to look, give it a value to search for, and it highlights the first place it finds that value. If that's not the one you want, use Locate Next to keep looking. Paradox keeps trying until it's out of records to check.

The process is quicker to do than explain, so try one and see how you like it.

1. **Before you can use Locate, you need to open your table and be looking at it on-screen.**

   If you need help with this initial step, refer back to "Opening the Table (Again)" in Chapter 7.

2. **Click somewhere in the field you want to search.**

   Locate only works on a single field, so pick your poison and continue.

 3. **Start Locate by clicking the Locate Field Value button on the ToolBar or by pressing Ctrl+Z.**

   This brings up the Locate Value dialog box, without which there could be no Locate command.

4. **In the Value field, type whatever it is you're looking for and then click OK to start the search.**

 Figure 8-4 shows a Locate dialog box that's ready to go. If Locate doesn't find the right record, click the Locate Next button on the ToolBar or press Ctrl+A. That tells Paradox to keep looking for the same thing it just found.

   You don't need to worry about capitalization, but *spelling* definitely counts. Keep the following points in mind:

   - You can search for part of an entry with *wildcards*. The most useful one is the double period (..). In Paradox lingo, it stands for any number of letters. Say you remember that a customer's name was Rick, but you don't know if he's in the database as Ric, Rick, or Richard. Type **ric..** into the Value box. Paradox will find the first entry in the table that starts with the letters *ric,* regardless of what comes after it.

   - The other wildcard is the @, which replaces a single letter. If you wanted to search a Year field for all the things that happened in the fourth year of each decade, you could type **19@4.** (Yup, I do that every day myself.) You probably won't ever use @, but at least you know it's there. Check out Chapter 12 for more about wildcards (and queries, too).

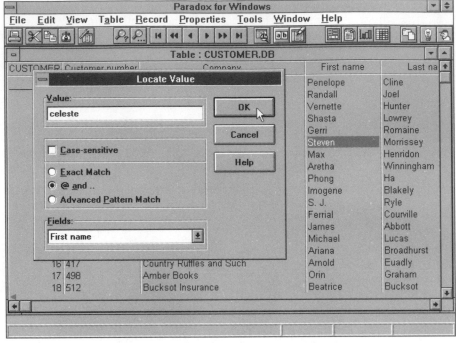

**Figure 8-4:**
In just a moment, Celeste won't be lost any more.

# Filtering Your Table for Cleaner Data

The latest version of Paradox adds something that's destined to make your life a whole lot easier. Without setting up a query or clicking through a bunch of Locates, you can quickly look at a select group of records. It's quick, it's easy — it's a *Filter*. Although it's much like a Query, it has some major differences that make it a powerful addition to your data analysis toolbox.

Possibly the nicest thing about a Filter is that it does what it says: Filters *filter* the data in your table. If you tell a Filter to display customers from Indiana, that's what you see. Want to look at the people who spent more than $15,000 with you last year? No problem. Filters even work with more than one field, so you can get as detailed as you want.

All is not nirvana, though. Filters only work with one table. You can't link two or three tables together and make some kind of pseudo-query. And Filters are temporary, too — you can't save them. Oh well, I guess you can't have everything.

You can create single-field filters on the fly as you're wandering through your table. One click with the Inspector and you're there. For more complex Filters, use the Filter Tables dialog box and build a gonzo whopper with lots of conditions. Both approaches are covered in the sections below.

Conditions are a point where Filters and Queries show their similarities. In a Filter, you can call for an exact match, a partial match (using wildcards), or a range of values (with the greater than and less than signs). In previous versions of Paradox, only Queries wielded this much flexibility. Filters are definitely the power tool of Paradox for Windows 5.

Table 8-1 shows what the different conditions look like in Official Paradox Filter Lingo (OPFL). If you need help with the comparison thing, check out Chapter 15. And don't worry about remembering the OPFL acronym — I made it up.

| Table 8-1 | Sample Filter Comparisons | |
|---|---|---|
| *Type of comparison* | *Example* | *Tips* |
| Exact match | IN or 46219 | Type the example entry carefully — data has to match *exactly* to pass the Filter. |
| Partial match | 462.. or ..Chi.. | Use the .. wildcard to match a portion of your data (like the first three digits of a zip code). One .. wildcard on each end of the example lets you find text in the *middle* of a field. |
| Range | >110, <=220 | Combine a greater than and less than with a comma (like the example) to see records between two extremes or use them individually to see everything above or below one point. Add an equals sign to include the example value in the range. |

# Single-field Filters

Creating a single-field Filter is a snap. In fact, you can make a bunch of them in the time it takes to read this sentence (let alone the following instructions).

1. **As with Locate, you must have the table open in the workspace before you can play the Filter game.**

2. **Click the field you want to filter, and then right-click and select Filter from the pop-up menu, as shown in Figure 8-5.**

   All this skulking around and clicking in the ether brings up the Field Filter dialog box.

   Paradox doesn't require you to click and then right-click to get the popup menu. By putting the cursor in the field *before* setting the Filter, you're protected if your Filter goes awry. Trust me on this one.

   If your right mouse button is out of order, click the field and press Ctrl+M to open the hidden menu, arrow down to Filter, and then press Enter.

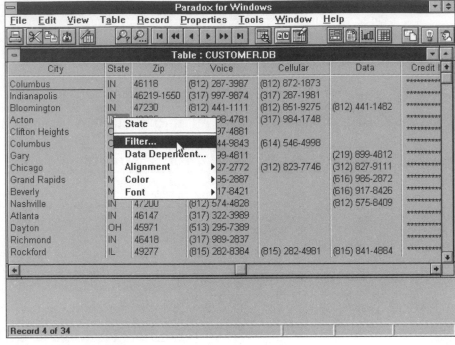

**Figure 8-5:**
Another
secret pop-
up menu
yields the
powerful
Filter
command.

### 3. Type the filter text into the Field Filter dialog box.

Figure 8-6 shows a simple exact match Filter. Only records where the State field is *IN* will pass through the filter and appear on-screen.

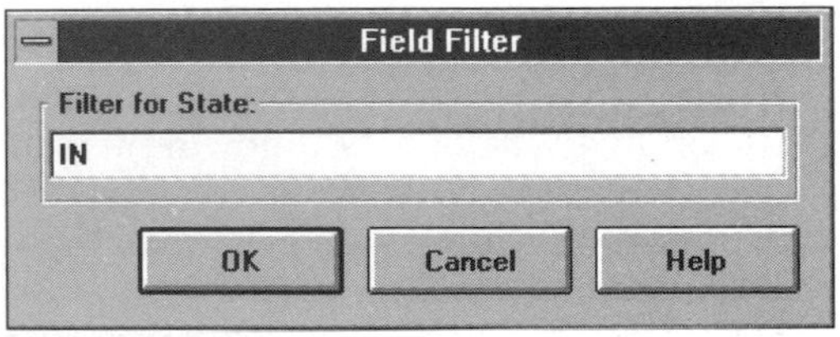

**Figure 8-6:**
A simple
exact match
Filter is born.

> **Field Filter**
>
> Filter for State:
>
> IN
>
> OK    Cancel    Help

### 4. Click OK to install the Filter.

The Filter takes effect immediately.

If all the data in your table vanishes (as in Figure 8-7), no matches exist for the Filter you created. If you followed my advice in Step 1 and clicked in the field before setting the filter, press Ctrl+M to bring up the field settings menu, and then select Filter. Press Del to remove the Filter text and click OK to save the changes. All your data reappears, safe and sound.

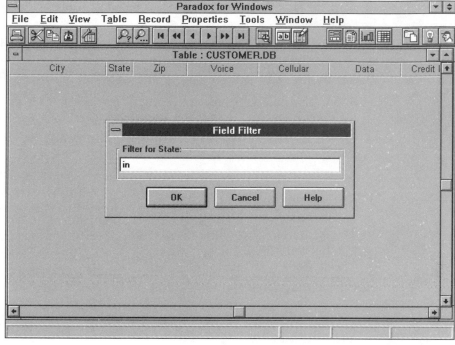

If you *didn't* take my advice, select File➪Close to send the poor table away, and then reopen it. Because Filters aren't saved, all your data is back in sight automatically.

5. **To delete the filter, repeat Step 2 to see the Filter text, and then press Del to make it go away. Click OK to be done with the whole sordid affair.**

If you want to limit your data even further, create some more single field Filters. They build on each other to truly strangle the flow of data to the screen.

## Multiple-field Filters

These are a little more complex than their simple siblings, so they're born in a more complicated way — through the Filter Tables dialog box. Getting started, though, is easier than ever:

1. **Open the table on the workspace.**

Yes, it's the normal prerequisite to all the really fun things in Paradox for Windows, come to visit you once again.

**2. Click the Filter button on the ToolBar or select T̲able⇨F̲ilter from the main menu.**

Either way, the dreaded Filter Tables dialog box enters and takes center stage (fade in eerie organ music).

**3. In the F̲ilters on Fields section, find the field you want to filter.**

If your table has more than 10 fields, use the vertical scroll bar to the right of the field list to get down to the other fields.

**4. Click in the Filter text box next to the field name and type your example.**

There's nothing to this — just type carefully and everything will be okay.

**5. Repeat Steps 3 and 4 for each Filter.**

In Figure 8-8, there are two Filters. The Zip field Filter allows records whose zip codes begin with 46. The more complicated one in Customer Number limits the display to customer numbers greater than or equal to 150 *and* less than or equal to 700.

**6. Click OK to put the filter into action.**

If all your data disappears, at least one of the filters didn't have any matches. Don't panic. Go on to the next Step and try deleting one (or more) of the filters you put in.

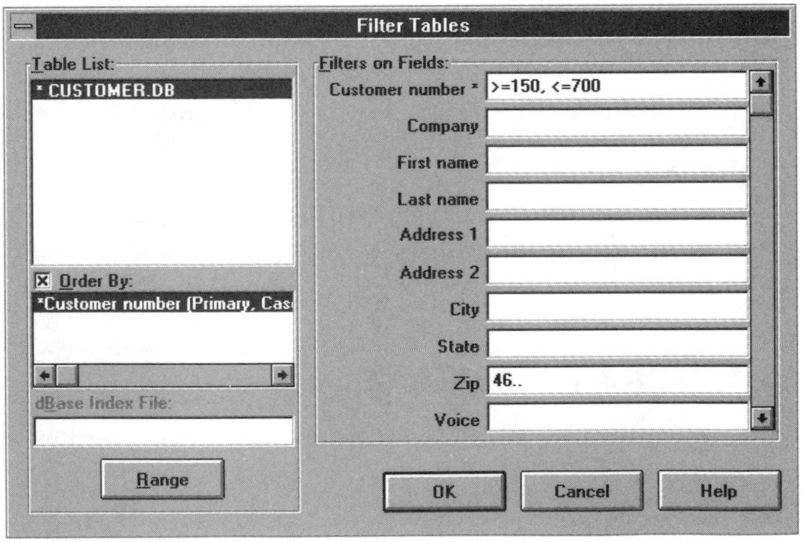

**Figure 8-8:**
Managing
multiple
Filters is as
easy as
you can
reasonably
expect with
the Filter
Tables
dialog box.

| Filter Tables | |
|---|---|
| **T̲able List:** | **F̲ilters on Fields:** |
| * CUSTOMER.DB | Customer number * >=150, <=700 |
| | Company |
| | First name |
| | Last name |
| | Address 1 |
| | Address 2 |
| ☒ O̲rder By: | City |
| *Customer number (Primary, Cas | State |
| | Zip 46.. |
| dB̲ase Index File: | Voice |
| | |
| R̲ange | OK   Cancel   Help |

7. **To delete a filter, click the Filter button (or do the Table⇨Filter menu thing) to bring up the Filter Tables dialog box. Find the filter you want to remove and click Filter text. Use the Del or Backspace key to remove every shred of text from the box. Click OK when your destructive rage is spent.**

Of course, you can remove *all* the filters by closing the table and reopening it, but that's kind of like killing a fly with a shotgun.

# When to Locate, Filter, or Query

The difference between an apprentice and a craftsman is knowing when and how to apply the right tool to a job. In the world of finding things in Paradox, your tools are Locate, Filter, and Query. The trick is knowing which one to use and when to use it.

✔ *Locate.* Great for finding a particular record *now;* lousy for analyzing anything that requires more than one or two records.

✔ *Filter.* The new tool of choice for a quick look at part of a table (and they work in reports and forms, too!); limited to working with one table, plus you can't save and reuse them.

✔ *Query.* The granddaddy of data inspection tools; takes time and effort to set up — and you *must* know what you're doing or risk getting wacky results.

Here's a craftsman's rule of thumb for choosing your analysis tool: just a record or two, use Locate; only one table, make a Filter; anything else, do a Query.

# Chapter 9
# Getting All Keyed-up

- - - - - - - - - - - - - - - - - - - - - - - - - - - - -

- - - - - - - - - - - - - - - - - - - - - - - - - - - - -

*Key* — what pops into your mind? Key ring, house key, car keys, driving to get pizza? Do the same experiment with Paradox and you only get one response: *key field.*

You and I both know that computer programs never were, well, *clever* about things like word games, so it's not really surprising that Paradox could only think of one reply. On the other hand, what it thought of is *primo* important to you as The Maker of Tables. That's why this Chapter explains the whole key field thing from start to finish. You might say it's a "key chapter." (I couldn't help myself.)

## What Is a Key Field?

The key field is a special field that *you* designate in each table. An individual record's *key* is the value in the key field. Depending on your data, a table can have one, several, or no key fields at all (there's more about that in the next section). The key field has two distinct jobs: to keep the records in order and to make sure that no two records have the same key.

✔ A table with a key field is called a *keyed table.* Currently, there is no acronym for this, but I'm sure someone, somewhere is working on one right now.

✔ Your table is automatically sorted by the entries in the key field. If the key is Customer Number, you see the records in ascending order by Customer Number.

✔ Searching a table by the key field is *very* fast because Paradox makes an index of the records by their key. This works just like the index of a book. When you ask for information on customer 4826, Paradox looks up that number in the index and *immediately* knows where to find the right record in the table. Otherwise, it has to look through thousands of customer records to find the one it needs (and that takes time).

✔ When you enter a new record, Paradox makes sure that no *other* record in the table already has that key. If it finds one that does, you have to change the key in the new record before Paradox will accept it.

Each record in a keyed table *must* have a unique key. For example, two customers can't have the same Customer Number — each one has to be different. Like I said, Paradox for Windows is quite stubborn about this rule.

## Picking the Right Field

Key fields are special, so not just *any* field can be the key. A good key field must be brave, truthful, and unselfish. No, sorry — that's how Pinocchio became a real boy. A key field needs to be unique *and* the first field in the table. Stay within those guidelines, and you can choose any field at all to be your key.

The main thing about a key field is that it's unique — you can't have duplicate values in the key field or Paradox has a conniption and stamps its little feet. What if your table doesn't have any one unique field? Are you sunk? No, you're still okay. You can either invent a unique field or look for two fields that are unique when they work together.

For example, last name is a lousy key by itself because too many people have the same last name. Using both last name and phone number as key fields would work, provided you only had one record per family. A better solution (at least from the computer's point of view) is to create a unique ID number for each record.

✔ Having unique values is the #1 requirement of a key field. If no single field has a unique value in each record, look for two fields that are unique when they're put together.

✔ This *unique value* requirement is why you live in a world of customer numbers, Social Security numbers, and all those other numbers that define who you are to the computers of the world. Computers don't like our pathetically nonunique names at all. (Obviously, the whole name thing *wasn't* designed by a computer — and it's a good thing, too.)

✔ Key fields can be these types: Alpha, Autoincrement, Date, Integer, Number, Time, and Timestamp. You can use the Money type for a key field as well, but I can't imagine why you'd do it.

✔ The key field must be the first field in the table structure. If you have more than one key field, that's fine, but they all must be at the top of the table structure. Beyond that, they can be in any order you want.

# Making a Key Field

At this point, the concept is completely driven into the ground and it's time to actually make a key field or two. Everything you need to know to turn existing fields into key fields is outlined in the following steps. If you're creating a new field as your key, check out the sidebar "All hail the new key" for some very important information.

✔ To add a key field to a new table or for general help creating a new field, refer to "It's (Finally) Time to Build the Table" in Chapter 6.

✔ For an interactive, step-by-step walk through keys and key fields, click the Coach button on the ToolBar and check out the Adding a Key in the Building a Database section. (Tell Coach that I sent you.)

## All hail the new key

If you're adding a special new field as your key (like the infamous *ID Number,* for example), you can't just pop the new field in, call it a key, and be done with it. If you do that, all of your records (except the first one in the table) immediately fall out into a table called KEYVIOL. This is *not* a good thing.

If this already happened to you, refer to the "Add and Subtract: Electronic Parallel Parking" section in Chapter 11 for a quick solution.

This is the *safe* way to make a new, custom key field:

1. Use Step 1 in "Making a Key Field" to start restructuring the table.

2. As soon as the Restructure dialog box appears, press Insert to make room for the new field.

3. Type in the field name, type, and size (if you're making an Alpha field).

4. Click Save to save the information about the new field.

Now edit the table and fill in values for the soon-to-be key field. Once every record in the table has a unique value in the new field, turn off Edit mode and go through all the steps in "Making a Key Field."

**1. To add a key, you need to restructure the table.**

Depending on where you are in Paradox, you can open the Restructure dialog box in different ways. Figure 9-1 shows the Restructure dialog box.

- *From the Project Viewer,* right-click the table you want to restructure and then select Restructure from the popup menu.

- *If you're viewing the table,* either click the Restructure button on the ToolBar or select Table⇨Restructure Table from the menu.

Whichever way you get there, the dialog box looks like Figure 9-1 once you arrive.

**2. Decide which is the new key field and move it to the top of the structure. Repeat the process if you're using two or more key fields.**

To move a field, click and hold the mouse button on the field number (the far left column in the Field Roster area). While holding down the button, move the field up to the top of the field list.

Because I'm making a composite key, I resettled two fields. The results of this moving experience are shown in Figure 9-2.

In case anyone asks you, two key fields working together are called a *composite key.* This information may come in handy around the coffee pot or at one of those fancy parties you go to all the time.

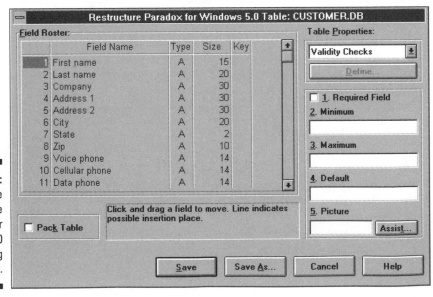

**Figure 9-1:**
The Restructure Paradox for Windows 5.0 Table dialog box.

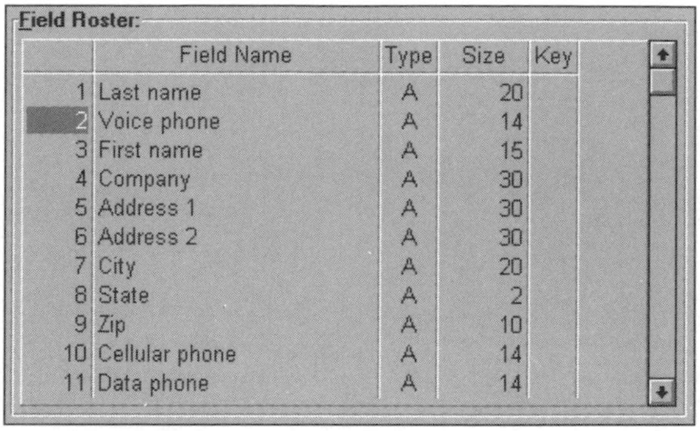

**Figure 9-2:**
The key
fields-to-be
(Last Name
and Voice
Phone) are
in place at
the top of
the
structure.

Field Roster:

| | Field Name | Type | Size | Key | |
|---|---|---|---|---|---|
| 1 | Last name | A | 20 | | |
| 2 | Voice phone | A | 14 | | |
| 3 | First name | A | 15 | | |
| 4 | Company | A | 30 | | |
| 5 | Address 1 | A | 30 | | |
| 6 | Address 2 | A | 30 | | |
| 7 | City | A | 20 | | |
| 8 | State | A | 2 | | |
| 9 | Zip | A | 10 | | |
| 10 | Cellular phone | A | 14 | | |
| 11 | Data phone | A | 14 | | |

WARNING!

If you're in the middle of adding a new field as your key, *stop right now* and read "All hail the new key." You can thank me later.

3. **Either click or Tab (depending on your preference) to the Key column of the prospective key field. Once there, double-click or press the spacebar to officially make it a key field.**

   Repeat the process if you're blessing two or more fields with *key* status.

   Figure 9-3 displays the finished product. Both Last name and Voice phone are now key fields. Figure 9-4 shows another way to make Customer a keyed table. Instead of reorganizing existing fields, I added a unique Customer number.

   Yes, it's one more thing for my customers to remember. Hopefully, they'll forgive me.

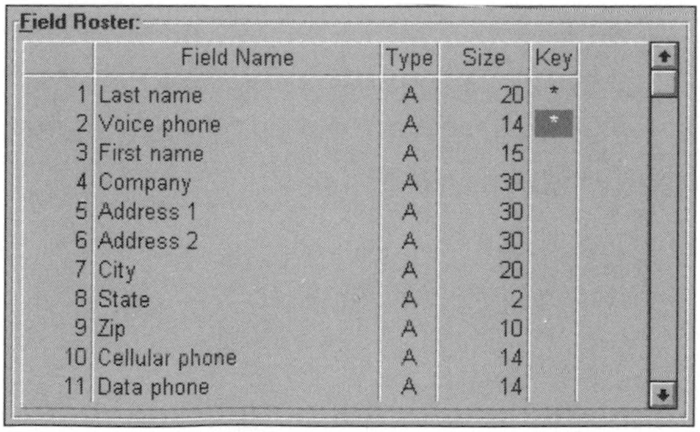

Field Roster:

| | Field Name | Type | Size | Key | |
|---|---|---|---|---|---|
| 1 | Last name | A | 20 | * | |
| 2 | Voice phone | A | 14 | * | |
| 3 | First name | A | 15 | | |
| 4 | Company | A | 30 | | |
| 5 | Address 1 | A | 30 | | |
| 6 | Address 2 | A | 30 | | |
| 7 | City | A | 20 | | |
| 8 | State | A | 2 | | |
| 9 | Zip | A | 10 | | |
| 10 | Cellular phone | A | 14 | | |
| 11 | Data phone | A | 14 | | |

**Figure 9-3:**
The deed is
done — all
hail the new
key fields!

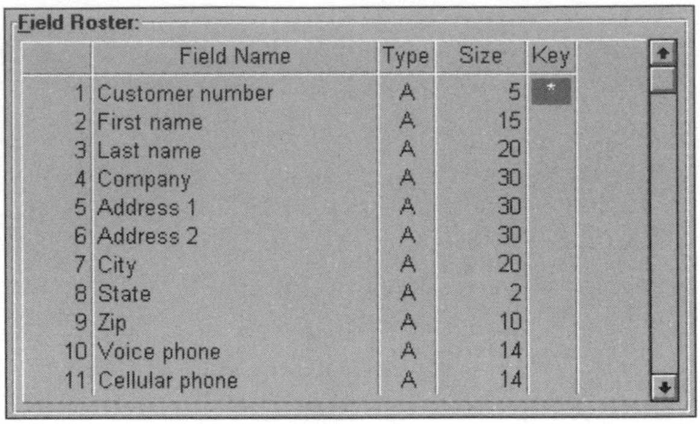

```
┌─Field Roster:─────────────────────────────────────┐
│         Field Name        Type  Size  Key    ▲    │
│      1 Customer number      A      5    *         │
│      2 First name           A     15              │
│      3 Last name            A     20              │
│      4 Company              A     30              │
│      5 Address 1            A     30              │
│      6 Address 2            A     30              │
│      7 City                 A     20              │
│      8 State                A      2              │
│      9 Zip                  A     10              │
│     10 Voice phone          A     14              │
│     11 Cellular phone       A     14         ▼    │
└───────────────────────────────────────────────────┘
```

**Figure 9-4:**
Here I
added a
field that's
specially
designed to
be the
perfect,
unique key.

**4. Click Save to make your work permanent.**

If you're immediately greeted with a table called KEYVIOL, there were some records in the table that even after all your hard work *didn't* have unique key values.

Close your eyes, breathe deeply a couple of times, and then look ahead to Chapter 11 for help putting the records back where they belong.

# Removing a Key Field

Compared to creating a key, removing one is a piece of cake. Nothing can really go wrong (but you might knock on wood just in case).

**1. Tell Paradox you want to restructure the table.**

Refer to Step 1 in the preceding section for the details.

**2. Click or Tab your way over to the Key column. When you get there, double-click or press the spacebar to turn off the Key marker.**

**3. Click Save to make the removal official.**

I told you it was easy.

# Chapter 10

# Making the Table Work for You

*T*eaching your dog to fetch is a human-canine bonding experience. Teaching the cat to do *anything* is an exercise in futility (the cat spends the whole time wondering when you'll catch on). Teaching your tables to think on their own is somewhere in the middle. It's not quite *bonding* material, but it's not feline head-banging either.

Paradox for Windows includes some simple, if well-hidden, tools to endow your fields with a stimulus-response level of intelligence. For example, your fields can know the difference between right and wrong, at least as the concepts relate to their tiny corner of digital reality. This chapter divulges the details of default values, edit pictures, and stuffy-sounding data-dependent properties. They're all here for your reading pleasure.

Don't worry if this stuff sounds a little technical right now — read to the end and everybody stays normal.

## Fields that (Sort of) Think

There's a lot to worry about when you're managing a table by yourself. It's up to you to make sure that the customer numbers are correct, the phone numbers don't have letters in them, and the zip codes all have five (or was that nine?) digits. If this stuff is stressing you out, I have some good news: there's a way to make the *table* carry part of the load. Is that great or what?

There are five different thought-inducing settings available for just about every kind of field in your tables. Table 10-1 describes these settings. Everything in the list lives in the Restructure Table dialog box, so you don't have to chase hither and thither through Paradox to use this stuff.

Logical fields can be Required and have a Default, but that's it. After all, when your choices are *true* or *false,* what does setting a minimum or maximum really do? (Memo and Formatted Memo fields can only be Required. No other settings are available.)

The official Paradox name for these settings is *Validity Checks.*

### Table 10-1  Settings in the Restructure Table Dialog Box

| Setting | Description |
|---------|-------------|
| Required | The field *cannot* be blank; it must have an entry in it. This is a particularly good setting for a key field. |
| Minimum | Sets the smallest possible value in the field. |
| Maximum | Sets the largest possible value in the field. |
| Default | This entry automatically appears in the field unless you put in your own value. |
| Picture | Creates a template for the field; limits what's acceptable and how the field is formatted. |

# Your Data Oughtta Be in Pictures

Most of the settings are pretty self-explanatory, but *pictures* could fill a book by themselves. Here's what you need to know about these little power tools:

- A *picture* is a collection of symbols with special meanings. Each symbol stands for a single character of one kind or another. Put them together and they limit what and how much you can type into a field.

- Some pictures let you type text into a field, but they automatically convert the lowercase letters into uppercase. You just can't turn your back on them for one minute, can you?

- Make sure that your field size agrees with what your pictures call for. Blessing the zip Code field with the ability to understand nine digit codes doesn't help if the field only holds five characters.

✓ Check out the sidebar for a quick lesson in the language of pictures. This is strictly help with *reading* the language, not *writing* it. Some of you may want to know what that gibberish in the picture code actually means. That's fine. But if you *don't* want to know, you don't need to learn — Paradox for Windows happily does it for you.

✓ Pictures are an extremely powerful tool, but they're a little scary to look at. Don't worry — they don't bite (very hard). Likewise, don't worry about creating your own pictures. Paradox includes the most common ones in a cool feature called Assist — you pick what you want and Paradox types it in for you.

In case Assist doesn't have *quite* what you're looking for, Table 10-2 describes some other useful pictures. Be careful when you type these picutres in — they have to be *exactly* the same as the example in order to work. Paradox is *very* sticky about this (you know how software gets).

| Table 10-2 | Paradox for Windows Pictures |
|---|---|
| *Picture* | *Represents* |
| *? | Any quantity of letters in either upper- or lowercase; no spaces |
| *& | Any quantity of letters; converts them to uppercase; no spaces |
| ###-##-#### | U.S. Social Security number; dashes fill in automatically |
| [(###)]###-#### | U.S. phone number with optional area code; dashes fill in automatically |
| #&@^*($* | I'm so mad I could just spit |
| ##/##/## | Date with automatic slashes (sounds like a bad horror movie) |

# *Setting the Settings*

Here's how to put these tools to work in your fields:

1. **Let Paradox know you want to restructure the table.**

   If you're in the Project Viewer, either right-click the table name and select Restructure from the pop-up menu, or just click the table name and select Tools⇨Utilities⇨Restructure from the main menu.

   If you're already looking at the table, click the Restructure button on the ToolBar or do the menu thing by selecting Table⇨Restructure Table.

## Picturing Frankenstein's monster in your fields

Pictures, for all their power, look like digital rejects from Dr. Frankenstein's laboratory. Who'd ever guess that *5#[-*4#] means *U.S. zip code (either 5 or 9 digits)?* It's certainly not the first thing *I* thought of this morning.

Like the monster in Shelly's story, though, pictures aren't bad — they just want to be understood. There are only seven symbols you need to know about. There are some other ones, but your local guru can explain them:

@     Accepts any character (letter, number, or symbol)

!     Accepts any character (letter, number, or symbol); converts letters to uppercase

?     Only accepts a letter

&     Only accepts a letter; converts it to uppercase

#     Accepts only a numeric digit (0-9)

*     Special — repeat the symbol that comes next an unlimited number of times (*& for example); if there's a number next to it (like *5), repeat only that number of times

[]     Special — anything contained in brackets is optional

To make a Paradox picture, string the symbols together like popcorn on a thread. Now that you know what the codes mean, here's another look at the little monster in the first paragraph. See if it makes more sense now.

*5# means accept five digits. Writing it with five pound signs (#####) is perfectly acceptable, too. In fact, I personally like it better that way because it's a *little* more intuitive (not much, but every little bit helps).

The brackets around [-*4#] mean this part of the picture is optional. It's fine if you want to type the data in, but you don't have to do it if you don't want to. Inside the brackets, the dash tells Paradox to *only* accept a dash after the first five numbers. *4# is old hat by now. It accepts four (and *only* 4) numbers.

When you put the whole thing together, the picture accepts either a five digit or a full nine digit zip code. If you're entering a nine digit code, it takes the remaining 4 digits *only* if you start with a dash (which is the right way to type a nine digit zip code, anyway).

All roads lead to the Restructure Paradox for Windows 5.0 Table dialog box (which is a good thing because you'd never fit all that on a street sign). Figure 10-1 is what you see when you arrive.

2. **The Table Properties box should say *Validity Checks*. If it doesn't, click in the down arrow next to the box and select Validity Checks from the drop-down list.**

   It should default to Validity Checks, but it never hurts to make sure.

3. **In the Field Roster area, click the name of the field you're putting to work.**

   Getting excited yet?

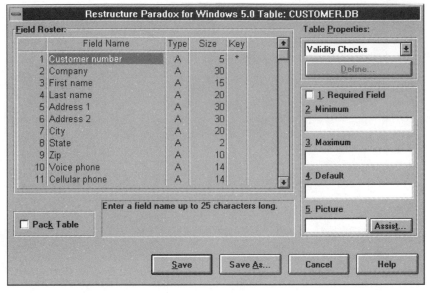

**Figure 10-1:**
The
Restructure
dialog box
stars in
another
episode of
Dialog
Boxes with
Names Too
Long to Care
About.

**4. Set any or all of the Validity Checks you want.**

Required Field, Minimum, Maximum, and Default are described in the following list. Pictures are covered in Step 5.

- If this is a required field, click in the Required Field checkbox or press Alt+1.

- To set a Minimum value for the field, click in the Minimum box (or press Alt+2) and type the value.

- To set a Maximum value for the field, click in the Maximum box (or press Alt+3) and type the value.

- To set a Default value for the field, click in the Default box (or press Alt+4) and type the value.

- To reach an operator, please stay on the line.

Figure 10-2 shows a field (in this case, table's key field) that's Required, has a minimum limit of 001, and tops out at a maximum of 99999. It looks like a Picture is in its future because the mouse pointer is hovering over the Assist button.

If you're not adding a picture, avoid the After-Picture Rush and skip ahead to step 9.

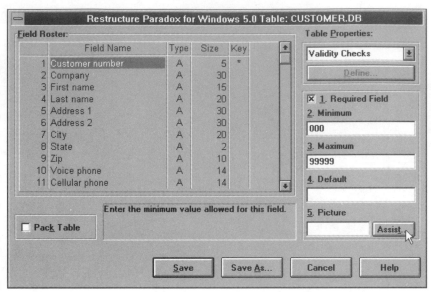

Restructure Paradox for Windows 5.0 Table: CUSTOMER.DB

**Field Roster:**

| | Field Name | Type | Size | Key |
|---|---|---|---|---|
| 1 | Customer number | A | 5 | * |
| 2 | Company | A | 30 | |
| 3 | First name | A | 15 | |
| 4 | Last name | A | 20 | |
| 5 | Address 1 | A | 30 | |
| 6 | Address 2 | A | 30 | |
| 7 | City | A | 20 | |
| 8 | State | A | 2 | |
| 9 | Zip | A | 10 | |
| 10 | Voice phone | A | 14 | |
| 11 | Cellular phone | A | 14 | |

Enter the minimum value allowed for this field.

☐ Pac**k** Table

**Table Properties:**

Validity Checks

Define...

☒ **1**. Required Field

**2**. Minimum

000

**3**. Maximum

99999

**4**. Default

**5**. Picture

Assis**t**...

Save    Save **A**s...    Cancel    Help

**Figure 10-2:** The Customer number field, its two validity checks, and a mouse caught in the act of adding a Picture through Assist.

TECHNICAL STUFF

5. **If you want Paradox to help you add a picture, click Assis_t_. If you want to use one of the examples in this book, click in the Picture box (or press Alt+_5_) and** *carefully* **type the picture code.**

   When you click Assis_t_, the Picture Assistance dialog box pops into view.

   You're not limited to just entering things from this book. Feel free to use your own pictures. (Are you some kind of masochist or something?)

6. **To see the list of ready-to-use pictures, click the down arrow next to Samp_l_e Pictures.**

   Brace yourself for a shock. As Figure 10-3 shows, this list is truly a peek at the sordid underbelly of Paradox for Windows.

7. **Use the up- and down-arrow keys to look through the list.**

   As you move from picture to picture, a brief explanation of the coded morass appears in the area direction above the Sample Pictures box.

8. **When you find the picture you need, highlight it and press Enter. Click _U_se to copy the sample into the _P_icture box. Click OK to escape this brush with mind-numbing techno drivel.**

   If all went well, your newly selected picture appears in the Picture box way down in the lower right corner of the Restructure dialog box, as shown in Figure 10-4.

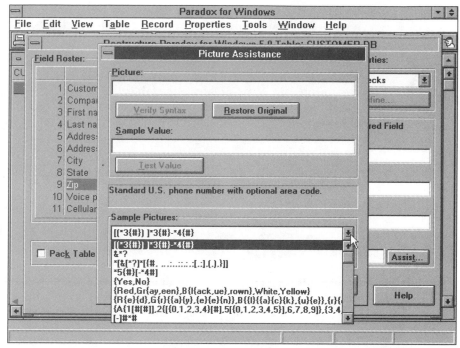

**Figure 10-3:**
The Sample
Pictures
drop-down
list is not a
pretty sight.

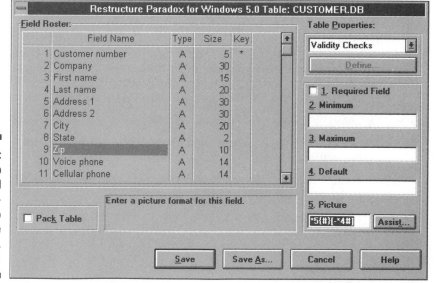

**Figure 10-4:**
The Zip
code field
has a long-
awaited zip
code
picture.
Hooray!

9. **If you want to inflict Validity Checks on any other innocent fields, go back to Step 3 and repeat the process. Otherwise, click Save to make all this stuff permanent.**

Don't panic when the Restructure Warning dialog box appears. Paradox wants to know if it should apply the pictures and other limitations you just created on data that's already in the table. Unless you have darn good reason, leave the settings as they are and click OK. Any records that don't pass your Validity Checks land in the special KEYVIOL table (which automatically shows up on-screen).

If you get slapped with a KEYVIOL table, flip over to Chapter 11 and check out the sidebar "Dealing with a ticket from the Data Cops."

# Fields that Really Sing

Intelligent fields aren't *nearly* as entertaining as fields that put on a show. This last section introduces a final hidden feature of Paradox for Windows: fields that change font and/or color depending on the data they contain.

Look at Figure 10-5. Quick — how many customers have credit limits above $20,000? Time's up. It wasn't easy to tell at a glance, was it?

Now try the same thing with Figure 10-6. Quite a contrast, isn't it?

The difference is *Data Dependent Properties*. Each field in a table has two properties, font and color, that can change depending on the field's value. In Figure 10-6, I told Paradox to change the background color to black, text color to white, and make the font bold in any field with a Credit limit greater than $20,000. *Poof!* The rest, as they say, is history. Here are some tips to keep in mind:

✔ Every field in your table, except Memo fields, has a Data Dependent Properties setting.

✔ Memo fields don't have Data Dependent Properties. Memo fields never get to do anything fun. (It's a conspiracy.)

✔ You can apply a data dependent rule to a single value ($21,682.53) or a range (greater than 10 and less than 20, greater than or equal to 5000).

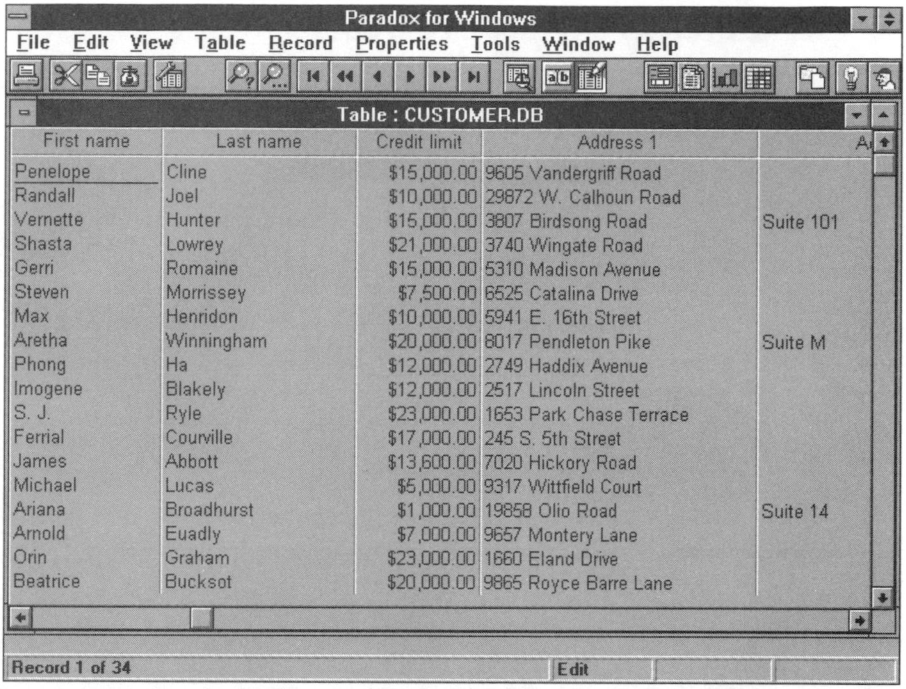

Paradox for Windows

File   Edit   View   Table   Record   Properties   Tools   Window   Help

Table : CUSTOMER.DB

| First name | Last name | Credit limit | Address 1 | A |
|---|---|---|---|---|
| Penelope | Cline | $15,000.00 | 9605 Vandergriff Road | |
| Randall | Joel | $10,000.00 | 29872 W. Calhoun Road | |
| Vernette | Hunter | $15,000.00 | 3807 Birdsong Road | Suite 101 |
| Shasta | Lowrey | $21,000.00 | 3740 Wingate Road | |
| Gerri | Romaine | $15,000.00 | 5310 Madison Avenue | |
| Steven | Morrissey | $7,500.00 | 6525 Catalina Drive | |
| Max | Henridon | $10,000.00 | 5941 E. 16th Street | |
| Aretha | Winningham | $20,000.00 | 8017 Pendleton Pike | Suite M |
| Phong | Ha | $12,000.00 | 2749 Haddix Avenue | |
| Imogene | Blakely | $12,000.00 | 2517 Lincoln Street | |
| S. J. | Ryle | $23,000.00 | 1653 Park Chase Terrace | |
| Ferrial | Courville | $17,000.00 | 245 S. 5th Street | |
| James | Abbott | $13,600.00 | 7020 Hickory Road | |
| Michael | Lucas | $5,000.00 | 9317 Wittfield Court | |
| Ariana | Broadhurst | $1,000.00 | 19858 Olio Road | Suite 14 |
| Arnold | Euadly | $7,000.00 | 9657 Montery Lane | |
| Orin | Graham | $23,000.00 | 1660 Eland Drive | |
| Beatrice | Bucksot | $20,000.00 | 9865 Royce Barre Lane | |

Record 1 of 34                     Edit

**Figure 10-5:**
A normal, boring table. You might get more entertainment value from a rock.

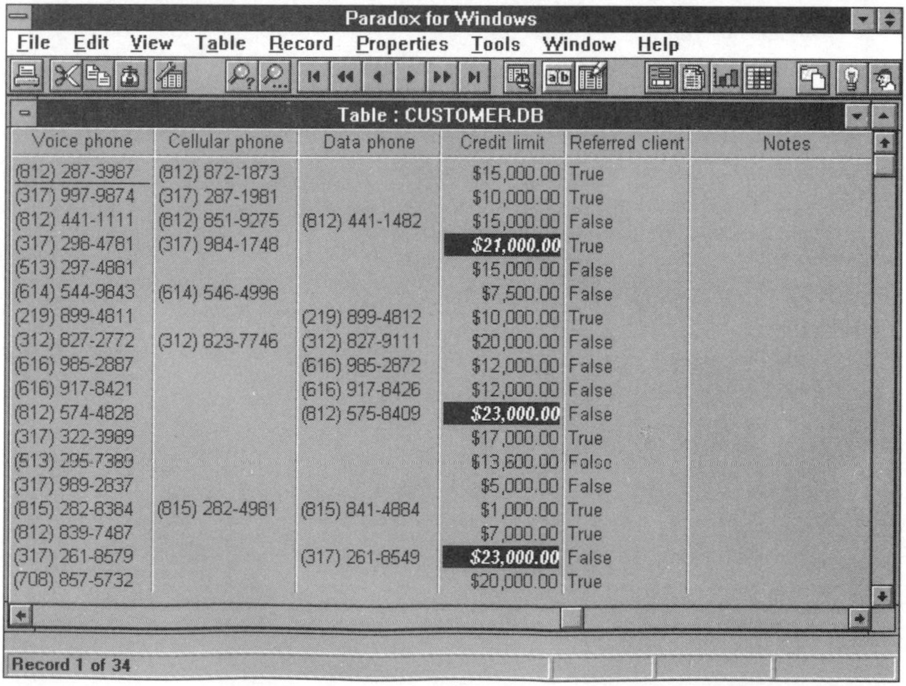

Paradox for Windows

File   Edit   View   Table   Record   Properties   Tools   Window   Help

Table : CUSTOMER.DB

| Voice phone | Cellular phone | Data phone | Credit limit | Referred client | Notes |
|---|---|---|---|---|---|
| (812) 287-3987 | (812) 872-1873 | | $15,000.00 | True | |
| (317) 997-9874 | (317) 287-1981 | | $10,000.00 | True | |
| (812) 441-1111 | (812) 851-9275 | (812) 441-1482 | $15,000.00 | False | |
| (317) 298-4781 | (317) 984-1748 | | *$21,000.00* | True | |
| (513) 297-4861 | | | $15,000.00 | False | |
| (614) 544-9843 | (614) 546-4998 | | $7,500.00 | False | |
| (219) 899-4811 | | (219) 899-4812 | $10,000.00 | True | |
| (312) 827-2772 | (312) 823-7746 | (312) 827-9111 | $20,000.00 | False | |
| (616) 985-2887 | | (616) 985-2872 | $12,000.00 | False | |
| (616) 917-8421 | | (616) 917-8426 | $12,000.00 | False | |
| (812) 574-4828 | | (812) 575-8409 | *$23,000.00* | False | |
| (317) 322-3989 | | | $17,000.00 | True | |
| (513) 295-7389 | | | $13,600.00 | False | |
| (317) 989-2837 | | | $5,000.00 | False | |
| (815) 282-8384 | (815) 282-4981 | (815) 841-4884 | $1,000.00 | True | |
| (812) 839-7487 | | | $7,000.00 | True | |
| (317) 261-8579 | | (317) 261-8549 | *$23,000.00* | False | |
| (708) 857-5732 | | | $20,000.00 | True | |

**Figure 10-6:**
Whoa — now that's what I call a table that talks!

Record 1 of 34

## *Setting the properties*

Compared to everything else in this chapter, setting the color and font properties is a piece of cake. Here's how to do it:

1. **Open the table you want to work with.**

   There are many ways to do this — more, in fact, than rational people really need. If you haven't settled on a personal favorite, flip back to the "Opening the Table (Again)" section in Chapter 7.

2. **Scroll across the table until you see tonight's target field.**

3. **When the field is in range, right-click it or just click the field and press Ctrl+M.**

   Whatever you do, one of those vaguely annoying menus that appear from nowhere promptly does its thing.

4. **Select Data Dependent from the menu, as shown in Figure 10-7.**

   The Data Dependent Properties dialog box takes over the screen.

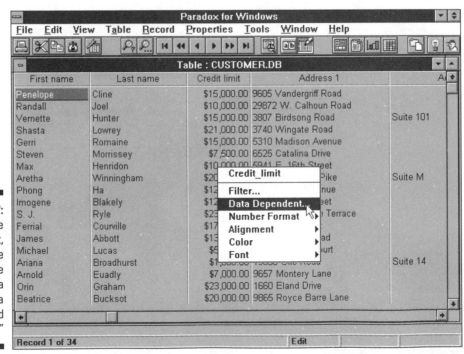

**Figure 10-7:** Getting here isn't a fight, but it sure sounds like one: "It's a right, then a left. And he's gone!"

5. **Click New Range to start the creative process.**

6. **Now it's time to define the range by putting entries in the Range Includes Values section.**

   For ranges using *equal to* (=), *greater than* (>), or *greater than or equal to* (>=), use the first three radio buttons and the upper text box. Click the radio button for the sign you want, and then double-click the **<blank>** entry in the upper box (next to the > radio button). Type in the value you want to test against.

   For ranges using *less than* (<) or *less than or equal to* (<=), use the lower two radio buttons and the text box next to them. Click the radio button for the appropriate sign, and then click in the text box and type your test value. Leave the **<blank>** value in the upper text box. It looks funny, but it's supposed to.

   To create compound ranges (such as **<=10 and >25**), fill in both entries.

   In the coming steps, keep your eye on the word Sample that's next to the Set Properties button. As you set the Data Dependent Properties, it changes to show you how the fields that match your range will look all decked out in their new finery.

7. **To change the field's color, click Set Properties, select Color from the menu that appears and then click the color you want from the pop-up color chart.**

   In Figure 10-8, I picked black because it stands out against the normal gray background.

   After I picked black as the background color, the Sample text became a huge black rectangle. If this happened to you too, don't panic yet. Paradox changed the color to black as you told it to. Since the text is *also* black, you can't see it right now. Continue with the next step and everything will be okay.

8. **To change the font typeface, size, style, or color, click Set Properties, select Font from the menu, and then click the option you want to change.**

   *Typeface* offers you all the different fonts Windows has to give. *Size* lets you change the size of the new font. *Style* covers bold, italic, strikeout, and underline. *Color* pulls up another color chart with your spectrum of choices.

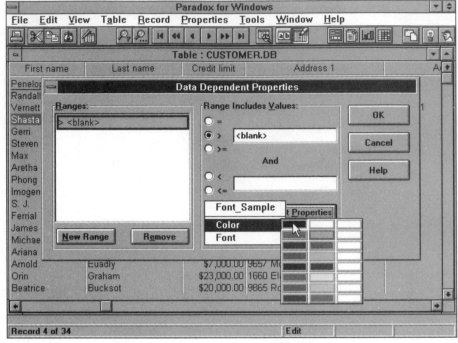

**Figure 10-8:**
It's not so
much a
color wheel
as a color
rectangle,
but it still
works.

- For the typeface, I suggest not changing it at all. If you *must* do something different, use Arial, Courier New, or Times New Roman.

- Leave the size setting alone as well. Paradox tables look a little strange with different size fonts in each record.

- Style is where I like to make my changes. Bold, italic, or both styles together really stand out in a table.

- Color is another favorite of mine. Choose a color that contrasts *very clearly* with your background color. White text on black, black text on yellow, and those same combinations reversed are very dependable choices.

9. **When all the properties are set and the range is ready, click Apply Changes to record all your work. Click OK to return to the table and see your labor in action.**

   Figure 10-9 shows the finished range ready for action. Notice that the description in the Ranges box shows both the range and the color and font settings. Pretty slick, eh?

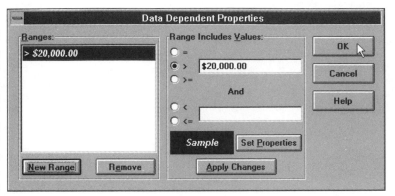

**Figure 10-9:**
The range is
set, the
properties
are in order
—one click
on OK and
this puppy is
done.

When you close the table, Paradox warns you that `The view properties for this table have changed`. It's talking about the work you just did. Click Yes to soothe its mind and make the dialog box go away.

You can set up several ranges for the same field, but they shouldn't overlap. To put a range on another field, right-click there and start the whole process over again.

## Removing Data Dependent Properties

Getting rid of the properties is easy — almost too easy to warrant its own numbered list:

1. **First, go through Steps 1 through 4 of "Setting the Properties" for the field whose properties you want to clear.**

2. **When the Data Dependent Properties dialog box appears, click the range you want to delete, and then click Remove.**

3. **Click OK to finish the process.**

   When you close the table, click Yes to tell Paradox it's okay that `The view properties for this table have changed`. You wouldn't *believe* how Paradox worries about stuff like this.

# Chapter 11

# The 10,000 Record Checkup: Looking under the Hood

- - - - - - - - - - - - - - - - - - - - - - - - - - - - - - - - - - - - - - - -

## In This Chapter

▶ Rummaging in the toolbox

▶ Taking the table in for a quick restructure

▶ Add and subtract: electronic parallel parking

▶ Changing the look and feel (fuzzy dice and all)

- - - - - - - - - - - - - - - - - - - - - - - - - - - - - - - - - - - - - - - -

*P*aradox tables are like high performance sports cars (you never noticed the resemblance?). When everything's just right, they're fun, fast, and pure pleasure to take out for a spin. But when you're not driving them, you always seem to be under the hood, trying to get everything just right so that it will be fun, fast, and pure pleasure the next time you take it for a spin.

Adding a field, copying a table, and salvaging records from the KEYVIOL table aren't particularly glamorous jobs, but they sure are necessary. That's what this chapter is all about: doing the stuff you have to do every now and then to make the stuff you do every day work like it's supposed to work. There you have it.

## *Rummaging in the Toolbox*

Paradox includes (at no extra charge) *five* different toolboxes for mucking around in your tables. One is under the Tools⇨Utilities menu (see Figure 11-1); the others pop-up when you right-click a table, report, form, or query in the Project Viewer (see Figure 11-2). That's way too many toolboxes to cover in one place, so this section handles the Utilities menu and the stuff in the table pop-up thingie inside the Project Viewer. The Project Viewer pop-up thingies for queries, reports, and forms are covered in Chapters 13, 19, and 25 respectively.

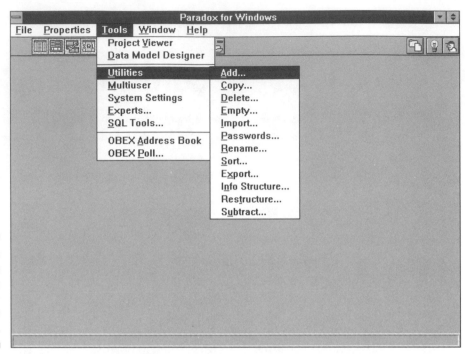

**Figure 11-1:**
Options
under the
Tools⇨
Utilities
menu.

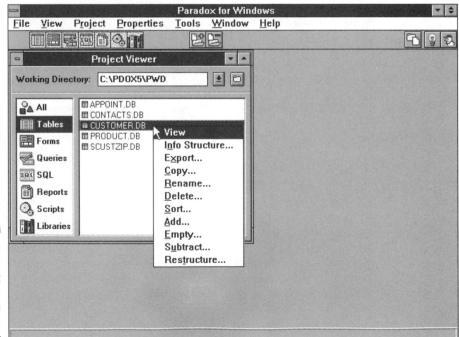

**Figure 11-2:**
Items in the
Project
Viewer pop-
up utilities
menu.

Lest you think Borland is giving you some incredibly great deal by including *billions* of utilities, most everything that's available in the main menu is *also* in the Project Viewer pop-up. The following listing shows what items live in which menu. Those few exceptions which are in just one place or the other are marked with an asterisk (but on-screen they look just like the others).

| *Tools⇨Utilities options* | *Project Viewer/Inspector options* |
|---|---|
| Add | View * |
| Copy | Info Structure |
| Delete | Export |
| Empty | Copy |
| Import * | Rename |
| Passwords * | Delete |
| Rename | Sort |
| Sort | Add |
| Export | Empty |
| Info Structure | Subtract |
| Restructure | Restructure |
| Subtract | |

In the interest of reducing your confusion about this whole thing, each utility has its own section (however brief) in the coming pages. Each section tells you briefly what the utility does, which menu it's on (if it's only in one place), and how to use it. Here are some things to keep in mind:

> ✔ If a utility is covered elsewhere in the book, you're referred there for help, and information — and because traveling is fun.

> ✔ In most cases, the instructions that follow explain how things work when you start from the *Project Viewer*. This is by far the easiest way to access the utilities — when Paradox tempts you with menus, just say "Inspector."

- Utilities started with the Tools⇨Utilities menu work the same way as their Project Manager brethren, but they always ask what table you want to work with. Because you have to right-click a table just to get the menu open in the Project Viewer, the utilities there already know which table you're imperiling. The menu options, on the other hand, either ask or guess which table to use (and I'm sure you'd rather Paradox ask for some guidance than try to discern any truth on its own).

- Paradox always asks for guidance; it would never think of guessing. It can't even guess its way out of a cardboard box (which is why you never see any copies of Paradox running loose in the local computer store).

## Add

This command takes the records from one table and inserts them into another table. You choose whether they're new records or updates of existing records.

Add is extensively covered in the section, "Add and Subtract: Electronic Parallel Parking," later in this chapter.

## Copy

This command makes a copy of a table and all the related files. In Paradox, one table may have an entourage of seven or eight files accompanying it.

Please, *oh please,* don't try to copy your Paradox tables with the Windows File Manager or (horrors!) from DOS. Take the extra minute or two and do it through Paradox. Otherwise, your copies may be more like a digital Dr. Jekyl than a hard working, industrious Mr. Hyde.

1. **In the Project Viewer, right-click the table you want to copy and then select Copy from the instant menu.**

2. **Type a name for the new table.**

   Although Paradox displays the name of the table you're copying, it's highlighted. As soon as you start typing, it disappears.

3. **If you want to put the copy somewhere other than the Working Directory, explain that to Paradox with some quick clicking in the Directories and Drive (or Alias) box.**

4. **Click OK when the new creature has both a name and a place to call home.**

# Delete

Ah, a self-explanatory utility if ever there was one. This sends your table to the Great Directory in the Sky. Delete trashes the table's whole retinue so that you don't have any more lost, useless files on your hard disk than Microsoft originally intended. You can't delete a table, it's open or otherwise in use. (If it's attached to a report, form, or query it's doing something.)

1. **In the Project Viewer, right-click the doomed table and select Delete from the pop-up menu.**

2. **Click Yes in the nearly hysterical dialog box that immediately appears.**

   That's it. The status line presents a brief obituary to let you know the process was a success.

# Empty

This is the little sister of Delete. Instead of completely annihilating the table, Empty just throws all the data out, leaving the structure intact.

1. **Right click the table you're emptying and select Empty from the pop-up menu.**

2. **Click Yes in the dialog box.**

   As with Delete, the status line reaffirms that everything went (out) well.

# Export

When it's time to share your data with the less fortunate (people who don't use the latest version of Paradox for Windows), Export is your tool of choice. You can send your data into the world in nine different formats, depending on the needs of the moment. For all the fascinating details, see Chapter 12, "Imports, Exports, and the Balance of Trade."

# Import

As you probably guessed, Import is the opposite of Export. When the order of the day is giving hapless data a clean and safe home, you need Import. The import command is only available through Tools➪Utilities in the main menu. The whole importing process is explained and expounded upon in Chapter 12.

## Info Structure

Sometimes you just want to see what makes a table click. You don't want to use Restructure because you might horribly mutilate something (like the whole table), but you *still* need to look under the hood. That's where Info Structure fits into the world. It shows the *same* information in the *same* dialog box as Restructure, but you can't change anything — it's for display *only*. This utility creates *great* documentation. Check out Step 3 below to find out how.

1. **Starting at the Project Viewer, right-click the table you're getting curious about, and then select Info Structure from the annoying pop-up menu.**

   The Structure Information dialog box appears, heavily laden with otherwise secret information about the table.

2. **If you're just looking, look to your heart's content and click Done when you're through.**

3. **To create a table containing all the structure information, click Save As, type a file name, and then click OK. Click Done to close the Structure Information dialog box.**

## Passwords

This gives you access to some of the interesting security features of Paradox for Windows. It's only available on the Tools➪Utilities menu.

If you're concerned about security, get your local guru's help. Do *not* hack around with this menu option on your own.

## Rename

Rename gives the selected table a new name — and perhaps a new location. Like Copy, it remembers all those other files that support your table so that it can do the wonderful things it does.

1. **In the Project Viewer, right-click the table that needs a new identity. Select Rename from the pop-up menu.**

2. **Type in a new name for the table. If you want to move it as well, choose a new drive and directory. Once the dust settles, click OK to make the changes happen.**

To move a table from one place to another and keep the same name, choose a new directory instead of typing a new name and then click OK.

## *Restructure*

This wins the award for Most Functionality in a Single Command. Sometimes it seems like you can't turn around in your table without needing Restructure to do it. If you're adding fields, establishing a key, putting in Validity Checks, or doing any number of things like this, you're doing the Restructure thing.

This command is absolutely *everywhere* in the book. Start with the section later in this chapter called "Taking the Table in for a Quick Restructure," and then flip back to Chapter 10 for information about Validity Checks. Beyond that, look in the index — it's tells you absolutely everywhere Restructure is mentioned (and that's a lot of places).

## *Sort*

Sort is useful — in a now-and-then kind of way. You tell it what order you want to see a table's records in, and it organizes them that way.

As you probably expect, there's a lot more to it than that, so turn to Chapter 8 for the details on searching and sorting.

## *Subtract*

This removes records in one table from another table. The tables *must* have the same structure for this to work right.

Oh, and there's something else: you can only subtract records *from* a keyed table.

Subtract, like its counterpart Add, can be found later in this chapter in the section "Add and Subtract: Electronic Parallel Parking."

## *View*

Here's a very simple utility. View displays the selected table. You probably won't use this much. You can do the same thing by double-clicking the table name in the Project Viewer. Why bother with the menu?

To use the View command, make sure that you are working in the Project Viewer. Right-click the table you want to see and then select View from the instant menu. The table miraculously appears in the workspace.

# Taking the Table in for a Quick Restructure

The concept behind the Restructure command is simple: sometimes (often?), you need to change the way a table is built. Restructure is one-stop shopping for all this and more.

Power always carries danger, and in Restructure the danger factor is high. You can woefully screw up an innocent table in no time at all. If you're in the Restructure dialog box and make a mistake, click Cancel *immediately.* Once you're out, go back into Restructure and try the process again. *There is no undo key when it comes to restructuring a table* — Cancel is as close as it comes. Once damage is done, it's done.

## Starting Restructure

It's easiest to restructure a table if you start from either the Project Viewer or the table view.

 ✔ *In the Project Viewer,* right-click the table name. Select Restructure from the pop-up menu.

 ✔ *If you're already looking at the table,* click the Restructure button on the ToolBar. If you want to do it the long-winded way, select TableÍRestructure Table from the main menu.

Whatever method you choose, the Restructure table dialog box appears.

## Doing various and sundry things

*To add a field in the middle of your table,* click where you want to put the field, and then press Insert. *Poof!* A blank line appears, ready and waiting for your new field. Fill in the Field Name, Type, Size, and Key information.

*If your problem is a field you don't need,* click the field name and press Ctrl+Del. It's outta there.

*Moving a field* is a cinch, too. Press and hold the mouse button on the *field number* (the first column on the left of the Field Roster area). When dark bars appear around the field (as in Figure 11-3), keep that mouse button down and move the mouse pointer to the field's new location. When you arrive, release the mouse button. The field instantly settles in.

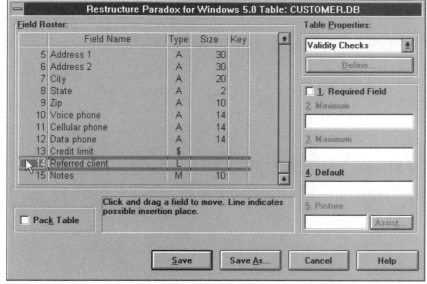

**Figure 11-3:**
The
Referred
Client field is
on the
move.

*If the Guru told you to pack the table,* click the Pack Table checkbox in the bottom left corner of the Restructure dialog box.

*When you're done,* click Save to make your changes permanent or Cancel to make them go away like a bad dream. Save As is somewhere in the middle, because it makes a new table with all the current settings and leaves the old one alone.

*When the clock says 5:00pm,* exit Paradox gracefully, close Windows, log off the network (if you don't have one, be thankful), and hit the trail. Tell your boss I said it was okay.

Here is some more helpful information:

✔ All those interesting boxes on the right side of the screen (Required Field, Minimum, and those others) are covered back in Chapter 10. Check them out — they do some really useful things.

✔ Remember the Save <u>A</u>s and Cancel buttons at the bottom of the screen. Of the two, Cancel is the more useful. At the first inkling of serious trouble, hit the Big C and get out of there while you still have data. If you think trouble is lurking but don't want to throw away all your hard work, use the Save <u>A</u>s button. It lets you save your changes in a new table, leaving the original table completely intact and untouched by your efforts.

What does *pack a table* mean, anyway? It's a basic maintenance step (which is why it's in this chapter) that squeezes extra space out of a table. Tables get flabby after a few hundred records come and go. Packing puts some tone in their electronic muscles by making sure the table is taking up only as much space on the disk as it should. Don't worry if nobody ever mentions this to you again.

# Add and Subtract: Electronic Parallel Parking

Although on the surface they're only common household utilities, Add and Subtract are important and powerful enough to warrant some special treatment. This section looks into using Add and Subtract and exposes some common pitfalls (which you can then avoid).

✔ The table with the records to add is called the *source table*. The table that's receiving the records is the *target table*.

✔ To work with Add, the tables need to have *identical structures*. They must have the same fields of the same Types in the same order for everything to work right.

✔ I didn't really lie in the previous bullet point, but I did kinda *simplify* the truth a bit. Tables don't have to be *identical* to work with Add, but they do have to be *compatible*. There are a whole bunch of rules about what *compatible* means, so if you need to use two not-quite-identical-but-quite-a-lot-alike tables together, get a guru to help you figure out the intricacies.

✔ When you subtract records from a table, only the two tables' key fields need to be identical. The other fields don't matter at all.

## Using Add

When it's adding records to a nonkeyed table (a table that doesn't have a key field), Add merely appends new records to the end of the table. *Borrrring.* If you're adding data to a *keyed* table, however, Add can insert records that aren't already there, update matching records, or do both at the same time.

When you add records to a keyed table, sometimes records don't *fit*—for one reason or another, Paradox can't figure out a good key for the record. When this happens, Paradox consigns these misfit records to a temporary table called KEYVIOL (for *key violations*). The records in here aren't bad; they just don't have good keys. See the sidebar "Dealing with a ticket from the Data Cops" for help incorporating these wayward souls back into your tables.

If Paradox gives you a table called PROBLEM instead of KEYVIOL, get your guru *now*. Something potentially bad is happening to your table and you need some expert help *pronto* to set things straight.

Actually adding two tables together isn't very hard at all:

1. **First, figure out which tables you want to combine. Then decide which one you're adding records *from*.**

   The other table is automatically the one you're adding records *to*. (That's the beauty of either-or things: make half the decision and you make the *whole* decision.)

2. **Change to the correct Working Directory.**

   If both tables are in the same directory, make that directory your Working Directory. Otherwise, change to the directory containing the table you're adding records *from* (the source table).

   For some tips about changing directories, see Chapter 3.

3. **Start the Add command.**

   *From the Project Viewer,* right-click the table you're adding records from. Select <u>A</u>dd from the pop-up menu to make the Add dialog box appear. The table name you right-clicked already appears in the <u>A</u>dd Records From box, so continue with Step 5.

   *Using the main menu,* select <u>T</u>ools➪<u>U</u>tilities➪<u>A</u>dd. The Add dialog box poofs into existence.

4. **If you started Add from the main menu, find the name of the table to add records *from* in the list on the left side of the dialog box. When you track it down, double-click it.**

   Paradox already did this step for those of you starting from the Project Viewer. Wasn't that sweet?

5. **Click in the T<u>o</u> box and then repeat Step 4 for the table you're adding records *to*.**

   You can change directories (if you need to) in the <u>D</u>irectories box and the D<u>r</u>ive (or Alias) pull-down list under it.

6. **If you're adding records to a keyed table, click the radio button describing how you want the records added (Append, Update, Append & Update).**

   The following options are available:

   - Append adds any records that don't already exist in the target table (the one that's receiving records).

   - Update replaces only records in the target table that have the same key as records in the source (the table that's providing records).

   - Append & Update appends new records and updates existing ones. This is the default setting.

   Paradox can only *append* records to an unkeyed table, regardless of which option you choose.

7. **To automatically see the table when the Add is done, click the View Modified Table checkbox.**

8. **You're done with the preliminaries, so click OK to make it happen.**

   Figure 11-4 shows a completed Add dialog box. It's set to Append new records from Old_Cust.DB onto Customer.DB and show the Customer table on-screen when its done.

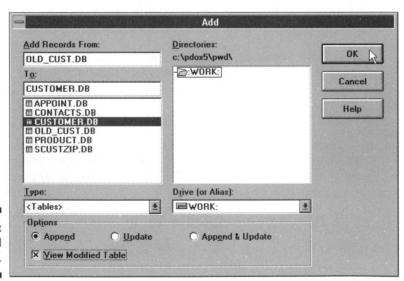

**Figure 11-4:** The Add dialog box.

## Dealing with a ticket from the Data Cops

Receiving a KEYVIOL table from Paradox is frustrating, mainly because it means that something went wrong with your Add command and you need to find out what happened before getting on with your work.

Fixing the records in the KEYVIOL table really isn't hard at all. All you have to do is find out why Paradox didn't like the value in the key field, edit the records in the KEYVIOL table to fix the problem, and then add the KEYVIOL table to the target table again.

There are two common things that cause key violations: a Blank key field and incorrect key values. If the key field is blank (not a good thing), type in a value. If there's already a value there, make sure that it's valid. If your target table has a Number type key field, you can't add records that have numbers *and* letters in their keys.

If there are records that Paradox for Windows *still* won't put into your table, throw up your hands in defeat and get some help. There's only so much you can do on your own.

## *Using Subtract*

Compared to Add, Subtract is short and sweet. It removes all the records from the target table with key fields that *exactly match* records in the source table.

✔ Subtract *only* works when the target table (the one you're subtracting records *from*) is keyed. If it doesn't have a key field, Subtract won't work.

✔ Only the key fields are important to the Subtract utility. As long as the key fields are identical in the source and target tables, everything works fine. None of the other fields have anything to do with the job — they're just along for the ride.

Here's how to subtract records in one table from another:

1. **Follow Steps 1 through 5 in the "Using Add" section — just substitute Subtract everywhere you see Add.**

   Almost everything about Add and Subtract is the same (except, hopefully, the results). The source table is the one with records to subtract; the target table is the one you're subtracting the records from.

2. **To automatically see the table once the Subtract is done, click in the View Modified Table checkbox.**

**3. Click OK when you're ready to do the deed.**

Figure 11-5 is a ready-to-go Subtract dialog box. It's removing records from Contacts.DB that match Old_Cust.DB. When it's done, the Contacts table will show up on the workspace.

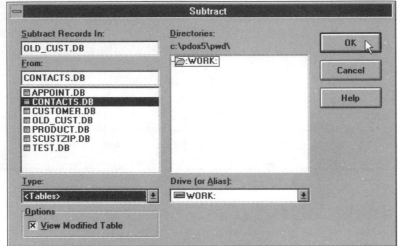

**Figure 11-5:**
The
Subtract
dialog box.

# Changing the Look and Feel (Fuzzy Dice and All)

Here are some quick and easy tricks to make your tables a little easier to interact with. Casually share these with your officemates and they'll think you're a Paradox Wizard (which may or may not be a good thing).

🖋 Everything in this section works when your table is in the workspace — when you're looking at the data and it's looking back.

🖋 None of these change the structure of the table. They only affect how it looks on-screen. Nothing in here can harm your data. It may look funny, but, like bad haircuts, such things are temporary.

🖋 You can also make changes to the grid (the lines between the fields), but I don't think it's that big a deal. If you want to try it, right-click any grid line and feel free to explore the menu options.

🖋 To save any of the changes in this section, close the table and click Yes in Paradox's *Golly, the View properties changed* dialog box, or select Properties⇨View Properties⇨Save from the main menu.

✔ To undo these changes after they're saved, open the table in the workspace and select Properties⇨View Properties⇨Delete. Click OK when Paradox asks whether you really want to delete the property file (that's where these changes are stored). The table is returned to its original pristine beauty.

## *Reorganizing the columns*

You can temporarily move whole columns of data when you're looking at a table. This is handy if you're analyzing a couple of fields that happen to be on opposite ends of your table.

1. **Move your mouse pointer up to the field name and hold down the mouse button.**

   If dark bars appear on either side of the column, that's a good sign. If your cat is floating around the house three feet off the ground, that's a bad sign.

2. **Keep the button down and move the mouse to the right or left — whichever way you want to take the column.**

   A dark bar goes with you — that's where the column will land when you let go of the mouse button.

3. **When you're *there* (wherever that is), release the button.**

   The column settles into its new home.

   You also can do this trick manually by pressing Ctrl+R. Move the cursor to the place you want the column to *end up,* and then press Ctrl+R until the column is there.

   This isn't a permanent change — you're just looking at the table in a different way.

## *Changing column widths*

Sometimes, you need to squeeze a little more stuff onto the screen. By adjusting how wide the columns look, you can do wonders with on-screen real estate.

1. **To the right of each field name, there's a line (the *grid*) that separates the fields. Put your mouse pointer on the right grid line next to the field name.**

   The mouse pointer becomes a horizontal, double-headed arrow when you succeed.

   You always adjust from the right side of the field. If you grab the left grid line, you're adjusting the field to the left.

2. **Press and hold the mouse button.**

   The whole grid line turns dark gray.

3. **While holding down the mouse button, move the mouse left to make the field look smaller or right to expand it. When it's the right size, release the mouse button.**

   If you change the width of a field and some of the data changes into asterisks, it's not a problem — it just means the field isn't big enough to show the data any more. When you regain consciousness, make the field wider and the asterisks go away.

## Setting the font

Paradox's default font is okay, but maybe it's just not *you*. If there's a font that reflects more of your style, grace, charm, or that's just easier to read, you can use it pretty easily.

1. **Right-click the field that's getting the new font.**

2. **Select Font from the pop-up menu.**

3. **From the submenu, set the typeface, size, style, and color of your dreams.**

If you're making several changes, click in the round button at the top of the submenu. That brings up a Font dialog box which lets you pick your typeface, size, and style without constantly going back and forth through the menus. When you're through, click the round button in the upper right corner of the dialog box to make it go away.

## Aligning everything just so

You can make the data line up to the right, to the left, or perfectly centered in every field with this handy tool.

1. **Right-click the out-of-alignment field.**

2. **Select Alignment from the popup menu.**

3. **Select either Left, Center, or Right from the submenu.**

   There are also options for Top, Center, and Bottom, but you can safely ignore them for now.

# Chapter 12
# Imports, Exports, and the Balance of Trade

• • • • • • • • • • • • • • • • • • • • • • • • • • • • • • • • • • • • • • • • • • •

## In This Chapter

▶ What it all means

▶ Import: reading new, exotic files (and understanding them)

▶ Export: sharing your stuff with the outside world

• • • • • • • • • • • • • • • • • • • • • • • • • • • • • • • • • • • • • • • • • • •

*S*haring data is practically a national pastime these days. Unfortunately, the data rarely seems to be in the right format for whatever grinder you want to run it through. *Sigh*. Oh, the frustrations of life with technology. (Remember: in the future you'll look back and call these the "good old days.")

Paradox for Windows addresses this format problem in a very 90's way: It's fluent in 8 different data languages. You supply the data, it makes heads *and* tails of it — pretty cool. This chapter explores the woolly world of sharing data. It covers getting data from those wretched souls who don't use Paradox for Windows and sending your stuff on excursions into the wild unknown. Until recently, this was strictly technoid material, but Paradox makes it easy.

## What It All Means

All this import and export stuff boils down to one thing: Paradox has this handy capability to read and write files that belong to other programs. Instead of retyping the stuff from your spreadsheet, Finance's off-brand database, or some far off mainframe computer, you can feed it directly to Paradox for Windows and let your software do the work.

The newest version of Paradox reads and writes eight different file formats. The following list provides a brief explanation of where each format hails from.

| | |
|---|---|
| Delimited Text | The most basic way to export data. Almost *everything* can read and write this. |
| Fixed Length Text | An oldie but goodie, this is mainly for salvaging data from aging mainframe computers. |
| Quattro Pro for Windows | This is a competitor of Lotus 1-2-3 and Excel (and it's a relative of Paradox). |
| Quattro Pro for DOS | The DOS version of this popular spreadsheet program. |
| Quattro | The antique relative of Quattro Pro. |
| Lotus 2.x | The Lotus 2.x format is the second most common format behind Delimited Text. (I think even an abacus can read Lotus files.) |
| Lotus 1.A | This is the *really* old Lotus file format, but there are still a few programs around that use it. |
| Excel 3.0/4.0 | In the Windows environment, reading and writing Excel is an absolute must — it's *that* popular. |

Paradox for Windows 5 can read and write in Paradox 4's file format. If you're sharing data with people using Paradox 4.x for DOS or Windows, it's good to know this format is available. (It's called *backward compatibility.*)

## Delimited text: the universal format

As frustrating as it is sometimes, Delimited Text is about as close to a universal data format as it gets these days. If it's software and it can export data, it probably supports Delimited Text, although the software may not *call* it by that name.

The most common names for this format are either *Comma Quote Delimited* or just *Comma Delimited.* If you look at how a Delimited file is put together (ooh — sounds like Data Biology 101), you discover that the fields are separated by commas. That explains the first part of the name, but what about this *quote* stuff? That part's because text (what Paradox puts in Alpha type fields) has quote marks around it.

# *Reading New, Exotic Files (and Understanding Them)*

Importing something to Paradox isn't bad at all—particularly when you consider the magnitude of what you're doing. Luckily, Borland pays people to consider such things, so you don't even need to think about that. Just focus your energy streams on how easy and simple the process is as you actually import some stuff during the following steps.

Figure 12-1 shows an Excel file that's ready for importing. Notice that the column names are in the first row of the spreadsheet. That's important to Paradox (and it's good spreadsheet formatting). By default, Paradox assumes that the column names are in the first row. If your column names aren't there, it's not a disaster, but I recommend that you get face-to-face help from your local guru instead of trying to import it on your own.

| | Microsoft Excel | | | | | | |
|---|---|---|---|---|---|---|---|
| File | Edit | Formula | Format | Data | Options | Macro | Window | Help |

A1     Product

**PRODUCTS.XLS**

| | A | B | C | D | E | F | G |
|---|---|---|---|---|---|---|---|
| 1 | Product | SKU | Cost | List | | | |
| 2 | Body Armor | 247887 | 300.00 | $400.00 | | | |
| 3 | Defense Spray (large) | 479119 | 20.00 | $35.00 | | | |
| 4 | Defense Spray (medium) | 479117 | 8.00 | $17.00 | | | |
| 5 | Defense Spray (small) | 479115 | 5.00 | $10.00 | | | |
| 6 | Flares (3/pkg) | 492765 | 3.00 | $12.00 | | | |
| 7 | Flares (case of 24) | 492767 | 20.00 | $30.00 | | | |
| 8 | Handcuffs, Plastic (100/pkg) | 199885 | 40.00 | $60.00 | | | |
| 9 | Handcuffs, Stainless | 199847 | 27.00 | $40.00 | | | |
| 10 | Nightstick | 88794 | 30.00 | $55.00 | | | |
| 11 | Nightstick, Collapsable | 88795 | 40.00 | $68.00 | | | |
| 12 | Nightstick, Enhanced | 88800 | 47.00 | $75.00 | | | |
| 13 | Plastic Tape (1000'/roll) | 492512 | 30.00 | $60.00 | | | |
| 14 | Plastic Tape (500'/roll) | 492511 | 20.00 | $40.00 | | | |
| 15 | Portable Fencing (1 foot) | 287394 | 1.20 | $1.95 | | | |
| 16 | Riot Helmet | 479288 | 410.00 | $550.00 | | | |
| 17 | Riot Shield | 479287 | 220.00 | $310.00 | | | |
| 18 | Security Shoulder Patch | 380297 | 0.95 | $2.50 | | | |

**Figure 12-1:** A Microsoft Excel spreadsheet as seen in its native habitat.

Ready                 NUM

1. **Before you begin, you need the name of the file you're importing, what kind of file it is, and the complete DOS path to its door.**

   Knowing this stuff up front saves you a considerable amount of frustration starting about two steps from now.

   The *complete DOS path* probably looks something like C:\FINANCE\STUFF\MORESTUFF. If you're on a network, the path may be even longer. (I'm sorry, but there's nothing I can do.)

   To *really* simplify your life, change the Working Directory before you go any further. Use the marvelously fascinating DOS path where the file of interest lives. Now, when you get to Step 4, the file you're importing will be sitting there nice and pretty, waiting for your call.

   If you're importing a spreadsheet that's not set up like Figure 12-1, you also need to know the addresses of the upper left and lower right corners of your stuff. Paradox needs this information much later so that it knows where to find the data you're interested in.

2. **Select Tools⇨Utilities⇨Import from the main menu.**

   The File Import dialog box pops to attention. By default, Paradox shows you available files in the Working Directory.

3. **Click the down arrow next to the File Type box to see a list of importable file types. Select the appropriate type from the list.**

   Figure 12-2 shows the mouse pointer in the midst of this very important process.

   - If you're not sure what file type you're dealing with, use this rule of thumb. If it's from a spreadsheet, try *Lotus 2.x* or *Lotus 1.A*. If it's from a *big* computer (the ones in the climate-controlled rooms with white robed technicians in constant attendance), try *Delimited Text*.

   - If you're importing from a database program and the file's name ends in DBF, don't use Import. Instead, try opening the file with the Project Viewer. The DBF extension means the file may be in dBASE format, which Paradox can read and write *without* formally importing the data.

   - Get help from the guru if all your attempts fail. At least you tried.

   The rest of the process depends on this step. If you pick the wrong file type, Paradox won't list your file (there are different extensions for each file type — .WK1, .WKS, .XLS for example).

4. **If your file isn't listed in the File Name area, you may need to change directories. Use the Drive (or Alias) and Directories controls to wind your way toward the obnoxious DOS path you wrote down in Step 1.**

- If the path is right but you're *still* not seeing the files, double-check the File <u>T</u>ype to be sure that Paradox is looking for what you think it's looking for. As a last resort, haul out that bag of munchies and call in your guru.     Don't you wish you'd changed the Working Directory back in Step 1?

If you're importing a lot of files, go ahead and create an alias for this directory. Next time, you won't have to slog through all the *drive this* and *directory that* stuff again. See Chapter 3 for help establishing a useful alias.

**Figure 12-2:**
Picking the
right file
type is more
important
than
brushing
after every
meal.

```
┌─────────────────────────────────────────────────────────────┐
│ ─                         File Import                         │
├─────────────────────────────────────────────────────────────┤
│ File Name:                  Directories:                      │
│ *.txt                       c:\pdox5\pwd\        ┌──────────┐ │
│                             ┌─☐:PWD:             │    OK    │ │
│                                                  └──────────┘ │
│                                                  ┌──────────┐ │
│                                                  │  Cancel  │ │
│                                                  └──────────┘ │
│                                                  ┌──────────┐ │
│                                                  │ Aliases..│ │
│                                                  └──────────┘ │
│                                                  ┌──────────┐ │
│ <Delimited Text>                                 │   Help   │ │
│ <Fixed Length Text>                              └──────────┘ │
│ <Quattro Pro Win>                                            │
│ <Quattro Pro DOS>                                           │
│ <Quattro>                                                   │
│ <Lotus 2.x>                                                 │
│ <Lotus 1.A>                                                 │
│ <Excel 3.0/4.0>            Drive (or Alias):                │
│ <Delimited Text>      ▼    ☐ PWD:              ▼             │
└─────────────────────────────────────────────────────────────┘
```

5. **In the <u>F</u>ile Name area, double-click the name of the file you want to import.**

   Don't panic when the File Import dialog box is abruptly replaced by a special import dialog box geared specifically toward whatever type of file you're importing. Figures 12-3 and 12-4 show the two most common dialog boxes: spreadsheets and Delimited Text files.

6. **To put the new Paradox table somewhere *other* than the current directory, use the alias (or the DOS path) and correct the information in the <u>N</u>ew Table Name box.**

   You can change the name of the new table by just typing a new name into the <u>N</u>ew Table Name box. That's a lot easier than using the Rename utility!

7. **Click OK to finish the import process and create the new table.**

   That's it — the import process is complete. If everything worked like it should, the status bar displays the happy message Import completed successfully.

Depending on where the data came from, you may need to make some manual adjustments to the field types Paradox selected for your data. View the table and restructure it if some fields need your loving touch.

If you're importing a spreadsheet and need to adjust the From Cell and To Cell addresses, do that before clicking OK (otherwise, it's a moot point). If something else happens (like a PROBLEM table appears), something didn't work quite right. Get some guru-type help before touching anything.

If a table already exists with the filename and DOS path you chose in Step 6, Paradox warns you of this horrible indiscretion. Further, it asks for your permission to blow away the existing table and replace it with your newly created masterpiece. If this whole thing is a surprise to you, click Cancel. If you anticipated it, click OK.

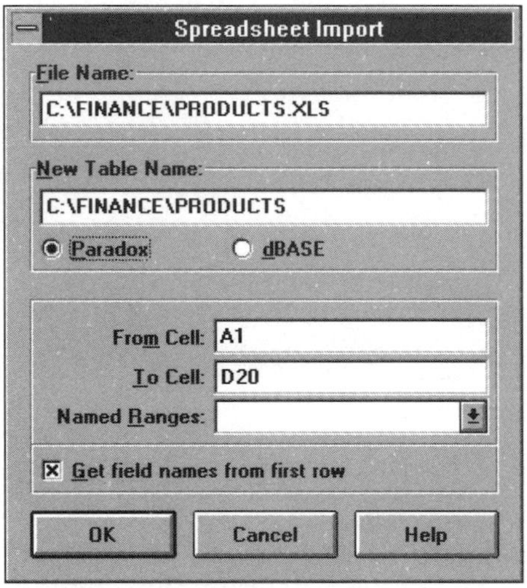

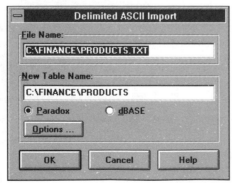

**Figure 12-3:** The Spreadsheet Import dialog box.

**Figure 12-4:** The Delimited ASCII (also known as Comma Delimited) Import dialog box.

# *Sharing Your Stuff with the Outside World*

Exporting files is a whole lot easier than importing them. And because Paradox is in control of the process and knows all about the data, there aren't too many things that can go wrong.

Not that I'm superstitious or anything, but please get out your *Paradox For Windows User's Guide* and knock on it three times with your left hand. Think of it as a good luck thing.

Although the process itself is simpler than importing, strange things can still happen. Memo fields are sometimes a problem because they're handled differently in other file formats. Don't be surprised if the field names in the exported file aren't *exactly* the same as your originals. dBASE, for example, has vastly different field naming rules than Paradox.

Before you begin, make sure that you know which file format to use for the Export. If you choose the wrong format, the other program won't understand the file you're making for it.

If you're really worried or wondering why you got into this at all, leap into the steps below before another questioning thought strikes. *Drink while the teapot is hot,* as my wife says so often.

1. **In the Project Viewer, right-click the file you're exporting. Select E**x**port from the pop-up menu.**

   This, as you might expect, starts the Table Export dialog box.

2. **Click in the down arrow next to the** E**xport File Type box. Select the appropriate file type from the drop down menu.**

   If you're making a Delimited Text file, skip this step. In Paradox for Windows, that's the default setting.

3. **Double-click the highlighted table name.**

   When you double-click, a new dialog pops onto the scene. Figure 12-5 shows the dialog box for a Delimited Text export. Figure 12-6 is the same dialog box when you're exporting to a Quattro Pro for Windows file.

   Some of the dialog boxes have an O**p**tions button. It leads to more advanced options. You *might* need to use this when you're exporting to a Delimited Text file (but even then, it's a long shot). Before piddling around with anything in this box, get some expert help.

4. **If you want to change the name of the exported table, do that in the New File Name box.**

5. **Click OK when you're collectively through.**

   You're through and the export is a done deal, at least if that's what Paradox says in the Status Bar.

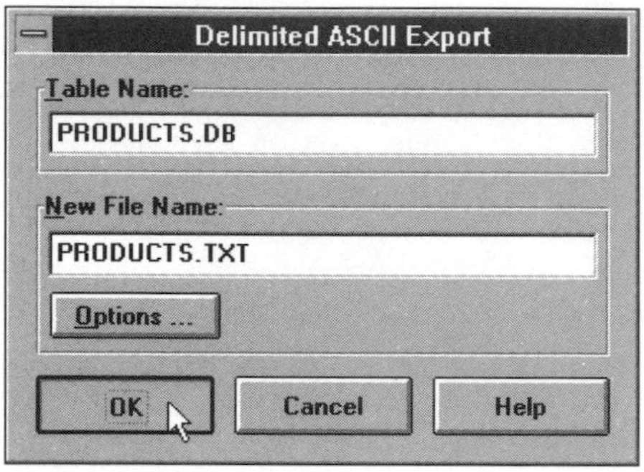

**Figure 12-5:**
The inap-
propriately-
named
Delimited
Text export
dialog box.

**Figure 12-6:**
The
Spreadsheet
Export
dialog box
isn't much
different
than ol'
what's-his'-
box shown
in Figure
12-5.

# Part III

## A Good Question Is
## Half the Answer

The 5th Wave     By Rich Tennant

"HEY DAD, IS IT ALRIGHT IF I WINDOW YOUR COMPUTER?"

# In This Part...

*Girls: But, who are you, sir? Speak!*
*Frederic: I am a pirate!*
*Girls: A pirate! Horrors!*

Act I, Gilbert and Sullivan's *The Pirates of Penzance*

Stuffing your amassed collection of data into a bunch of tables is nice, but unless you can ask good questions, it's pretty useless. One of Paradox's strongest features is Query By Example (QBE). This part dissects queries from stem to stern. It's a long trip, but the trouble's worth it in the end.

# Chapter 13
# The Quest Begins

*T*his is it — your big chance to be an electronic Sherlock Holmes. Find that clue, discover a link, and dodge those poison darts (you *did* dodge, didn't you?) on your way to fame, fortune, and (most importantly) the answer your boss wants by 5:00 p.m.

Queries are probably the most powerful and flexible tools in Paradox. And sometimes they're an infinitely frustrating tool, particularly at first. This chapter uncovers the basic mysteries of the query process. It explains what queries do and how *you* can do it without getting eaten alive in the process. It introduces wildcards that let you ask half a question and get lots of answers back. Overall, it gets you going with queries.

(It *doesn't* take you out for a malted after you're through, so don't get your hopes up.)

## What Queries Are All About

Queries are the Big Kahuna Tools of Paradox. They answer questions, edit tables, and generally make your data sit up and bark like a chicken (which is no small trick).

Because it would be way too simple to have only one name for something this useful, queries are also called Relational Queries, Query by Example, Relational Query by Example, and RQBE.

My favorite name is *Query by Example* because that's the essence of how the process works. You start out with a table (or two) and explain to Paradox what you want to know. The electronic witch doctors swing a few old computer manuals over their heads and mystically divine a response your question. That last phrase deserves a replay: queries respond to what you *ask* regardless of what you really *want*.

Paradox for Windows *still* isn't psychic (although I've repeatedly asked the programmers for this feature); it only does what you *tell* it. This is the most important thing to remember about queries: If you don't ask the right question, you don't get the right answer.

# Asking a Simple Question

These days, even simple questions aren't *that* simple. A simple query really has two parts: the question you're asking and the fields you want to see in the answer.

You ask Paradox to find certain records in the table by typing in examples of what it should look for (that's why they call it Query by *Example*). If you want to see all the customers in Indiana, type **IN** in the State field. To see everyone in the 46226 zip code, type **46226** in the Zip field.

Telling Paradox which fields you want in your answer is easy. In the query, click in the little white box under each field you're interested in. When you do that, a green checkmark appears in the box. Paradox is telling you that particular field will be in your *Answer* table — that's where Paradox temporarily puts what it discovers during a query. If there's no checkmark for a field, it won't be in the Answer table.

- When you're typing a number, include only a decimal point and negative sign (dash), if necessary. *Don't* put in commas, currency signs, or parentheses.

- Chapter 16 describes *Example Elements,* which are more advanced example values. Don't confuse an example value that you type (such as 46226) with an Example Element — they're very different things.

- You aren't just limited to looking for a single value (like people inside one five digit zip code). See the section called "Wildcards" later in this chapter to learn more about wildcards and what amazing things they can do for you.

- Paradox automatically sorts the Answer table in alphabetical order starting with the first field you checked (the one farthest to the left). It uses the other fields to break any ties it finds.

✔ If you want some serious electronic warm fuzzies about the whole Query thing, there's a Coach who can show you the ins and outs. It's called Creating a Query and you can find it in the Queries, Forms, and Reports section of the Coach menu.

The steps to doing a query in Paradox are painstakingly outlined for you below. Good luck and all that. Although this is an old refrain, I present it to again: make your life a little easier by changing the Working Directory before making your query. When it's time to pick a table, the one you want will be right there on the list.

1. **To start the query process, right-click the Open Query button on the ToolBar and select <u>N</u>ew from the pop-up menu, or select <u>F</u>ile⇨<u>N</u>ew⇨<u>Q</u>uery from the main menu.**

   Figure 13-1 shows how it's done from the ToolBar. If you're a menu person, I have faith you can do it without visual aids. The Select File dialog box appears.

**Figure 13-1:**
Here's the sneaky way to make a new query. It took me months to discover this.

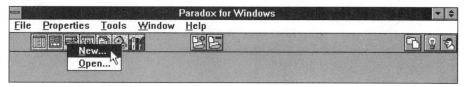

2. **In the <u>F</u>ile Name list, double-click the name of the table you want to query.**

   A blank query appears across the middle of the screen.

   Sit with your back straight and take a deep breath. Hold it for a couple seconds, and then let it out slowly. Doesn't that feel good?

3. **Fill in the example you want Paradox to find. Scroll through the query until you get to the proper field. Click in the space under the field name and type the example text.**

   In Figure 13-2, the State field has I N as an example. Only records from Indiana will appear in the Answer table.

Figure 13-2:
The first
example
value is in
place inside
the State
field.

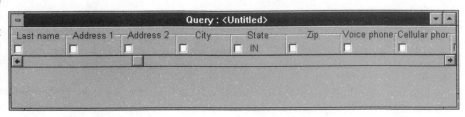

- The example text *must exactly match* what's in the field before Paradox puts the record into the Answer table. Example IN won't match values like In, in, or iN — only IN.

- If you want to match examples in two different fields, scroll over to the next field and type in the example. Paradox automatically knows to look for records that meet *both* criteria.

- You can include more than one example *in one field* by using OR. To find records in two states Indiana and Illinous, for example — use the example IN OR IL. OR tells Paradox to accept records that match either value in the eexample. Is this slick or what?

- That OR thing is a topic unto itself, but I wanted to sneak you a peek at it here. Look it up in Chapter 15 to get all the facts.

4. **You're almost done. Scroll through the query and click in the white box of each field you want in the Answer table.**

   - When you click, a green checkmark appears to confirm your request. If you check the wrong field, just click that field's box again and the checkmark goes away.

   - When you click, a pop-up menu appears with several different kinds of checks. Don't let it worry you. The other kinds of checkmarks are explained in Chapter 14, "Checking Up, Checking Down, and Sorting All Around"

   To quickly include *all* the fields, click in the black box way to the left side of the query (under the table name).

 5. **Start the query by clicking the lightning bolt button on the ToolBar or by pressing F8.**

   A bar chart appears briefly (or longer if it's a big query) to let you know how the query is doing. When it's done, the Answer table takes the stage.

   - Paradox puts the Answer table in your Private Directory. The alias for this area is :PRIV:.

   - There are several tricks you can play with Answer tables, like having Paradox sort the records into the order *you* want or automatically naming the table something *other* than Answer. Chapter 14 explains the sorting thing; Chapter 15 uncovers the Answer table's properties.

- To save your Answer table (if you're particularly fond of it), while you're viewing it on-screen, select Table⇨Rename. Type **:WORK:** and then the new name. Don't put any spaces between the Working Directory alias and the table name or Paradox complains bitterly. This process moves the Answer table from the Private Directory to the Working Directory and assigns it the new, useful name you chose.

- If the Answer table is blank (as in Figure 13-3), Paradox didn't find any records that matched your examples. Make sure that you typed the example correctly and that it's in the right field (an embarrassing mistake, but one I've made myself).

6. **If you like the query and want to use it again, select File⇨Save from the main menu. Type a name for the query in the cleverly titled New File Name box, and then click OK.**

   Your query is saved in the Working Directory. Paradox automatically tacks the extension QBE onto the file name. (I'll give you three guesses where they came up with *that* extension.)

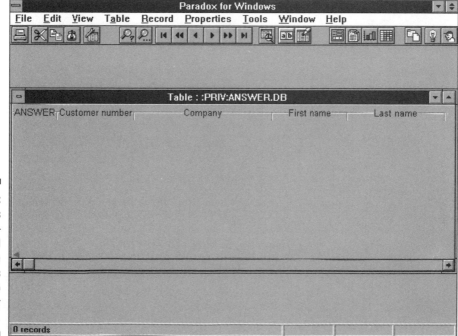

**Figure 13-3:**
The news isn't good — I'm afraid none of the records made it to the Answer table.

# *Wildcards*

Using precise examples is great, but sometimes you need to ask a less specific question. *Wildcards* give you a simple way to do this.

Thanks to wildcards, you can find all the zip codes starting with 462, company names ending in Inc., or anything in between. They're flexible, powerful, and (best of all) there are only two of them: .. and @.

To indicate "any quantity of any character, or nothing at all" use the .. wildcard. The example **Jo..** finds *Jon, Johnson, JoBeth's Fishing Supplies, Job 9482,* and just plain *Jo.* You can put the wildcard anywhere in your example, although it often goes at the end.

To indicate "any single character," use the @ wildcard. This wildcard is handy for narrow searches. **J@n** matches *Jon* and *Jan* but not *Jo* (because it doesn't end with *n*). **199@** matches any year in the 1990s. It matches **199** too, because when the @ comes at the end of the example, it means "any single character or nothing at all." You can also stack a whole bunch of @'s together and look for a specific number of characters, such as **J@@n** for *John, Joan,* or *Jenn.*

You can even combine the wildcards in the same example for some really fancy searching. **J@n..** finds *Jon, Janus Moving and Storage, Jane,* and *Jenny's Crafts.*

Table 13-1 shows you some wildcards in action. To use them in your queries, type a wildcard example instead of a specific example in Step 3 of the section "Asking a Simple Question."

| Table 13-1 | Wildcards in Action |
| --- | --- |
| *Wildcard* | *Matches* |
| Pe.. | Pete, Peterson, Pedro's, Penny, Pen and Ink |
| ..y | Andy, Jenny, Central Refinery, Harlington Haberdashery |
| Pe..y | Penny, Pearl of the Sea Livery, Penzo Arany |
| ..Company.. | Company Woman, The Balloon Company, Blasto Company Inc. |
| J@n | Jon, Jan, Jen |
| Mar@@ | Marie, Marge, March |
| R@@k..y | Rockland Company, Rook's Cabinetry, Rocky Andriony |

# *Using the Query Again*

Your query works and it's saved, but how do you ever find and run it again? There are a couple different ways depending on your preference.

If you're heavily into the Project Viewer, click the Queries option to list all the query files in the Working Directory. Open your query (to look at it or make changes) by right-clicking its name in the list; run the query (and create an Answer table) by double-clicking or selecting Project⇨Open Current Item from the menu.

For the ToolBar people, open your query by clicking the Query button and then double-click the name of the query in the File Name list.

## There are query utilities, too

The Project Viewer has a button to list your queries by name and a cool pop-up menu with five clever utilities for annoying them. By right-clicking a query file in the Project Viewer, you can quickly access each of these options:

**Run**  Run the query you clicked on. This is the same as opening the query and then clicking the lightning bolt.

**Open**  Put the query itself up on-screen so that you can marvel at it or change it as you will.

**Copy**  Make a copy of the clicked-on query.

**Rename**  Change the query file's name or move the file to a new location on your disk.

**Delete**  Completely remove the query file from your disk drive. *Zoop!* Gone for good.

# Chapter 14

# Checking Up, Checking Down, and Sorting All Around

**W**ell, Sherlock, your first queries ran swell, but now the Boss wants more and she wants it sorted *her* way. The Check can't help you this time — what you need is a Super Check.

As luck would have it, Paradox has some of those Super Checks to get you out of this bind. Of course, Borland would probably call them SuperChecks because they're trying to conserve spaces, but that's a different issue. This chapter covers the basic Check, CheckDescending, and CheckPlus. The Chapter also details the Answer Sort option (which *I* think should be Sort Answer, but nobody ever *asks* me), which gives you control over how the Answer table is sorted. It's good stuff (and it makes you shine for the Boss, too).

Paradox *still* doesn't have CheckIn and CheckOut (for travelers), or MonthlyCheckUp (for Doctors), but I'm sure they're coming in a future version.

There's one check I didn't include in this chapter: the GroupBy Check. You only use it in SET queries (which are real techno-wizard stuff). If someone recommends a SET query to solve a particularly hairy problem, seek guidance, help, and assistance from your guru.

# A Quick Review of the Basic Check

☑ Here's what you (probably) already know about the basic Check in a Paradox query (hey — I said quick and I meant quick):

Default choice — Paradox automatically uses the plain, vanilla Check when you click a field to include it in the Answer table.

Unique values — The Answer table includes only *unique* records. If you ask for a list of cities and the table you're querying has Chicago listed three times, Chicago will appear only *once* in the Answer table. But if you check both City and Customer number, Paradox gives you a table with all the *unique combinations* of the two fields. If Customer 344 has locations in both Chicago and London, the Answer table has two entries for that customer — one for each city.

Ascending sort — Records in the Answer table are put in alphabetical (ascending) order by the first field from the left. If there are two identical values in that field, Paradox looks through the other fields until it can break the tie.

(*That's* what I call quick.)

# Go from Big to Small with CheckDescending

☑ CheckDescending is the *going-my-own-way* twin of the basic Check. It does exactly the same things that Check does (includes only unique values and sorts the Answer table), with one important exception: it sorts in *descending* order, not ascending.

Figure 14-1 shows two query results. The one on the left (Ascend) was made with basic Checks; the other (Descend) used a CheckDescending in the City field and a basic Check in State. The city names in Ascend are, in fact, sorted alphabetically. Likewise, in Descend, the CheckDescending did its job and put the city names in reverse alphabetical order.

Notice the highlighted entries in each table. The records that have identical city names (Columbus) are in order by State. Because the State field had a plain Check, Paradox used *ascending* order when it broke the tie between the two Columbus records. If both fields used CheckDescending, Columbus, Ohio, would be first in the list. Such is the way of life.

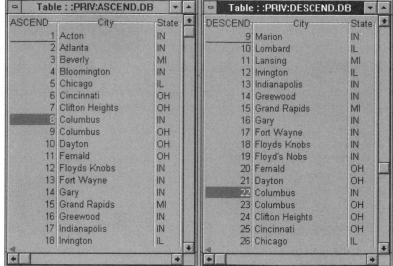

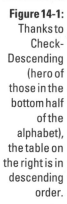

**Figure 14-1:**
Thanks to
Check-
Descending
(hero of
those in the
bottom half
of the
alphabet),
the table on
the right is in
descending
order.

✔ Like the simple Check, CheckDescending includes only unique records in its Answer table. Even if there were 1000 records with a particular value, CheckDescending only throws one into the Answer.

✔ The field with the CheckDescending is sorted in *descending* order.

✔ Paradox sorts the Answer table starting with the leftmost field and moving right as it needs tie breakers. If the field you put the CheckDescending in is way over to the right, Paradox probably won't ever get there to ask about sort order. You can get around this problem by telling Paradox what order to sort the fields. Check out the last section of this Chapter, "It's Your Answer, So Sort if You Want to," for all the details.

# Find Everything with CheckPlus

There are times when you just want to see *everything* and you don't *care* about the order it's in. That's why Borland included the CheckPlus option for your continued querying enjoyment.

Both the basic Check and its relative, CheckDescending, take great pride and care in selecting only the best in unique records for their Answer tables. Once selected, these records go through a tough sorting process until they're in either ascending or descending order according to your preference.

Comparatively speaking, CheckPlus is the lazy slob of the group. Does it make sure that its Answer table records are unique? No. Does it bother to sort the records in *any* direction at all? It doesn't. CheckPlus just slaps every record that matches the criteria into an Answer table. It shoves them in there in whatever order it finds them, too.

It's not elegant, but it gets the job done. Figure 14-2 shows the results of an ignoble but complete and accurate query using CheckPlus.

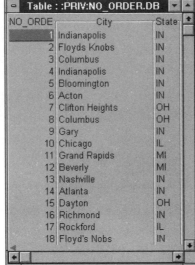

**Figure 14-2:**
The results ain't beautiful, but CheckPlus sure finds all the records, duplicates or not.

| NO_ORDE | City | State |
|---|---|---|
| 1 | Indianapolis | IN |
| 2 | Floyds Knobs | IN |
| 3 | Columbus | IN |
| 4 | Indianapolis | IN |
| 5 | Bloomington | IN |
| 6 | Acton | IN |
| 7 | Clifton Heights | OH |
| 8 | Columbus | OH |
| 9 | Gary | IN |
| 10 | Chicago | IL |
| 11 | Grand Rapids | MI |
| 12 | Beverly | MI |
| 13 | Nashville | IN |
| 14 | Atlanta | IN |
| 15 | Dayton | OH |
| 16 | Richmond | IN |
| 17 | Rockford | IL |
| 18 | Floyd's Nobs | IN |

Table : :PRIV:NO_ORDER.DB

Here are some things to remember:

✔ CheckPlus *overrides* the other checks in your query. You can't have one field calling for *unique records in descending order* while another one doesn't care who shows up or where they sit. With CheckPlus, it's *any way* or the *highway.*

✔ CheckPlus puts all the records that match the query into the Answer table —even duplicates.

✔ The Answer table is in no special order. The records land there in whatever order CheckPlus finds them.

---

## Stop the tragedy: donate your excess spaces now

I'm making this appeal to you on behalf of millions of innocent query checks all over the world. Due to the overwhelming popularity of Paradox for Windows, Borland (the software's publisher) has completely run out of spaces for their names. As a result, these poor creatures are forced out into the world without a simple space between their first and last names. They're condemned to go through life as peculiarly named outcasts, forced to forever wonder whether CheckAscending goes in the First Name or Last Name blank on the job application form.

It's a wretched existence when you lack something so simple, so *basic* as a space to call your own. They're not asking for a middle initial — just a space to make a name (well, *two* names) for themselves.

If you have extra spaces at the office or at home (or if you see one discarded along the road), please donate them to *SpaceForChecks* at 800-4-SPACES.

---

# It's Your Answer, So Sort if You Want to

It's great that Check and CheckDescending sort your Answer table, but Paradox *still* chooses which field to sort first. As a result, you can CheckDescending until you're blue in the mouse, and watch Paradox wander off and do its own thing. It's enough to make you stamp your feet.

You can still have the last laugh though, thanks to Paradox's Answer Sort tool. Answer Sort (or *troS rewsnA* if you hold this page up to a mirror), is a sweet little feature that lets you tell Paradox *precisely* how to organize the Answer table. You tell Paradox what field to sort first, second, third, and so on. When Paradox goes to the field, it sorts in whatever order *the Checks* tell it to.

To use Answer Sort, follow these steps:

1. **Create your query, complete with examples and checked fields.**

   Because Answer Sort works hand in hand with Check and CheckDescending, you have to set up the query *before* Paradox lets you worry about the sort order.

 2. **Click the Sort Answer Table button on the ToolBar or select <u>P</u>roperties⇨Answer Sort from the menu.**

The Sort Answer dialog box pops up.

Only checked fields appear in the Available Fields section, so make sure all the fields you're interested in are Checked (or CheckDescending'd or CheckPlus'd).

3. **In the Available Fields list, double-click the first field you want to sort by. Repeat the process for any other fields you want to specify.**

   When you choose a field, it hops over to the Sort By box. Figure 14-3 shows a complete Sort Answer dialog box. Paradox will sort the Answer table by the State field in descending order (there's a CheckDescending in the State field at the bottom of the screen), and then sort by City for all records in the same State.

   Paradox sorts the fields in the order you choose them. It sorts by the first field in Sort By and uses the other fields only as tie breakers. If you choose the wrong field, double-click it in the Sort By list and watch it hop away. If one of the Sort By fields is out of order, click it, and then use the up and down arrow buttons to put it in the correct spot. If you're hungry, get something to eat.

4. **When the sort order is in order, click OK.**

   That's it.

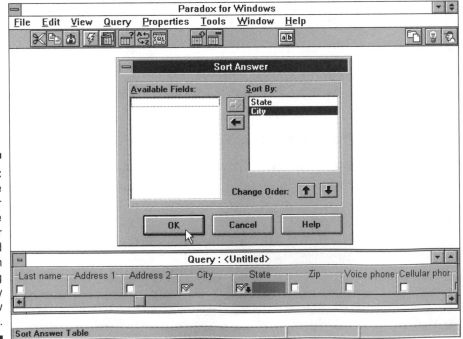

**Figure 14-3:**
Without the Sort Answer option, the Answer table would come out in ascending order by City. How sad.

# Chapter 15

# Just Like This, but Different (Mr. Boole Strikes Again)

*T*here's more to queries than black and white questions. Sure, there *are* times you need to find all the customers from Michigan or see what sweatshirts are available in Cleveland (for such things are important, particularly in Cleveland). But life's not always so cut and dried.

Maybe you have a complex question like "Last year, who bought mouse pads, lives in either Indiana or Ohio, and has a credit limit greater than $7,500?" Solving *that* requires more than a simple example. You need comparisons, logical operators, and the smarts to put the whole thing together without loudly wondering why mouse pad purchases are even part of the issue. Oooh — sounds tough (especially the last part).

If you're up to the task, Paradox is ready to stand with you. It has a full complement of tools for building any kind of comparison — and they're all explained in this chapter. As a special added bonus, there's even a section in here on how to make the Answer table more useful by reorganizing the columns and (best of all) naming it something *other* than Answer.

## Finding Things that Aren't Like the Others

*They* say you can't compare apples to oranges. I say you *can,* provided you're using the right operator.

*Comparison operator* is a fancy term for the symbol that fits into the middle of a comparison — you know, like the ones in the list below. They're the workhorses that define *how* to compare whatever is it that you're comparing.

| | |
|---|---|
| > | Greater than |
| < | Less than |
| >= | Greater than or equal to |
| <= | Less than or equal to |
| <> | Not equal to |

Using these operators is a real trip back to elementary school (where, incidentally, I never could remember which one was *greater than* and which was *less than*). There, you compared what was on one side of the operator with what was on the other (6 > 4, for example).

In Paradox, things are a little different. When you use a comparison in a query, you leave off the first part of the comparison and type in the rest (> 4 instead of 6 > 4). Since you're putting this into a particular field of the query, Paradox assumes you want to use the values in that field to fill in the missing part of the equation. The answer is always true or false (which, in computer lingo, are 1 and 0). The query plugs every field value into the equation and smiles on those that come out *true*.

Figure 15-1 shows some comparisons in a sample query. It's asking for all records with a Customer number less than 700, a Credit limit greater than or equal to $15,000, and a company name that ends in *Inc*.

You can have more than one comparison in a query. You can even combine comparisons with wildcards as shown in Figure 15-1.

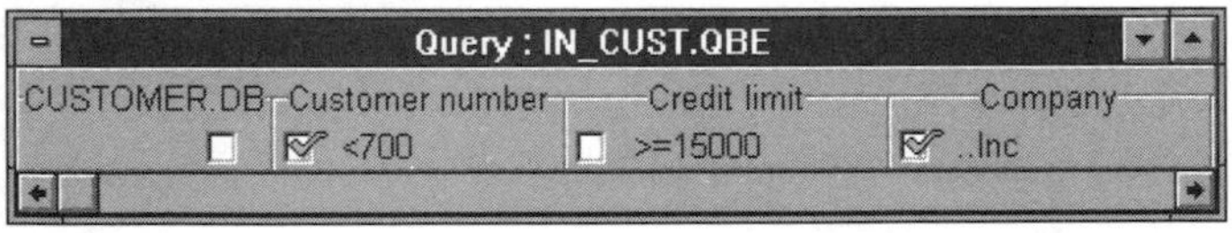

**Figure 15-1:**
Two wrongs don't make a right, but two comparisons and a wildcard certainly make a query.

| Query : IN_CUST.QBE | | |
|---|---|---|
| CUSTOMER.DB—Customer number | Credit limit | Company |
| ☐ ☑ <700 | ☐ >=15000 | ☑ ..Inc |

# *Building Better Queries with Knots, Oars, and Commas*

Okay, so I took some poetic liberties with the section name, but the concept is right. This section explores better querying through Boolean operators: NOT, OR, and comma.

*Comma?!?!* Yes, the comma. In Paradox queries, the quiet comma is actually *AND* — protector of the innocent and combiner of multiple expressions.

Each one of these operators works a little differently and it's important (one might go so far as to say "like, it's righteously critical, dude") to understand how they do what they do. As luck would have it, here's a table that does just that — whoa, too cool.

| | |
|---|---|
| Comma (And) | This is Paradox's version of the *And* operator. It joins two comparisons together like this: **>100, <250.** The whole thing is true only if *both* comparisons are true. If you feed the value 375 to this sample, it passes the first test but fails the second, so the whole shebang is *false*. |
| OR | It's like the And operator, but with a twist. OR joins two comparisons, just like And. But OR is *true* when *either* one or both of the comparisons are true — that's where it differs from And. Here's what OR looks like in action: **<100 OR >250.** If you run 375 through this sample, it fails the first test (375 is greater than 100), but passes the second. Because this is an OR operation, the whole thing is *true* because at least one comparison was true. |
| NOT | Say hello to Mister Contrary himself. NOT reverses the value of whatever you attach it to. **NOT > 100** shows NOT doing its thing. If you annoy the number 375 for one final time, this comparison starts out *true* because 375 is greater than 100. Then NOT gets in the act and reverses the value, giving a final value of *false*. |

Here are some things to keep in mind:

✔ Although I wrote OR and NOT in ALL CAPITAL LETTERS, Paradox doesn't care one way or the other about case. Heck, TyPE tHEm iN MIxeD CaSe if you want to and Paradox *still* won't care (although your coworkers may begin — or continue — to wonder about you).

- When you're working with And, make sure that *one* answer matches *both* comparisons. Setting up a query for a Customer number **<100, >500** won't get you anywhere, because you can't have something that's less than 100 and greater than 500 at the same time.

- By replacing the errant And in example above with an OR, you get a perfectly valid equation. Really, you do.

- You can combine NOT with the other two operators and come up with some truly complicated equations, but I don't recommend it. The best rule is still *keep it simple*.

- Yes, I made that rule up on my own. How did you know?

- Logic only works if you're outside the government. It works sporadically in city or state offices, but it's been gone for *years* at the national level.

---

# A portable logic class for the road

There's nothing like a few examples to take along as you start the journey toward better queries. The ones below show you how the operators work together and as individuals to meet even the hairiest of needs (and I've met some pretty hairy needs in my day). Use them to find answers to your questions and to build up your own elaborate tributes to Mr. Boole (the 19th century logician who refined all this logic stuff).

| | |
|---|---|
| 4 > 10 | False. There isn't much more to say about this one. It just *is*. |
| 6.4 < 7 | True. As long as it's even a *little* smaller, it still counts. |
| 6.4 <= 6 | False. Watch out for values with decimal places when you're using *less than or equal to*. If your data has decimals, it's better to use a simple *less than* instead of something more complicated. |

| | |
|---|---|
| NOT 5 <> 5 | True. It's a stumper, isn't it? Five *is* equal to five, so the expression itself is false. But then old, contrary NOT turns that into *true*. |
| 10 > 5, 4 > 27 | False. And (remember, that's the comma) is only true if *both* sides of the equation are true. Since the second half of this one is experiencing a distinct *lack* of truth, the entire thing is false. |
| 10 > 5 OR 4 > 27 | True. Here is the basic difference of OR: only one side has to be true for the whole thing to be true. Since 10 is still greater than 5 (at least it is here in Indiana—I can't speak for the more free-thinking areas of California, though), the entire affair is true. |

# Customizing the Answer Table

Answer tables are great (your queries just wouldn't be the same without them), but they still have a few faults. For one thing, they're always called *Answer*. And Paradox gets to choose the field order — I have no input in the decision whatsoever. Geez, I *bought* this program; you'd think it would at least have the courtesy to ask my opinion (even if it disregards what I say).

The newest version of Paradox *finally* gives you easy-to-use control over both the name and organization of the Answer table. Compared to how things *used* to be, well, there's just no comparison.

All this power is consolidated in one place: the Answer Table Properties button on the ToolBar. Click this button and the Answer Options dialog box pops into existence. There, arranged for your comfort and pleasure, is everything you need to customize the heck out of your Answer table.

And here's how to do it:

1. **With a query on the workspace, click the Answer Table Properties button on the ToolBar or select Properties⇨Answer Options from the menu.**

   The Answer Options dialog box appears, looking equally resplendent on-screen, as shown in Figure 15-2.

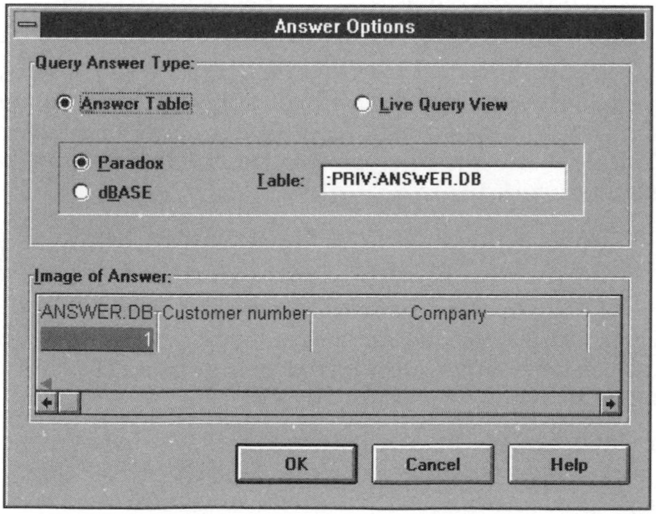

**Figure 15-2:** The Answer Options dialog box, looking amazingly like itself.

---

**Answer Options**

Query Answer Type:

⦿ Answer Table          ○ Live Query View

⦿ Paradox
○ dBASE          Table:  :PRIV:ANSWER.DB

Image of Answer:

ANSWER.DB Customer number          Company
                    1

[ OK ]     [ Cancel ]     [ Help ]

2. **To change the name of the Answer table to something vaguely more useful, double-click in the Table box and type a new name.**

If, for some reason, you want the Answer table to be in dBASE format instead of Paradox format, click the dBASE radio button. It's to the left of the Table name box.

Remember to include an alias with the table name. If you don't have a special alias you want to use, at least type in **:WORK:,** which is Paradox's alias for the Working Directory.

Don't mess with the radio buttons at the top of the dialog box marked Answer Table and Live Query View. The Live Query View is something new to this version of Paradox, but I'm unconvinced about how useful it is to normal people.

3. **To change the order of the fields in the Answer table, first find the field you want to move in the Image of Answer section (you may have to use the horizontal scroll bar to do it). When you find it, put the mouse pointer on the field name, press and hold the mouse button, and then move the mouse left or right to move the field. Release the mouse button when the field is where you want it.**

That's a lot of instructions for something that barely takes five seconds to do. It probably took you longer than that just to read about doing it.

You can repeat this exhaustively (or is that *exhaustingly?*) described process as many times as you want. If you're patient enough, you can move every field in the whole table, but with a big table, that requires some serious patience. But if you're that patient, you ought to be doing other things with your time (like transcribing this book onto a grain of rice).

4. **If you want to get *really* wild, right-click the fields in the Image of Answer area. You can set data dependent properties, alignment, color, and font for your yet-to-be-created Answer table right here, before it even hits the workspace.**

*Ewww.* This smacks of genetic engineering to me. Oh well, I guess the cat's out of the bi-helical bag, now isn't it?

Despite the fact that you *can* set a filter on the Answer table, I don't recommend it. That's a little arcane for my taste — and too easily overlooked six months from now when you're trying to figure out why some of the records are missing.

For more about data dependent properties, see "Fields That Really Sing" in Chapter 10. Alignment, color, and font are covered in Chapter 11's "Changing the Look and Feel (Fuzzy Dice and All)" section.

*Bi-helical* is a term I made up to play off the paragraph's reference to genetics. The study of genetics focuses on the famous double helix protein structure that makes each of us who we are (see — now you know who's to blame). My wife (who took genetics in college and occasionally reminds me that I *didn't*) completely missed this bit of humor. I just wanted to make sure that those of you out there with backgrounds similar to hers *would,* in fact, get the joke.

5. **When you're done, click OK to close the dialog box.**

6. **Try running your query and see how the changes look.**

   If you like the new, improved Answer table (or whatever you called it), be sure to save your query so all the custom answer stuff gets written down somewhere.

# Chapter 16

# Query Magic for the Reasonably Brave

*T*here's a lot you can do with Checks, examples, and Mr. Boole's logical operators, but that's only one side of querying. There's still a mysterious world out there of data that doesn't exist, things that appear from nothingness, and magic field names that change before your very eyes.

Welcome to the *other* side of queries.

This chapter explains calculations, example elements, and some other magical tricks for your queries. There's a lot of power in here, so tread carefully, but have a good time.

## Finding Stuff That's Not There

Just because you're looking for something in a table doesn't mean it has to be there. What if you wanted to see the records that didn't have *anything* in a particular field? Can it be done? If so, how?

Yes, there *is* a way to look for things that aren't there. Thanks to the BLANK keyword (that's *really* its name — I didn't beep out an expletive there), you can explain to Paradox that you're looking for data that doesn't exist. And isn't that what the Boss always wants, anyway?

Use BLANK in your query just like any other example text. Just type the word **BLANK** into the field as you see in Figure 16-1. Rather than finding the word *blank,* Paradox recognizes that it's supposed to find blank *fields.* Pretty slick, huh?

**Figure 16-1:**
Use BLANK
to find data
that isn't
there.

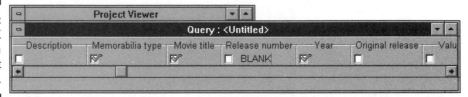

Combine BLANK with the NOT operator to look for fields that are "NOT BLANK."

Paradox doesn't care about whether it's typed *BLANK, blank, or bLAnK.* It's the word *inside* that counts — not the fancy packaging.

# Changing Field Names on the Fly

This is a useful trick, but it kinda defies easy organization. Out of sheer desperation, it landed here. With that fascinating introduction, let me acquaint you with the AS operator.

AS lets you change a field's name for the Answer table. If that explanation sounds complicated, just hang on — this is one of those things that's a bear to explain but really easy to do.

For example, say there's a field in your query called `95PGIO`. It (hopefully) means something to someone, but absolutely nothing to you. In the Answer table, you'd rather call it `Proj Income`. To accomplish this feat, type **AS Proj Income** into the field. Figure 16-2 shows the little fellow in action.

Notice that, as usual, capitalization doesn't matter. You can use either *AS* or *as* in the query and it works.

To combine AS with something else (like example elements or other such things), put a comma between the example and the AS statement.

Figure 16-2:
Thanks to
the AS
operator,
each field
gets a new
name in the
Answer
table (and
it's a good
thing, too).

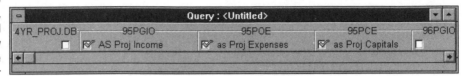

Figure 16-2:
Thanks to
the AS
operator,
each field
gets a new
name in the
Answer
table (and
it's a good
thing, too).

# *Making an Example of Your Data*

Example elements serve two main purposes: they're fodder for calculations and chains to link tables together. This section is a quick explanation of how to create example elements; info on *using* them is elsewhere in the book.

Specifically, calculations are covered in the next section, "Calculating Your Way to Fame and Fortune." Linking tables in a query resides in Chapter 17, "Dancing the Two Table Polka."

An example element is nothing more than a label you type into a query field. What changes it from mundane text into an *example element* is the magic F5 key. Before typing your text — er, example element — press F5 (the Example key). It says "Yo, Paradox — I'm typing an example element, so get ready." You immediately know whether Paradox heard you because example elements show up in a different color.

The following paragraph is a *severe* techno-junkie experience. Any of you with faint hearts or weak stomachs should skip it entirely.

If you remember any of your computer programming courses (assuming that you were silly enough to even *have* some programming courses), you can think of example elements as *identifiers* or variables. It's an arbitrary name you attached to a query field. Once attached, you can use it to represent the data in that field.

Here are some rules to keep in mind:

- ✔ Press F5 *before* typing your example. Otherwise, Paradox misses its cue.

- ✔ Use only letters and numbers for your example elements. Spaces aren't allowed (so don't even try).

- ✔ Limit your example elements to 10 characters or less. Although they can *legally* be almost any length, they get cumbersome if they stretch much beyond 10.

The example element can say anything. I like to use the field name as the example element because then I definitely know what field I'm playing with.

# Calculating Your Way to Fame and Fortune

Query calculations are the final thing on this chapter's *wow-this-query-stuff-is-too-incredibly-neat* feature list. And they truly are incredibly neat.

With calculations, you can do basic math, plus some interesting math-like things, with the fields in your table. The results pop into a new (not available in stores, but only through this TV offer) field in your Answer table. You can't miss the new field because it always has a silly name; Paradox uses the actual calculation as the field name. Yeech.

To give you an idea of the power that query calculations put at your disposal, the list below displays all the operators you can use in a calculation. They run the gamut from simple math to simple statistics.

| | |
|---|---|
| +, -, *, / | All the classic math things, from addition to multiplication |
| SUM | Totals all the values in a field |
| AVERAGE | Calculates the average value in a field |
| COUNT | Counts the number of matching records |
| MIN | Finds the smallest value in a field |
| MAX | Finds the highest value in a field |

For some people, it just doesn't get better than this, but it probably will for you because you're not a computer weenie. Here are some more rules:

- ✔ Calculations work with all field types except the really weird, esoteric ones (like OLE and Binary).

✔ Use the AS operator to make normal, useful field names for your calculations. See the sidebar for more information.

✔ Query calculations work with an example element (or two). If you're not familiar with example elements, jump back to the previous section for just a moment.

✔ You don't have to Check the field with the query calculation in it. Paradox *automatically* includes the query calculation in the Answer table. Put a Check in the field if you want to include *that field* in the Answer table.

✔ When it's looking at a mathematical calculation, Paradox does it one piece at a time, from left to right. First, it completes anything in parenthesis, then does all the multiplication and division, and finishes up with addition and subtraction. For example, when Paradox evaluates the equation 3+5*4, it does the multiplication first and comes up with 20, and then adds 3 and gets 23.

✔ When in doubt, use parentheses to make sure more complex calculations are done in the right order. Because Paradox always works through things in parentheses first, you can force Paradox to do the calculation just the way you want. Back to the 3+5*4 example, you could make Paradox do the additon first by adding parentheses: (3+5)*4. Now the answer is 32 rather than 23.

Actually using calculations in your queries isn't too hard at all. Here's what to do:

1. **Open your query.**

   If should be staring at you from the screen even as you read this.

2. **If you're doing a math calculation, click in the field you're calculating with, press F5, and then type your example element. If you're doing a statistical calculation (SUM, AVERAGE, MIN, or one of the others), skip ahead to step 3.**

   Repeat the process if your calculation needs two fields (or if you just like making example elements). Figure 16-3 shows two example elements ready and waiting to be part of a calculation.

**Figure 16-3:**
There's query coming; I can feel it. Looks like Cost and List are gonna be in it, too.

| PRODUCTS.DB | Product | SKU | Cost | List |
|---|---|---|---|---|
| ▓ | ☐ | ☐ | ☐ cost | ☐ list |

Query : <Untitled>

The preceding section, "Making an Example of Your Data," tells you more about the example element thing.

3. **Find the field where you're going to put the calculation and click there.**

   If the field is empty, you're in business — continue to the next step. If there's already something in there (such as an example element), double-click in the field to get the blinking toothpick cursor, and then press End to move to the right side of the example element. Type a comma and space to separate the example element from the calculation.

   By now, your query fields are probably getting a little crowded, but keep using those commas to separate everything and you'll be fine. See the sidebar for examples of how incredibly packed query fields can get (and how to survive the experience).

   Math calculations can go in *any* field because they use example elements to find their data. Statistical calculations (SUM, AVERAGE, and the others) don't use example elements, so they have to be *in the field they're calculating.*

4. **Type the keyword** CALC **followed by your calculation.**

   Repeat this step for however many calculations you're driven to include in the query. Table 16-1 has some ready-made sample calculations for you to choose from or use as models for your own creations.

5. **Check any other fields you want to include in the Answer table.**

   Check (or CheckPlus, if you prefer) Figure 16-4 to see a complete, ready-to-run query.

   AVERAGE, COUNT, MIN, MAX, and SUM work best if either no fields are checked or something other than the key field is checked.

   This would also be a good time to change the query properties or the sort order, if you're so inclined. Chapter 14 guides you through the basics of the query sort. Look in Chapter 15 for everything you want to know about changing the innocent Answer table's properties.

**Figure 16-4:**
A calculation and a couple of fields ready for liftoff.

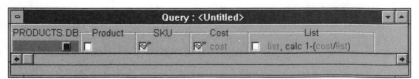

6. **Run the query by clicking the Run Query button on the ToolBar or by pressing F8.**

With some careful planning, blind luck, and the proper number of sun spots, your Answer table appears (perhaps looking a little like Figure 16-5).

If your calculation fields came out with names as flaky as Figure 16-5 did, check out the sidebar for help using AS to rectify the situation.

## Table 16-1 Sample query calculations

| Calculation | Explanation |
|---|---|
| CALC MIN | Doing a statistical calculation. |
| CALC *cost/ list* | Using two example elements in some simple math. |
| CALC *cost* * 1.15 | More simple math, but now between an example element and a number. |
| CALC ( *cost* * 1.15 ) - *list* | Combining the whole thing, complete with parentheses. |
| CALC 1 - ( *net/ list* ) | A standard calculation to find the discount of a sale. |

**Figure 16-5:** Ta-da! Here's the Answer table, funny field names and all.

| Paradox for Windows |
|---|

File   Edit   View   Table   Record   Properties   Tools   Window   Help

Table : :PRIV:ANSWER.DB

| ANSWER | SKU | Cost | 1 - Cost / List |
|---|---|---|---|
| 1 | 88794 | $30.00 | 45.5 % |
| 2 | 88795 | $40.00 | 41.2 % |
| 3 | 88800 | $47.00 | 37.3 % |
| 4 | 199847 | $27.00 | 32.5 % |
| 5 | 199885 | $40.00 | 33.3 % |
| 6 | 247887 | $300.00 | 25.0 % |
| 7 | 287394 | $1.20 | 38.5 % |
| 8 | 380297 | $0.95 | 62.0 % |
| 9 | 380872 | $45.00 | 25.0 % |
| 10 | 479115 | $5.00 | 50.0 % |
| 11 | 479117 | $8.00 | 52.9 % |
| 12 | 479119 | $20.00 | 42.9 % |
| 13 | 479287 | $220.00 | 29.0 % |
| 14 | 479288 | $410.00 | 25.5 % |
| 15 | 492511 | $20.00 | 50.0 % |
| 16 | 492512 | $30.00 | 50.0 % |
| 17 | 492765 | $3.00 | 75.0 % |
| 18 | 492767 | $20.00 | 33.3 % |

Record 1 of 18

# Doing it all together

All the tips and tricks in this chapter give you some really powerful (and good looking) calculations, but first you have to bring them all together. Here's how to do it.

If your query fields are getting a little crowded, they get bigger as you type. To enlarge them by hand, click and drag the separator bar to the right of the field.

Separate example elements and query calculations with a comma. That keeps them safe and happy.

Use AS to give your query calculations useful names. Just tack the AS statement onto the end of the calculation like this:

**CALC 1 - ( net / list ) AS Profit**

# Chapter 17
# Dancing the Two Table Polka

• • • • • • • • • • • • • • • • • • • • • • • • • • • • • • • • • • • • • • • • • • •

## In This Chapter

▶ Working with a group of related tables

▶ Teaching old example elements new tricks

▶ Building multitable queries

• • • • • • • • • • • • • • • • • • • • • • • • • • • • • • • • • • • • • • • • • • •

*A*lthough you may not know how to *build* a fancy bunch of tables that all link together, more than likely you have to *use* related tables in your work. More and more companies put their raw data out on a network and expect you to play Paradox like an instrument, sifting through that data, pulling information out of the digital chaff.

The good news is you don't need to be a database expert to work with related tables. This chapter tells you what you really need to know about the whole relational database thing in order to do your job. It explains how tables link together and how to explain those links to Paradox in a query.

There's a lot more to know before you create your own related tables. For that information, see Chapter 28.

## See the Amazing Siamese Tables

A *relational database* is just a bunch of tables that work together. Each table contains different kinds of data, but they all share a field or two that links them together.

Most of the time, the links look like knots on a string — to go from one end of the string to the other, you have to go from knot to knot. Because the string only goes from one knot to the next, you can't skip a knot without getting off the string. In the database world, one field in the first table (the first knot) links to the second table (the second knot); a different field in the second leads you to the third (I'll let you guess which knot it is). To connect the data in the first table to related stuff in the third, you *have* to go through the second table — otherwise, you can't make a link.

Is this as technical as you expected? (I hope not.)

To use a group of related tables, you have to know what fields link them together and how the links make it happen. If you have three tables called Customer, Invoice, and LineItem, you need to know that Customer links to Invoice by the Customer Number, and that Invoice is tied to LineItem by the Invoice Number. There's no direct way to link Customer to LineItem without involving Invoice.

You have to know all this stuff to know which tables to use to get the information you need. The links are *vital* because without them, you're stuck with three uncooperative tables that simply refuse to talk among themselves.

> ✔ Related tables are linked together by fields. These linking fields are identical in each table (for example, the Customer Number field is the same type and size in both the Customer table and the Invoices table).
>
> ✔ Tables often don't directly link together. You may have to link both to a third table — kind of a digital arbitrator — to get the information you're looking for.
>
> ✔ If this whets your appetite to make your *own* relational tables, get one of those do-it-yourself nerd test kits. If you pass, it's safe to check out Chapter 28, "Deliberately Using Two (or More) Tables."

# *Teaching Old Example Elements New Tricks*

Example elements reared their contrastingly-colored heads in the realm of query calculations, but they're back with a vengeance in multitable queries.

You use example elements to build the links between tables. For now, just remember that you have to type *exactly the same example elements* into each linking field, or Paradox doesn't catch on that you're making a link. The specific hows and wheretofores are in the next section, so I won't completely bore you with them here only to rebore you with them there.

 Before sending you on, though, there's a new tool you need to meet. When you have a query on-screen, the Join Tables button is an easy way to put in matching example elements without worrying about typing errors.

When you have both tables in your query (don't worry — that's covered in the next section as well), click the Join Tables button. Click the linking field in the first table, and then click on its mate in the second. Paradox automatically puts a cleverly named example element called *Join1* into the two fields you clicked. If you need another link, use the tool again. This time it puts in *Join2*. Is this slick or what?

- ✔ In addition to using the Join Tables button on the ToolBar, you can always manually type your examples (just like the good old days).

- ✔ The example elements must be spelled *exactly alike* for the links to work. Remember: Paradox isn't terribly clever, so you have to lay everything out *just right* or it doesn't catch on.

- ✔ If your example elements aren't the same, Paradox often complains that the `Query appears to ask two unrelated questions`. If you get that error, double-check the example elements and make sure of your spelling.

# *Arranging Blind Dates for Your Data*

Lonely tables are sad tables, and you don't want a bunch of morose tables moping around your disk drive. Setting up a nice query is a great way get them talking. Here's how to build the best in multitable queries.

1. **Find out which fields link the tables you're interested in and how those links work.**

    This is not a time for guessing. If you don't know specifically how the links work between your tables, ask your guru for help. That's a lot better than trying to explain to your boss why your numbers say the company hasn't sold anything at all in the last three years.

2. **Open new query window.**

    When Paradox wants to know which table to use in the query, click the first of the related tables you're using. If you have any luck at all, a normal looking query window appears on the workspace; an innocent harbinger of bigger things to come.

3. **To add the next table to the query, click the Add Table button on the ToolBar or select Query⇨Add Table. Double-click the table name in the File Name area, as shown in Figure 17-1.**

    The query window now shows the fields from both tables.

- If you include the wrong table, click the Remove Table ToolBar button or select Query⇨Remove Table. In the Remove Table dialog box, double-click on the name of the table you don't want. It's summarily thrown out of your query.

- Although queries can have lots of tables linked together, Paradox *really* starts dragging with more than three linked tables in a query. If your question is *that* complicated, split it into several questions and do smaller, simpler queries to solve them.

4. **Click Join Tables button on the ToolBar. Click in the linking field of the first table, then click in the same field of the other table, as Figure 17-2 shows.**

   A pair of matching example elements appear in the fields. Repeat this step if you have to set up more than one linking field.

5. **Carry on like it's a plain vanilla query.**

   Now that the link's established, you can calculate, Check, and example until you're all calculated, Checked, and exampled out.

   Figure 17-3 is a finished multitable query. It pulls the Customer number and Company name from the Customer table. Current balance and Credit limit come via the link to the Credit table. The two tables are linked by Customer number.

   For more help with queries, check the other chapters in Part 3.

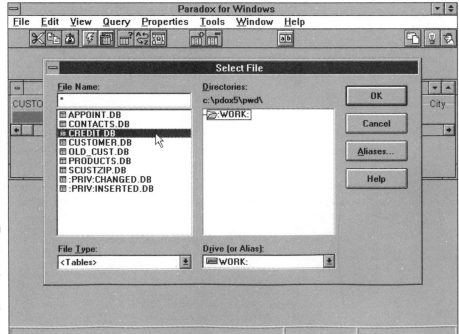

**Figure 17-1:**
Adding another table to a query is child's play.

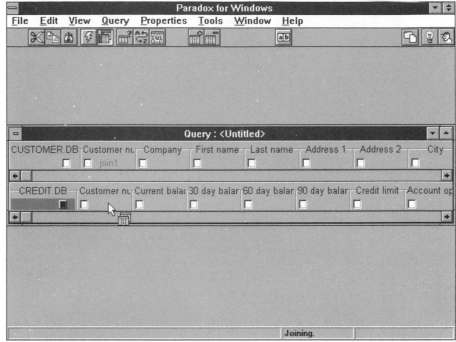

**Figure 17-2:**
With the Join Tables button, you can relax and leave the example element typing to Paradox.

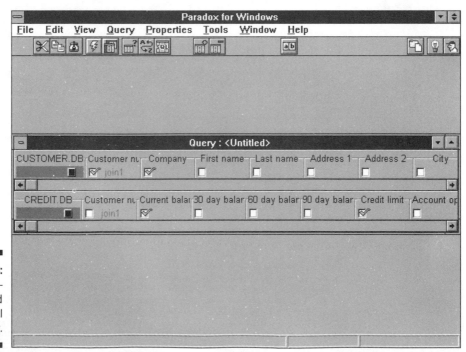

**Figure 17-3:**
Here it is — the finished relational query.

# Chapter 18

# Bulldozing the China Shop (Changing Tables with Queries)

*In This Chapter*
- ▶ Inserting a whole slew of records
- ▶ Deleting data you don't need
- ▶ Changing it all in one easy step

*T*oday's sprawling data tables are too big to really mangle if you do it one record at a time. When you need to add new records, delete old ones, or "make a few changes" (notice how the boss smiled when she said that?), you might be dealing with thousands of individual records. Like the china-hating bull, you need a technological boost to meet today's bigger challenges.

Paradox gives you that boost with INSERT, DELETE, and CHANGETO queries. These let you identify a group of records and do *nasty* things to the whole lot of them. But why am I telling you here? Read on, for that's what the whole chapter is about.

If you're not particularly sure about this whole query thing, *don't try this Chapter by yourself.* These are power tools that can trash an entire table in one little click. Don't turn this page unless you feel comfortable with queries in general and with two table queries from Chapter 17 ("Dancing the Two Table Polka") in particular. Please, believe me — INSERT, DELETE, and CHANGETO queries are the Paradox equivalent of remodeling your house with high explosives. Proceed with caution and get help from your local guru if you're at all unsure.

Take it from me (being the ex-guru that I am): gurus prefer that you call for help *before* the catastrophe occurs. It's easier on them to invest five minutes up front and help you the first time or two than to take a couple hours later and help you reassemble the now shredded table.

# *Inserting a Whole Slew of Records*

INSERT comes in handy when you have a bunch of records in one table and you need them to be in another table. Why not use Add? Because Add only works if both tables have the same fields in the same order. The tables I'm thinking of, alas, share some fields, but to call them *identical* is to seriously challenge the traditional definition of the word.

You build a query with the Source table (the one with records to add) and the Target table (the one shaking like a leaf over there next to the red and white bullseye). Using example elements, you explain to Paradox which fields go together. Press the Run Query button and you're done.

The results of an INSERT query are much like very fast typing. All the data that *can* go into the new table goes there, except for records that cause key violations or otherwise irk Paradox for Windows. It's just like you typed and typed and typed all the stuff into your table. Pretty cool, huh?

The process makes one or two temporary tables, depending on your success. The one it usually makes is called (brace yourself — this is a killer) :PRIV:INSERTED. The other table, :PRIV:ERRORINS, is for records that Paradox couldn't insert.

So much for the glowing introduction — here's what to do and how to do it.

1. **Compare the two tables and figure out which fields go with which.**

   Write down two columns of fields: one column for Source and the other for the matching Target. Include all the fields from the Source table that are destined for new homes in the Target.

   If you're not sure about some of the fields, either ask someone who knows about such things in your organization or compare the structures of the two tables.

   Examining a table's underlying structure is exactly what the Info Sturcture command is for. If you're not familiar with what it is or does, hold your place and flip over to Chapter 11 and go "Rummaging in the Toolbox" to find out.

2. **Start a new query using either the Source or Target table.**

   It doesn't matter which one you use first. Eventually (during the next step, in fact), the other table jumps in with gusto.

   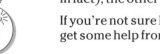

   If you're not sure how to make a new query, *don't try using INSERT.* Instead, get some help from your friend, sister, guru, or support line.

3. **Add the other table to the query with the Add Table button on the ToolBar button or by selecting Query⇨Add Table from the menu.**

When the Select File dialog box comes up, double-click the name of the other table involved in today's adventure.

4. **Put the mouse pointer under the name of the Target table (the one you're adding records *to*). Press and hold the mouse button until a pop-up menu appears. Select Insert from the drop-down menu (like Figure 18-1), then let up on the mouse button.**

The word Insert appears below the Target table name, just like you want.

 5. **Use the join table button to match up the various fields you identified in Step 1.**

Figure 18-2 shows the ponderous procedure in progress.

Don't put Check marks *anywhere*. INSERT queries don't like Check marks — and you don't want to worry the INSERT query.

Refer to Chapter 17 for information and pleasant conversation about linking two tables together in a query.

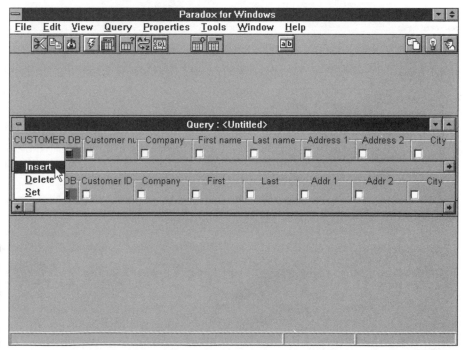

**Figure 18-1:**
Picking
Insert off
the drop-
down menu.

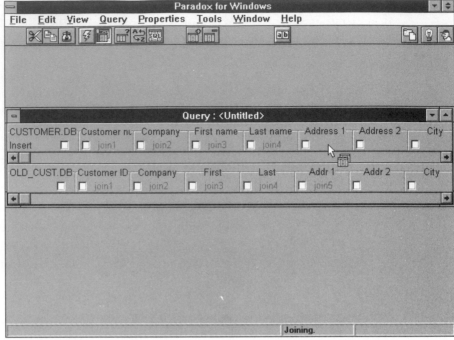

**Figure 18-2:**
It's the most
incredibly
tedious part
of an
INSERT, but
there's no
way around
doing the
example
elements.

  6. **When everything's ready, click Run Query on the ToolBar or press F8.**

Depending on your degree of success, either the :PRIV:INSERTED table appears alone or with company (the :PRIV:ERRORINS table).

7. **Check your work to see whether it all happened like you hoped.**

If you have an ERRORINS table, Paradox couldn't insert some of the records. Examine the records that didn't work, fix them in the Source table, and then try the INSERT query again.

To completely undo the Insert, subtract the INSERTED table from the Source.

# Deleting Lots of Things You Don't Need

The next time you think of complete, wholesale, mass data destruction, think of a DELETE query. With that pleasant thought, allow me to introduce the next of Paradox's special query operators.

DELETE is a great tool for removing a group records from your tables. It works best for mass deletions where the records have something in common. You specify that something in a query, set your phaser on DELETE, and fire. The records are blown right out of your table into a temporary system table called :PRIV:DELETED.

Compared to some other things in Paradox, creating a DELETE query is a piece of fresh spice cake with made-from-scratch caramel frosting served next to two scoops of homemade vanilla ice cream drizzled with fresh chocolate sauce right off the stove. (You're hungry too? What a coincidence.)

1. **Decide which records you need to delete and figure out how to uniquely identify them.**

   Don't feel like a failure if you have to do more than one query to get them all. That's a whole lot better than getting *really* fancy with your criteria and deleting half the table in the process.

   You *are* deleting records, so be careful. Slow and easy is the name of the game.

2. **Open a new query based on the table you want to clean out.**

   The query window appears, blissfully unaware of the carnage to come.

3. **If you need information from another table to find the deletable records, add that table to the query and put in the example elements to link the two.**

   If you're unsure about this step, get some help. You don't want to accidentally delete records from the wrong table.

4. **Put the mouse pointer just below the name of the table you're deleting records from, and then press and hold the mouse button. Select **D**elete from the drop-down menu (see Figure 18-3).**

   To prove that it was listening, Paradox puts the word Delete in the space.

5. **Type whatever examples describe the soon-to-be-dead records.**

   You can use regular text examples, example elements that link to another table, or a combination of the two. In Figure 18-4, if a record's zip code *doesn't* start with 462, the record gets tossed.

   Don't put *any* Checks, CheckPluses, or CheckAnythings in your query.

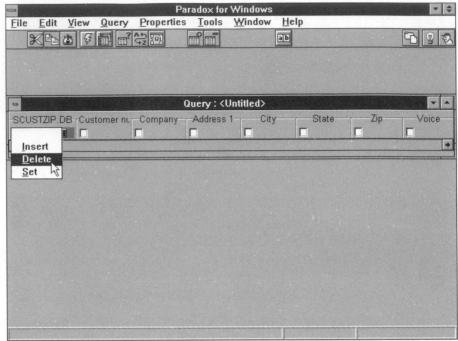

**Figure 18-3:**
Selecting
DELETE from
the drop-
down menu.

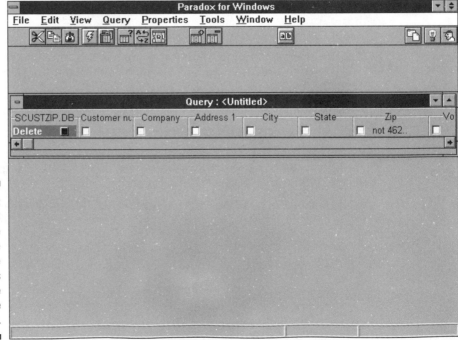

**Figure 18-4:**
The digital
guillotine
hangs above
all the
records
outside the
462 zip code
area.

6. **Double-check everything one last time, particularly the table name and the criteria.**

Speaking from personal experience, it's a bummer when you trash four or five hundred records and find out you're working with the wrong table. A *real* bummer.

 7. **Run the query.**

If all went well, the DELETED table appears. Check it carefully to make sure that you only deleted the records you thought you were deleting.

If something went wrong and you mowed down some truly innocent records, use the Add utility to put all the records in DELETED back into the original table. Look over your query to find out what happened, correct your query, then try again.

 When I delete a bunch of records from an important table, I rename the DELETED table to something like SAFEKEEP. After I'm absolutely sure that everything worked and my table is fine without those old records, I erase the SAFEKEEP table. On the other hand, if I find out some records were accidentally deleted, I just add the ones I need from my SAFEKEEP table.

# Changing It All in One Easy Step

Sometimes you need to make a change or two to a whole mess of records. Laboriously typing all the changes by hand is utterly out of the question. But you might be able to use a CHANGETO query, *if* (and that's a mighty important *if*) you can find some way to uniquely identify *only* the records you want to change.

If you want all the records from a particular day, with a particular value, or within a particular range, CHANGETO is a timesaving gift from above. If the changes are pretty random (any way you look at it there's no identifiable block of records), CHANGETO won't do you much good at all. Sorry.

Provided your problem fits CHANGETO's requirements, you can do just about anything with this query operator. Change a field's value to a particular constant (like 516.5 or the word *Discontinued*) or use a calculation to come up with a more custom solution. Whatever you do, Paradox copies all the records it changes into the :PRIV:CHANGED table so that you can check your work and quickly undo it if you must.

 Adding a percentage to the current value is a common CHANGETO request. Figure 18-5 shows a calculation that adds 15% to the list price of everything in the table.

Don't Check any fields in a CHANGETO query. Paradox gets really wigged out about stuff like that and will spit error messages at you like little digital hairballs.

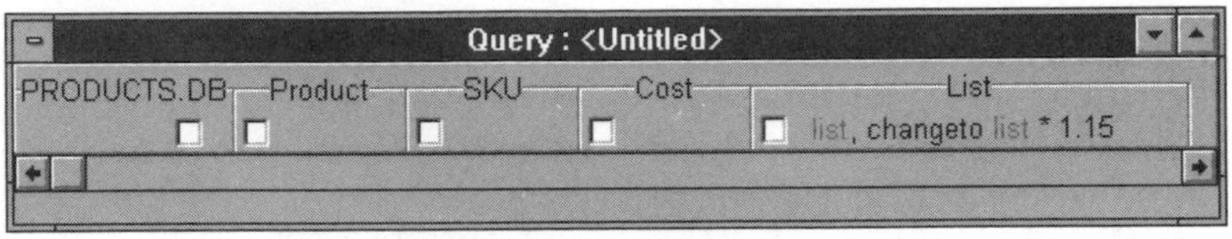

**Figure 18-5:**
When in doubt, raise prices. (That's why I'm not in retail sales.)

| PRODUCTS.DB | Product | SKU | Cost | List |
|---|---|---|---|---|
| | ☐ | ☐ | ☐ | ☐ list, changeto list * 1.15 |

*Query : <Untitled>*

### 1. Identify the group of records you want to change.

You're looking for some unique way to find *all* the records that need changes and *none* of the records that don't. If you have to do a couple of CHANGETO queries to get everything, that's fine. Don't feel like you've failed or anything.

### 2. Open a new query with the table containing the nasty errors.

You can do this in many ways, but my favorite is to quickly right-click the ToolBar's Query button.

### 3. If you need data from another table to fix everything, add that table to the query and link the two with example elements.

Link the two carefully (as I'm sure you always do). Above all, make sure you put the CHANGETO in the right table. It's embarrassing when you don't. (Yes, that's another observation born of personal experience.)

Refer to Chapter 17 for the details on linking tables together in a query.

### 4. Type in the criteria you discovered to find all the records that need a tune-up.

Depending on what you're doing, you may not have *any* criteria. The query back in Figure 18-5 is changing *all* the records in the table, so it doesn't need any criteria at all.

Carefully double-check what you type. Typos are, disappointing when you're doing mass changes.

5. **Click in the particular field that's getting a new value. Type** CHANGETO, **press the Spacebar, and then type the new entry.**

   This can be a constant value, a calculation, or a combination of both, depending on your needs.

6. **Double-check your handiwork once more.**

   No, it's *not* that I don't trust you — you're doing a great job. I just want you to *keep* doing a great job.

7. **When you're mentally prepared, start the query by clicking the Run Query button on the ToolBar or pressing F8.**

   Check everything carefully (yes, again — but this is the last time).

If the changes didn't work like you planned, add the CHANGED table back into the original table, repair your query, then try it again. (And be glad you're on *this* side of the screen.)

# Part IV
## Truth is Beauty (and These Reports Look Great)

"THIS REPORT IS REALLY GOING TO GIVE OUR PRESENTATION STYLE."

# In This Part...

*Oh, is there not one maiden here*
*Whose homely face and bad complexion*
*Have caused all hopes to disappear*
*Of ever winning man's affection?*

Act I, Gilbert and Sullivan's *The Pirates of Penzance*

Beauty may be more than skin-deep, but truth is pretty near the surface. Part 4 introduces Paradox's Report capabilities — plastic surgery for your data. A few fonts here, some colors and text areas there, and pretty soon you can proudly take your data out in public. This part is your key to everlasting printed (and on-screen) beauty.

# Chapter 19

# A Simple Report Is Better than None

- - - - - - - - - - - - - - - - - - - - - - - - - - - - - - - - - -

## In This Chapter

▶ Understanding reports

▶ Creating a (really) basic report

▶ Visiting the Report Designer

▶ Embellishing your report

▶ Saving your work for posterity

▶ Opening the report again

▶ Poking around in the Report toolbox

- - - - - - - - - - - - - - - - - - - - - - - - - - - - - - - - - -

*T*here comes a point in every table's life when it's time to stand up and be printed. Yes, despite the constant talk about computers bringing a *paperless office,* reality says you refill the printer several times each week. Database printing is notorious for keeping the paper companies in business.

Paradox's report tools are useful whether you're doing traditional paper reports or fancy, on-screen, ecologically correct creations. This chapter covers a lot of ground, from creating that first simple report to rummaging around in the Project Viewer's Report toolbox. Don't worry if you want more specifics — that's why there are *other* chapters in this part of the book.

## *Reports from the Front*

Reports are Paradox's main tool for looking at your data either on paper or on-screen. The key word in that sentence is *looking,* because that's all you can do with a report.

No additions, changes, or substitutions are allowed with a report. All records are shown as is, with no explicit or implicit warranty. The decision of the judges is final, except in California and Oregon. (Reality is a little bent there.)

Paradox for Windows has three basic report styles: single record, tabular, and multi record. Of the three styles, *single record* is probably the most popular. It aligns all the fields vertically on the page, as shown in Figure 19-1.

The *tabular* style lays your table out like a table (what a novel approach). It's fine for *small* tables, but big tables (anything with more than five or six fields) roll right off the side of the page. Figure 19-2 shows a tabular report looking pretty, uh, tabular.

*Multi record reports* are a more special need kind of thing, but they're good at packing lots of stuff into a small space. They put two or more records onto a single page. In Figure 19-3, two records are laid out vertically. Keep the following in mind:

- ✔ Reports *display* your data on-screen. You can't make any changes to what you see.

- ✔ To see your data in a beautiful format on-screen *and* make changes to it, you need a *form*. That, you see, is what forms let you do.

- ✔ Forms are covered in Chapter 25.

- ✔ If you want an interactive introduction to the whole report thing, click the Coach button and go through the section Creating a Standard Report section in the Queries, Forms, and Reports section.

**Figure 19-1:**
A single record report.

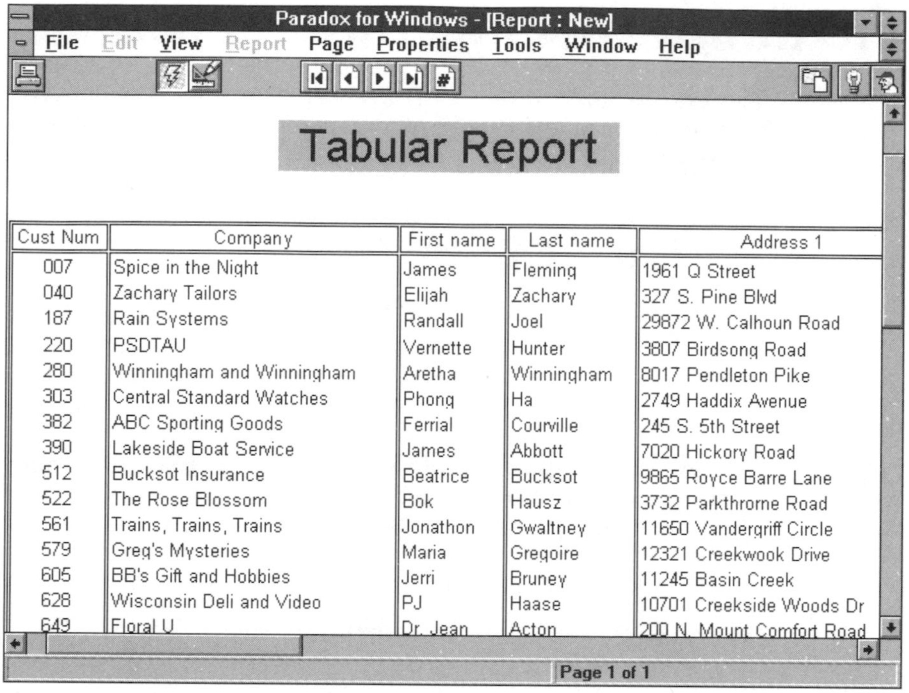

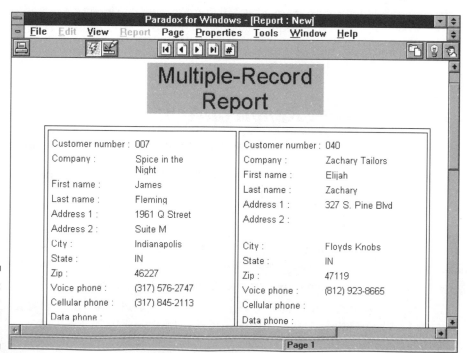

**Figure 19-2:**
A tabular
report.

**Figure 19-3:**
A multi-
record
report.

# Creating a (Really) Basic Report

There are a couple ways to make a report, depending on where you are in Paradox. Both have their advantages, so I feel obligated to tell you about each of them.

## The Instant Report button

 When you're looking at a table on-screen, there's a really neat button available to you. It's way over on the right side of the ToolBar. Looks innocent enough. But its name belies its power: Instant Report. One click on that button and Paradox spits out a ready-to-use tabular report for your table.

 I recommend using the Instant Report as a fast starting point for creating your masterpiece. At the very least, change its design from tabular into single record. The section called "Visiting the Report Designer" tells you how.

1. **View your table on-screen.**

   Double-clicking the table name in the Project Viewer is a good way to do this.

 2. **With your table in plain sight, click the Instant Report button.**

   Paradox puts up a little dialog box to let you know it's thinking *very hard* about your request. A moment or two later, you have a report.

   Granted, the report it creates isn't much to look at, but it *is* a quick way to start the process.

## The New Report button

From the Project Viewer, you have more traditional ways to create a report.

 1. **Right-click the Report button and select New from the popup menu (as shown in Figure 19-4) or do it the main menu way by selecting File⇨New⇨Report.**

   Whatever you do, you're met with the New Report dialog box.

2. **Click the honking big Data Model/Layout Diagram button at the bottom of the dialog box to continue your quest toward the ultimate report.**

   This summons forth the Data Model dialog box.

3. **In the File Name area, double-click the name of the table for the report and then click OK.**

**Figure 19-4:**
Inspecting
your way to
a new
report.

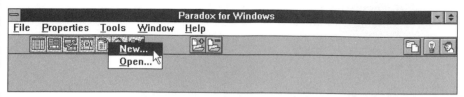

When you double-click, the file name leaps into the big open area on the right of the dialog box, as you can see with riveting detail in Figure 19-5.

After clicking the fateful OK button, the Data Model dialog vanishes, only to be replaced by the Design Layout dialog box. Egad — will these dialog boxes never end?

**4. It's time to choose a layout for your report. Click the Single Record, Tabular, or Multi-Record radio button to make your pick.**

The big window displays a thumbnail sketch of what your report currently looks like.

**5. Click OK to build the report.**

Paradox automatically leaves you in Design mode.

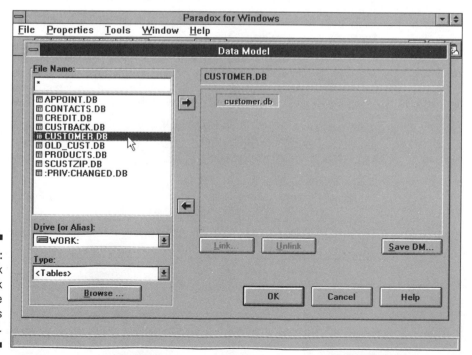

**Figure 19-5:**
A quick
double-click
and the
table moves
right slick.

To run the report, click View Data button or select View⇨Run Report from the menu. If you're *really* feeling lazy (I prefer to think of it as *conscious energy conservation*), just press F8.

# *Visiting the Report Designer*

Paradox has two different modes for reports: View and Design. In an amazing show of useful thinking, they're actually named according to what they do.

 *View mode* is for viewing a report all decked out with your data. When you run a report or click the famous Paradox Lightning Bolt ToolBar button, Paradox flips into View mode.

 *Design mode,* on the other hand, is where the fun stuff happens. To get here, click the Design button. In Design mode, you work with the framework of the report. Instead of seeing the *data*, you see the design objects that *hold* the data.

Figure 19-6 shows a report in Design mode. It's kinda funny looking, but if you know a few landmarks, you won't get lost. Table 19-1 describes the important ones to look for.

| Table 19-1 | Important Landmarks in Design Mode |
|---|---|
| *Landmark* | *Description* |
| Rulers | These show where the various fields and other *design objects* (lines, boxes, and such) are on the page. When something on-screen is selected (such as the *Corporate Customer List* box in Figure 19-6), the rulers turn dark gray to show that object's precise position. |
| Bands | These are the wide, dark bars that cut across the page. The three in the Figure are labeled *Report, Page,* and *Record.* |
| Special field | Special fields display things like the time, date, page number, or table name. |
| Table field | Here's your data — or at least where the data goes. Each of these fields corresponds to a field in the table. |
| Text field | Titles, notes, and other stray text go in text fields. You add these fields yourself. |

Rulers  Text field  Special field  Bands

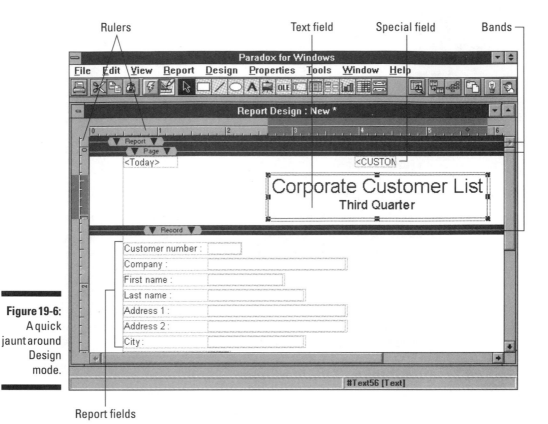

**Figure 19-6:**
A quick
jaunt around
Design
mode.

Report fields

# Embellishing Your Report

It's pretty plain right now — just a bunch of fields and names. It's not that I'm against *plain* or anything, but it would look nicer (and maybe tell you more) if it had just a *few* things added. Just a couple of points:

▶ To make changes in your report, you have to be in Design mode. So there.

 ▶ If you're viewing data in the report right now, click the Design button on the ToolBar to flip into Design mode.

## *Getting in style*

If you started with the Instant Report and want a single record or multirecord layout, now's the time to do it. Here's how.

*Don't do this* if you've customized the report with titles, summaries, or such as that. Changing the report layout through the Design Layout dialog box *completely replaces* your report; you're starting over from scratch with a new field layout. If you don't care about the titles and summaries, then do the Design Layout thing and trash 'em all.

1. **Select <u>D</u>esign⇨Design <u>L</u>ayout from the menu.**

   The appropriately named Design Layout dialog box pops into view.

2. **In the Style section on the left of the dialog box, click the radio button for either Single Record or Multi-Rec<u>o</u>rd layout.**

   When you choose a new layout, the sample report area shows you roughly what everything will look like.

3. **Click the OK button to accept the new field style. Click <u>Y</u>es when Paradox sets off the emergency warning sirens about changing the design.**

   You're replacing the *whole* report layout with a new one. This throws out titles, new groups, and summaries, too.

## *Endowing it with titles*

Every report needs a title — it's just the way life is. Adding a title isn't hard, but it does take some getting used to.

Titles usually go between the *Page* and *Record* bands in the report.

1. **Click the Page band.**

   It immediately changes color. That's its way of saying "oooh — that tickles."

2. **Move the mouse pointer down to the Record band. When the pointer is near the top of the band, it turns into a double-headed arrow. Once the cursor does its quick-change act, press and hold the mouse button, drag Record band down about an inch (see Figure 19-7), and then let go of the button.**

   Now there's room for the title. Hooray!

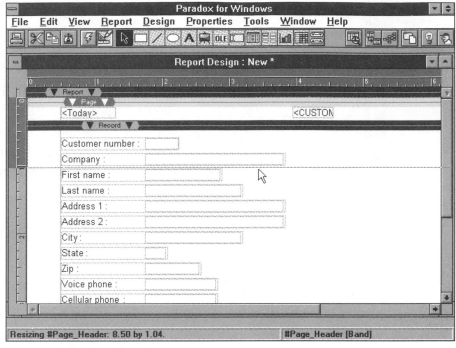

**Figure 19-7:**
The dotted line at the tip of the mouse pointer is where the Record band will land when I release the mouse button.

 **3. Click the Text tool from the ToolBar.**

The Text tool turns black and the cursor changes into a plus with a capital A next to it. Something's afoot.

**4. Click at the upper left corner of where you want the title. While holding down the button, drag across to the lower right corner of the area and then left go of the button.**

Figure 19-8 shows the text area nearing completion. When you're done, there's a box with a blinking toothpick cursor inside. That's as much of a *come right on in* as Paradox can muster for your text.

 **5. Type your title.**

If you want a two-line title, press Enter at the end of the first line. The cursor drops to the next line so that you can start anew.

**6. Click the View Data button on the ToolBar to see your work in lights.**

Well, there's your title. Of course, it looks a little puny and squished to one side, but Chapter 20 tells you all about how to change that.

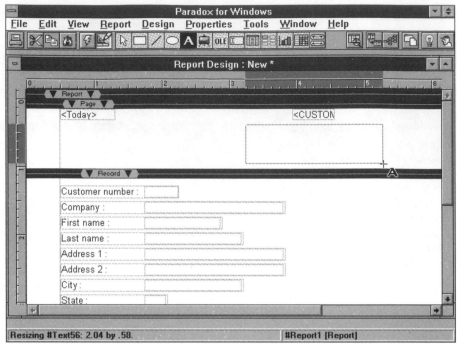

**Figure 19-8:**
The text box
is almost
done.

## Fixing field names

You don't want to see names like Q4ProjExp when you're looking at a report.
That's why Paradox for Windows lets you change the field labels pretty easily.
The best part is that Paradox doesn't care what you put in place of the field
names, so let your imagination run free.

1. **Click three times on the field name you want to change.**

    This puts a toothpick cursor inside the text area inside the field.

2. **Change the text however you want.**

    At this point, it's just like using a word processor. Use Del and Backspace
    to erase letters; use Home, End, and the arrow keys to move around.

3. **Click somewhere outside the field to save your new entry.**

# Saving Your Work for Posterity

Here's an interesting little tidbit to keep in mind: Paradox doesn't save your reports automatically. Safeguarding your work is *your* responsibility in the world of reports. Don't get in a big panic about it, though. Saving a report isn't a big deal.

Save your reports regularly because Paradox doesn't automatically save report changes like it does when you edit your tables.

1. **When it's time to save the report, select File⇨Save from the menu.**

   If the file's been saved before, you're done.

2. **For new reports, the Save File As dialog box appears. Type a name for the report into the New File Name box.**

3. **Click OK to finish the job.**

# Opening the Report Again

There are several ways to pull your reports kicking and screaming back to work. Here are the easiest ones:

*From the Project Manager,* click the Reports icon to see the report files in the Working Directory. To view data with the report, double-click it. To put it in Design mode, right-click the name, then select Design from the pop-up menu.

 *With the ToolBar,* click the Open Report button. In the Open Document dialog box, double-click the report name to view data with it. To go into Design mode, first click the Design radio button in the Open Mode area, then double-click the report name.

*Via the menu,* select File⇨Open⇨Report to get the Open Document dialog box. From there, it's just like using the ToolBar button.

## Poking around in the report toolbox

You can manage reports with the Project Viewer the same way you manage tables there.

Click the Reports button (insert figure of report listing) to see a list of all the reports in the current directory.

When you right-click a report name, the report utilities super popup toolbox appears. Here are the options on it:

| | |
|---|---|
| View Data | This is the same as double-clicking the file name. It opens the report in View mode. |
| Print | Print the report using your data. |
| Design | Opens the report file in Design mode. |

| | |
|---|---|
| Print With | This lets you print the report with data from another table. |
| View With | Like Print With, except it opens the report in View mode. |
| Copy | Make a copy of the report. |
| Rename | Change the report's file name. |
| Delete | Erase the report. |

Both Print With and View With are covered in Chapter 24, "Recycling Your Work."

The Copy, Rename, and Delete options work just like their brethren in the Tables pop-up utility menu. See "Rummaging in the Toolbox" in Chapter 11 for the details.

# Chapter 20
# Formatting Fireworks

· · · · · · · · · · · · · · · · · · · · · · · · · · · · · · · · · · · · · · · · · · · · · · · · ·

### In This Chapter
▶ Lighting a fire under your fields
▶ Shuffling some fields
▶ Setting trivial page details

· · · · · · · · · · · · · · · · · · · · · · · · · · · · · · · · · · · · · · · · · · · · · · · · ·

*P*aradox for Windows sets up some pretty uninspired reports when left to its own devices. Oh, the fields are all there and it works, but you just don't feel like standing up and saluting, if you know what I mean. After all, it's *just* a report.

This chapter is dedicated to the premise that all Paradox reports are created equal, but there's no reason to leave them that way. Hey — this is Windows, after all. Let's have some of those glitzy fonts! Bring on the colors! Make your information leap right off the screen and into the reader's mind. *That's* what I want see from your reports!

## Lighting a Fire Under Your Fields

Fields aren't too exciting right out of the gate. Truth be told, they're kinda boring. To help your fields communicate better, try changing their characteristics. Tweaking things such as the font, background color, and border can *really* make your data stand out (or simply be legible).

To change all these varied and wondrous options, call on the Object Inspector. Right-click the report field you're tuning to see the pop-up menu shown in Figure 20-1. Don't let the number of menu options daunt you — you don't care about a lot of them.

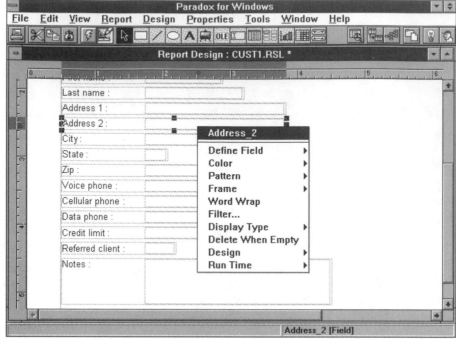

**Figure 20-1:**
The Inspector's pop-up field menu looks confusing, but you can beat it into submission.

The most common procedures are explained in the following sections. Each description assumes you're starting from a report in Design mode (because that's the only place you can change a report).

## Setting the font

You can change the font used in both the label text or the data area of a field. You can do the same thing to any extra text areas you added (such as a title or other on-screen missives).

1. **Select the field or text block you want to change.**

   If you're changing *both* the label text and data area of a field, click the field and then Ctrl+right-click it. This is the special handshake that tells Paradox you want change everything in the field. Paradox responds with the special pop-up menu shown in Figure 20-2. (Does it feel like you just joined a secret society?) You can skip ahead to Step 3 because you already have the menu open. On the other hand, if you're changing either the label text or the data area, see "A brief work about fields, mice, and natural selection" for help.

## A brief word about fields, mice, and natural selection

Most report fields are actually *three* fields in one: the label text, the data area (or *edit region* as Paradox likes to say), and the big box containing the other two pieces. Each of the three has its own properties, so it's important to make sure that you're clicking the right part of the field.

The first time you click a field, you select the big box that's around both the label text and the data area. That's great for moving the field, but does you no good if you're out to change the font or number format.

To set properties for either the label text or data area, select the area you want to change by *double-clicking* directly on it. Finally, right-click to bring up the properties menu.

**2. Right-click the area you're changing.**

This opens the mysterious, disappearing pop-up menu.

**3. Select Font to open the super submenu and then click in the funny button above the word Typeface to open the secret panel.**

It's a visual thing, so look at Figure 20-3 to get a picture of what you're doing. If you're successful, the Font dialog box appears.

To change the color of the type, select Color from the submenu instead of clicking the funny button. Click your choice of colors from the ensuing palette.

**4. In the Font dialog box, pick the typeface, size, and style you want.**

The Font dialog box in Figure 20-4 has typeface settings in the upper left side, font size in the far right, and style settings along the bottom half of the box.

To make something stand out, try changing the font style to bold or italic. If that's not enough, make the text bigger. Change the typeface only as a last resort.

**5. Close the Font dialog box by clicking the button in its upper right corner.**

The font is changed. Ta-da!

Don't panic when the cursor changes to a miniature interpretation of the common sand dollar just before you click the button — that's what it's programmed to do. I *would* say the behavior is normal, but I'm not sure that it is.

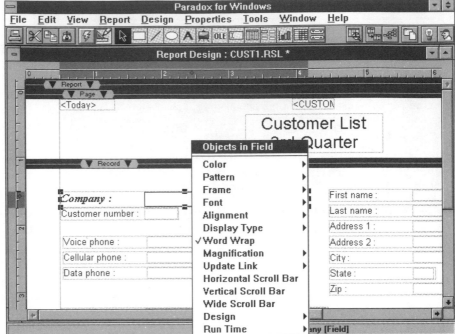

**Figure 20-2:**
Welcome to the Mysterious Order of the "Hidden Menu Accessible with Ctrl+Right-click."

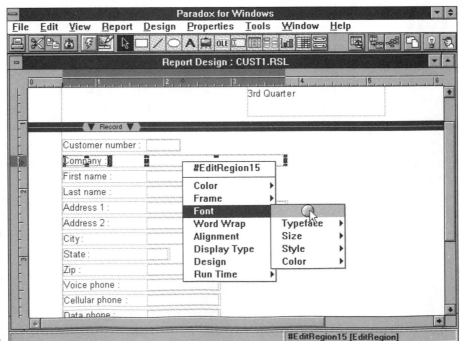

**Figure 20-3:**
Press the button to reveal a hidden panel.

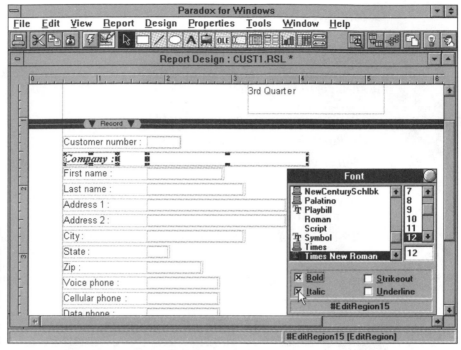

**Figure 20-4:**
The Font
dialog box is
Formatting
Master
Control.

# *Framing your fields*

A friend of mine once told me that the best way to make sure that people see
something is to draw a box around it. Paradox for Windows must think the
same thing, because you can put a frame around just about anything. Here's
how:

1. **Right-click the field you want to frame.**

   You can frame a whole field (the *big box*) or just the part you're interested
   in. It looks great if you frame just the data area of a field, though. It's slick
   — *really* slick.

2. **From the pop-up menu, select Frame⇨Style.**

   Options are also available for color and thickness, but you can explore
   those on your own after you're comfortable with the frame thing.

3. **Click your choice of the various frame styles Paradox offers (see Figure
   20-5).**

   Start out with the simple line frames and work your way up to the 3-D ones
   at the bottom of the bar.

To remove a frame, use the same steps but click the blank space at the top of
the frame styles menu bar. It's just below the thumbtack button at the very top
of the bar.

# *Changing alignment*

Nothing (and I mean *nothing*) annoys me quite so much as a bunch of data that's not aligned correctly. I like centered text and right justified numbers. It's just how I am. Luckily, Paradox lets me indulge my craving for visual order with the Alignment option.

1. **Double-click the data area of a field to select it.**

2. **Right-click to get the pop-up menu.**

3. **Select Alignment and then your choice of Left, Center, Right, or Justify (as shown in Figure 20-6).**

   Any of these options work for text. Titles look best when they're centered. Numbers (for the most part) should be right-aligned.

   If the field values don't seem to be paying attention to your alignment settings, double-click the data area of the field, and then right-click to bring up the properties menu. Select Run Time⇨Fit Width from the submenu. Now try the report again. The fields should be fine.

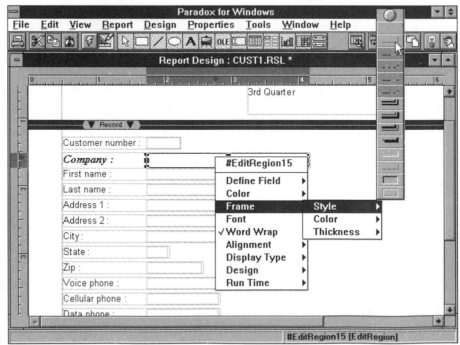

**Figure 20-5:** Simple frames are at the top; advanced, neat looking ones are near the bottom.

## *Adding some color*

Like the Frame options, you can apply color to a whole field or just its individual parts. Go easy with colors, though. It doesn't take much to turn a mundane report into something that's clashingly dreadful.

1. **Right-click the field you want to color to open the pop-up menu.**

   If you're touching up just *part* of a field, double-click that part first and then right-click to start the pop-up menu.

2. **Select Color from the menu.**

3. **When you're presented with the color palette, click your pick.**

   The color of choice is immediately applied to your field.

   Make sure that you can still read the text with your new background color. If you can't, refer to "Setting the Font" earlier in this chapter.

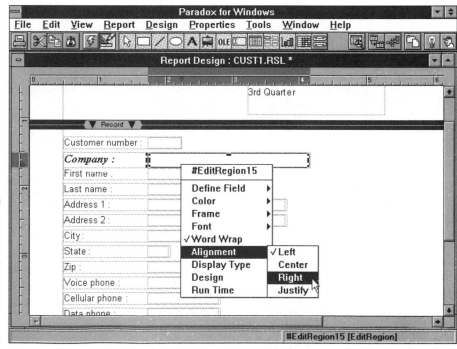

**Figure 20-6:**
The default is Left, but I want Company Name to be right-aligned.

## *Applying a filter*

Reports can have data filters, just like tables. The concept is exactly the same. If you're not clear on the Filter thing, check out Chapter 8 for a complete explanation.

1. **Right-click the field to filter.**

   The pop-up menu goes *poof!* and appears from nowhere.

2. **Select Filter from the pop-up menu.**

   This brings up the Field Filter dialog box.

3. **Type your filter text into the Field Filter dialog box. Click OK when you're done.**

Please, for your own sake, document your report filters. They're really handy little animals, but they're *very* easily forgotten. If something terribly evil ever happens to your report, the mind your documentation saves could be your own.

# *Shuffling Some Fields*

When Paradox slaps your fields into a report, it's not particularly artistic about the whole thing. It takes them all and unceremoniously drops them onto the page. Oh, they're all there, but the layout won't make anyone catch their breath.

To make your reports easier to read, easier to understand, and easier on the eyes (always a welcome feature), consider moving some of the fields around. You don't have to go wild and reorganize everything, but putting things in simple groups often does wonders for even the most boring data.

The point of all this isn't merely to beautify the report. The ultimate goal is to make the report easier to read and understand.

Organizing your fields in the report is actually kind of fun. I know that sounds sick, but the process appeals to my artistic side. Here's what to do.

1. **Figure out what you want the report to look like.**

   You don't need to have a complete plan written down or anything, but it helps if you have a general idea of what you want to do.

2. **With your report open in Design mode, select View⇨Zoom⇨Fit Width from the main menu.**

This squishes your report so that you can see the entire page width at once. It's really helpful when you're flinging fields around.

3. **Click a field to select it.**

To move several fields at the same time, you have to select them all (as in Figure 20-7). Click the first one, and then hold the Shift key down and click any others you want to bring along for the ride.

4. **Aim the mouse pointer at one of the selected fields, and then click and drag the field (or fields) to the new location.**

As you move the fields, a bunch of nondescript gray boxes show where the fields go. In Figure 20-8, the name and address fields are on the move.

Use the rulers to find out precisely (well, pretty precisely) where you are on the page.

5. **When everything is just the way you want it, release the mouse button.**

Paradox for Windows drops the fields onto the page.

If you don't like where everything landed, *immediately* select Edit⇨Undo from the menu or press Alt+Backspace. This tells Paradox to turn back the clock and pretend you didn't do the last thing that you did. The limitation is that you have to catch the error right away, otherwise you can't undo it.

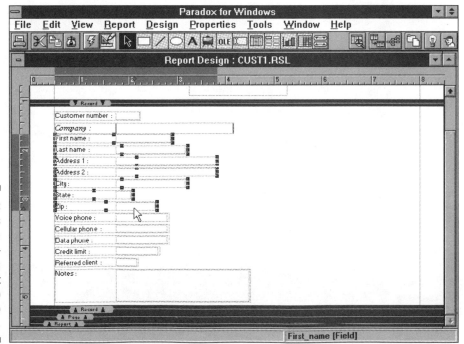

**Figure 20-7:**
It's practically a migration— everything from First Name to Zip is ready to move out.

# *Setting Trivial Page Details*

In addition to all the fun things you can do *on* the page, Paradox lets you do things *to* the page as well. You can create reports sized for the screen or printed page, adjust the margins, and, if you're committing the report to paper, choose the paper size and orientation.

The Page Layout dialog box shown in Figure 20-9 is your Master Control Panel for all this page stuff. Getting there is, as they say, half the fun, so hop on your mouse and gallop off into the following steps.

1. **With your report in Design mode (for this is how** *all* **good instructional steps seem to start), select** <u>R</u>**eport⇨**<u>P</u>**age Layout from the main menu.**

   Aha! So *this* is what starts the Page Layout dialog box. Now you know!

2. **In the** <u>D</u>**esign For area, tell Paradox whether this report is destined for the** <u>P</u>**rinter or** <u>S</u>**creen by clicking the appropriate radio button.**

   If you choose <u>S</u>creen, some of the other options in the dialog box become gray. It's okay — that's what they're supposed to do.

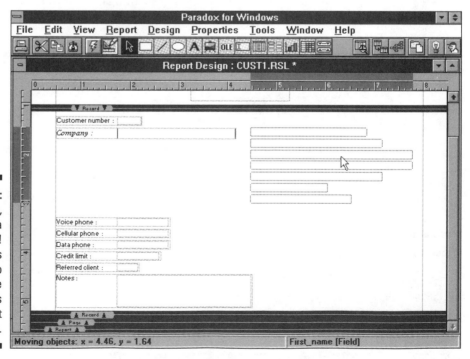

**Figure 20-8:**
Giddyap, data doggies! The herd's headed to the wide open spaces on the right of the page.

3. **For paper reports, you can choose a page Orientation. Click the radio button for Portrait or Landscape.**

   The little page icon in the Orientation box actually shows you how the page will look with the current setting.

4. **For the paper-based among you, turn your attention to the area in the middle of the dialog box labeled Paper Sizes. If you want to use something other than standard Letter paper, make your selection here.**

   In the upper right corner, Paradox lets you enter a custom paper size. Stay away from this option — stick with the standard page sizes.

5. **Margins lets you change Paradox's default half inch all the way around margin settings. Double-click in the margin box you want to change and then type a new margin.**

6. **When you're through with your page changes, click OK.**

   Save your report!

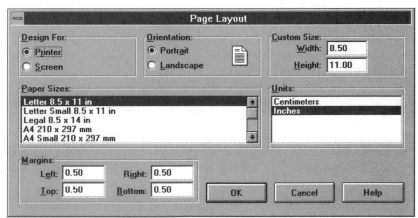

**Figure 20-9:**
The Page
Layout
dialog box.

# Chapter 21
# Separating Apples and Broccoli

. . . . . . . . . . . . . . . . . . . . . . . . . . . . . . . . . . . . . . . . . . . . . . . . . . . . . .

. . . . . . . . . . . . . . . . . . . . . . . . . . . . . . . . . . . . . . . . . . . . . . . . . . . . . .

*I* have a confession to make: I must have space between all the foodstuffs on my plate. I just can't stand having different foods *touching* each other. I don't know how I acquired this particular twist, but this chapter is an appropriate place to disclose it. This chapter, you see, is all about keeping thing organized, apart, and generally separate.

Often, you want see records that are alike grouped together. Paradox gives you that ability with report *bands*. You get several *other* abilities along with that, but you find out about those in the next section, so why spoil the surprise?

# Big Bands and Report Bands Are Not the Same

The world moves fast these days, too fast to keep up with every little development. So, as a public service, here's the information you need to prevent an embarrassing technological faux pas about Paradox report bands.

## Big bands

Big Bands are almost *nothing* like Paradox. The bands had 10 to 12 players organized into instrumental sections instead of being treated as a single group. Count Basie, Duke Ellington, Benny Goodman, and Glenn Miller led some of the best-known bands. Big Band music reached the height of popularity during the Swing Era (1935 to 1945), but was overtaken by the looser Bop style in the 50s. It was rediscovered in the 1970s and remains popular today.

## Report bands

Report bands, on the other hand, have nothing to do with music. Even if they *wanted* to play, their absolute lack of musical talent is augmented by a complete inability to hold an instrument. In the words of someone who probably said many such things, "it just ain't gonna happen."

You only find report bands in Paradox. They tell Paradox where to print the fields (er, *objects*) in the report. Each band governs a different area of the report. Altogether, there are four different report bands. Each one's area of concern is explained in the following list.

| | |
|---|---|
| Report | Governs the beginning and end of the report. |
| Page | Controls the top and bottom of each report page. |
| Group | Optional. You add Group bands yourself — as many as you want, need, or feel led to include. They set the order your records appear in the report. |
| Record | Where the data hangs out. When you print the report, this section repeats for each record in your table. If you're creating a big, fancy miltiple-record report, this band is called *All records*. (Just something *else* to remember.) |

Here are some tips to keep in mind:

- It's easy to find the bands in Figure 21-1 — they're the dark horizontal bars emblazoned with clever things like *Report, Page, and Record*. The report title *(Customer List)* is in the Page band; the Zip field is in the Zip Group band.

- The bands at the top of the report are the *headers*. Things in the header section are printed at the beginning of the report, the top of the page, or just generally before stuff in the Record band.

✔ At the bottom of the report, there's another set of bands with the same labels. These are the *footers*. Footer items are printed, well, you can probably guess where. (In case you just *don't* guess, they appear after the Record band, on the bottom of the page, and at the end of the report.)

✔ If two bands are touching (*ewww* — cooties!), Paradox for Windows ignores that section. In Figure 21-1, the Report band is right on top of the Page band, so Paradox omits it entirely.

# *Moving the Bands*

When you're working on a report, it seems like you're forever taking the report bands out for a drag to make more space for the stuff in your report. Moving them around isn't *hard,* but it is frustrating until you get the hang of it (much like writing your name one letter at a time in those tiny spaces on insurance forms).

1. **Click the band you're changing.**

   The trick to this whole thing is to *click the band you're working in,* even if it's not the exact one you want to move.

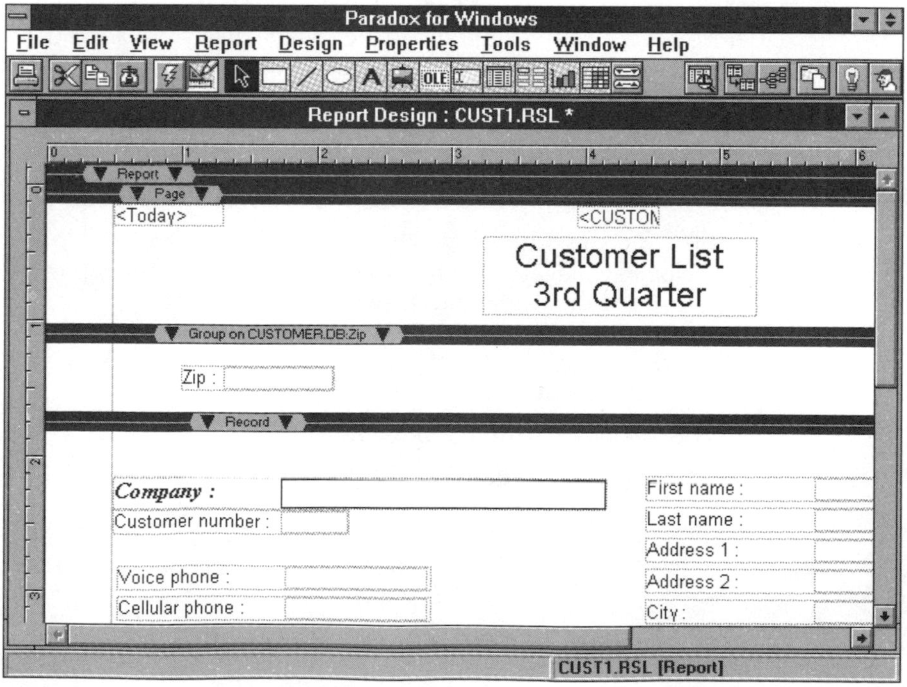

**Figure 21-1:**
Dig those *crazy* report bands. They look great, but you just can't dance to 'em.

To make space between the Report and Page bands in Figure 21-1, for example, you start by clicking the Report band, even though you're going to *move* the Page band.

2. **Position the mouse pointer over the band you want to move. When it turns into a double-headed arrow, press and hold the mouse button and then drag the band to its new home. Release the button when you get there.**

This is the most confusing part of the process. It drove me nuts for a while, but I finally caught on and everything was okay. (They even let me leave Happy Dale and move back home permanently.)

Depending on the circumstances, you might move the band you clicked on or the band right next to it. When the Report band is highlighted, the Page band represents the bottom of the Report band's space. Likewise, when the Page band is highlighted, the Record band is at the bottom of its space.

Continuing the example from Step 1, the Report band is highlighted, but you click and drag the *Page* band down to make more Report band space.

# Starting Your Own (Group) Band

Compared to moving the bands around, making a new one is a piece of cake. Before going through the steps, decide which field you want to use for the band. Once you make up your mind, continue on with the process. Keep in mind:

✔ Planning ahead simplifies your life, even when you're working with computers.

✔ You can have just one Group band, several, or none at all. The choice is yours.

✔ If you have several bands, Paradox starts sorting the report with the one closest to the Page band and works in from there.

 1. **Click the Add Band button on the ToolBar or select <u>R</u>eport⇨Add <u>B</u>and from the menu.**

The Define Group dialog box appears from nowhere.

2. **Double-click the field you're interested in as shown in Figure 21-2.**

The dialog box runs for the disk drive as your new group appears on the report (see Figure 21-3).

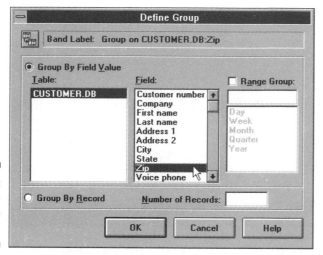

**Figure 21-2:**
The Define
Group
dialog box.

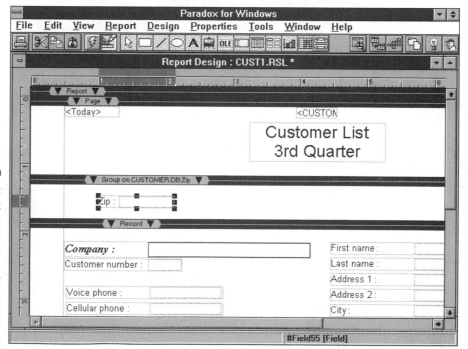

**Figure 21-3:**
Paradox
made the
group and
included a
copy of the
field — at
no extra
cost. Wasn't
that sweet?

## Group band inspection opportunities

Like everything else in Paradox for Windows, every band has a secret pop-up properties menu. To see the menu, just right-click the band itself. Of all the report bands, Group bands have two useful properties, which are listed following this paragraph. The other property settings are pretty much techno-weenie stuff, so I recommend you steer clear of them.

Define Group — Tells Paradox to use a different field for the group. Just pick the new field from the pop-up list and you're done.

Sort Order — Lets you specify the direction your records are sorted in the report. The default is ascending.

# *Ordering Groups Around*

If you're *really* adventuresome and have more than one Group band in your report, you can change the order of the group bands themselves with some clever clicking and dragging.

Paradox uses the groups in the order it finds them. If the Customer number group is first, followed by the Zip code group, Paradox sorts the report by Customer number and uses Zip code as a backup in case there are two identical Customer numbers.

There's only one step, so don't blink or you'll miss it.

1. **Click and drag the Group band you're moving past the other Group band in your report. Let go of the mouse button when the band is in position.**

As soon as you start moving the band, it disappears from sight and is replaced by two dotted gray lines. Just drag the lines past the other band and Paradox gets the idea (see Figure 21-4). When you release the mouse button, the band pops back into sight.

# *Disbanding Your Groups*

When a band has outlived its usefulness, delete it. No hemming and hawing, no pussyfooting around the issue — just delete it. But keep the following in mind:

- When you delete a band, Paradox deletes *everything* in the band. You lose all the fields, lines, graphics, and whatever else you packed in there.

- If you want the band to work with a different field, don't remove it completely and put in a new one — just tell Paradox which field you'd rather use. See the sidebar for more detail.

- Shed not a tear in sorrow, but look forward to the bright new day of a reconfigured report.

Deleting a band is a snap. Here's how you do it:

1. **Click the band you want to delete.**

   The unsuspecting band is highlighted. Click carefully so you don't arouse any suspicion.

2. **Press Del.**

   It's history.

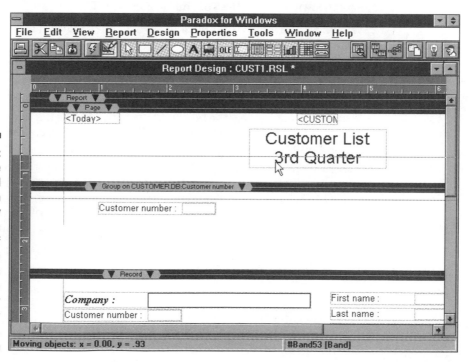

**Figure 21-4:**
The zip code Group band (which currently looks like a couple of dotted lines) moves ahead of the Customer number Group.

# Breaking Up the Page

Paradox collaborates with Windows to decide where the page breaks should go in your report. They analyze the various headers and footers in the report, look at all the data you're packing onto the page, and consider the page size before issuing a final decision.

Take heart, though. This duo of software giants invariably comes up with at least one page break that's in precisely the wrong place for your purposes. Oh, the agony of it all.

Luckily, you can take control of this whole messy affair by putting page breaks right into your report. Use the exceedingly short instructions that follow and soon you'll have a page break to call your very own.

Page breaks work and play well with Group bands. I recommend putting them in the band footer for the best results.

1. **Scroll down to the bottom of your report.**

2. **Wherever you want to put the page break, click way out at the left side of the Paradox window.**

   When you click, a funny little box appears along with a bold red line that cuts across the page. The whole thing looks remarkably similar to Figure 21-5, but yours is probably in color.

   To move it, just point at the box, hold down the mouse button, and drag the break up or down to its new home. When you're there, release the mouse button.

   If you want to get rid of a page break you inserted, pretend you're moving it, but drag it to the right instead of vertically. Release the mouse button when you're past the ruler, and the break is gone for good.

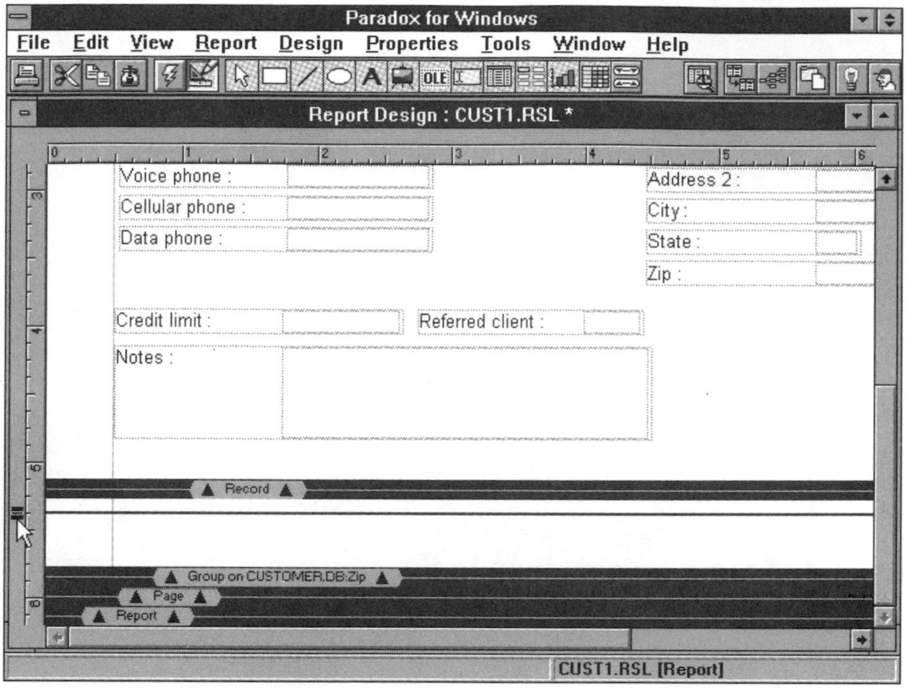


**Figure 21-5:** (Click) Whoa — it's a page break!

The 5th Wave    By Rich Tennant

"YES, WE STILL HAVE A FEW PROBLEMS WITH THE PRINTER. BY THE WAY, HERE'S A MEMO FROM MARKETING."

# Chapter 22
# Sublime Summaries and Crazy Calculations

- - - - - - - - - - - - - - - - - - - - - - - - - - - - - - - -

## In This Chapter

▶ Understanding summaries

▶ Adding a stray field

▶ Making it a summary

▶ Calculated craziness

▶ Creating the calculation

- - - - - - - - - - - - - - - - - - - - - - - - - - - - - - - -

*W*hat do you do when your data isn't telling you what you want to know? You go get some data that *does*. In Paradox report lingo, what you need are Summary and Calculated fields. These do the tallying, ciphering, counting, and other *ings* to create the vital information you need for whatever important things everyone at the office thinks you do all the time. This chapter explains how these tools work and shows you how to apply them.

## Whatza Summary?

You know what a summary is: It's the point where you start waking up during a presentation so you can be bright-eyed for drinks after it ends.

Well, in a Paradox report, a *summary* is a special kind of field. It does many of the same things that a Calculated field does in a query. For both of them, you tell Paradox what you want summarized and then sit back to see what happens.

Table 22-1 describes the ten available. Not every Summary is available for every type of field, so don't come unglued if you don't see all the options in your menu. Paradox only displays what you can use. Isn't that thoughtful?

| Table 22-1 | The Ten Summaries |
| --- | --- |
| **Summary** | **Description** |
| sum | Sums all nonzero values |
| count | Counts all nonzero values |
| min | Finds the smallest value |
| max | Finds the largest value |
| avg | Averages all values |
| std dev | Calculates the standard deviation |
| variance | Calculates the variance |
| first | Returns the first value |
| last | Returns the last value |
| previous | Returns the previous value |

You don't use the last five very often at all.

The most common summaries (sum, count, min, max, avg) often work hand in hand with a Group band of some kind or end up in the Report band footer. Although you can put summary fields anywhere in the report, be careful because you might get strange results depending on exactly where you put things.

If you're experimenting with a, shall we say, *unique* place for a summary field, check the report on-screen and make sure that Paradox is giving you the answers you're expecting.

# Adding a Stray Field

When you create a report, Paradox automatically includes fields for everything in the table. To make calculated or summary fields (and *special* fields too, which are covered later in this chapter), you need an extra field that's not attached to anything. I like to call these *stray fields,* because they wander around the report doing whatever they want, without any responsibilities. Well, they have no responsibilities until you *give* them some, but that's in the next section. Here are some things you should know about stray fields:

- ✔ A stray field can grow up to be a summary, special, calculated, or even a table field.

- ✔ Once you put it on the report, you can move the field into any band you choose.

▶ The only caveat about putting your new field in *any* band is that some calculations and summaries don't expect to be in the Record band. Putting the field there can cause erroneous values.

▶ No, you're thinking of the word *erogenous*. Erroneous means *untrue*.

The technique for adding a stray field is the same regardless of how you ultimately press it into service.

1. **Start the process by clicking the Field tool on the ToolBar.**

   The mouse pointer changes to a delightful cross hair with a small replica of the Field tool surgically attached to its backside. All things considered, it's a nice effect.

   There are no two ways about this one: you *have* to use the ToolBar. No alternate keystrokes, no menus, no deposit, no return, significant penalty for early withdrawal, offer not valid with other database programs or in the state of Vermont.

2. **Scroll through the report until you get to where the field goes. Stop there.**

3. **Position the cross hair where you want the upper left corner of the new field. Click and drag the mouse down and to the right to make a rectangle that's about an inch long. Release the mouse button when you're there.**

   Your new stray field pops into place, complete with a label that says (cleverly enough) LABEL. It doesn't look any better in Figure 22-1.

   Don't worry about getting the exact size for your field right now. Paradox changes the size when you officially make it a summary.

4. **Give the field something to do before it gets bored and wanders off on its own.**

   To make it a Calculated or Summary field, continue through the chapter to the appropriate section. To create a special field, read "Using special fields" and *then* the next section.

   Whatever way you go, you're stuck reading the next section so you might as well get on with it.

# *Making It a Summary*

So now you have a field. It's just a stray, a digital mongrel in the electronic pound of computerized life. It has no meaning, no purpose — yet.

Giving your field a goal in life takes just a couple of mouse clicks. Everything you need to do is described in the following steps. Proceed carefully (I'm sure you will).

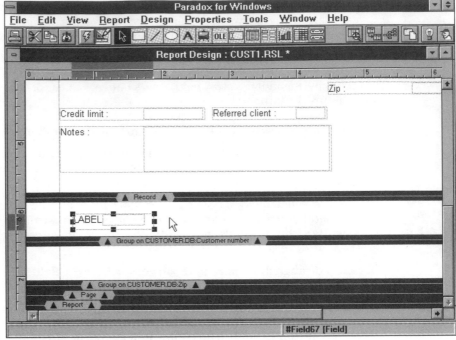

**Figure 22-1:**
A stray field
looks for a
home.
Maybe, just
maybe, it
will find one
soon.

1. **Create a new field for your summary calculation.**

   See the preceding section, "Adding a Stray field," for the details of this fun and enjoyable procedure.

2. **Right-click the lucky field that's destined for summarydom.**

   This opens the pop-up menu.

3. **Select Define Field⇨... (ellipsis) from the menu.**

   The Define Field Object dialog box takes center stage.

4. **Click in the down arrow next to the table name to open a list of table fields. Double-click the field you want to summarize.**

   The field name appears in the big area at the top of the dialog box.

   Scroll through the list if you need to. There's no reason to be ashamed that your field is way down at the end of the list. All the same, don't go around telling everybody.

5. **Click in the down arrow next to the Summary box. This reveals a list of the different summaries available for the type of field you selected. Click your choice (see Figure 22-2).**

The big box that previously held the field name now contains *both* the field name and the summary operator. Pretty techno-looking, isn't it?

Don't panic if the summary you want to use isn't in the list. Take your hand off the mouse, breathe deeply for a moment, and then make sure you clicked on the right table field. Paradox only shows you summaries that work with the type of field you selected — you can't try to Average your customer names, so it won't even let you try.

6. **Click OK to accept your work.**

When you return to the regularly scheduled report, a sight much like Figure 22-3 meets your eyes. There is the new Summary field, bright and shiny, full of promise and possibilities. Of course, it was christened with a rather uninspired name, but you can fix that.

If you're not sure *how* to do field name surgery, refer to "Embellishing Your Report" in Chapter 19 for the gory details.

# Calculated Craziness

If your stray fields don't end up as Summaries or special fields, you can always make them Calculations. And who knows — in the process of giving an unloved, unfocused field a new purpose in life, you might even learn something new about your data.

A Calculated field is just that: a field whose value is derived from calculation, usually involving other fields in the report. Like the Summary field, Calculated fields draw their roots from the query's CALC statement.

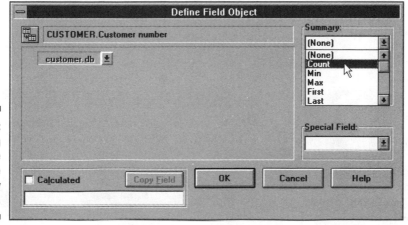

**Figure 22-2:**
Picking Count as the appropriate summary type.

## Using special fields

Although they're not exactly summaries, Paradox has five special fields you can use in your reports. Because you create them in much the same way you make a summary field, this seemed like as good a place as any to include them. So there.

The special fields display specific values. The five possible kinds are listed below along with a brief explanation of what each does.

| | |
|---|---|
| Today | Today's date |
| Now | Current time |
| Timestamp | Today's date *and* the current time |
| Page Number | Current page number |
| Number of Pages | Total number of pages in the report |

To add a special field to your report, create a field as if you're making a summary (you know you're not, but Paradox doesn't — that's okay). Right-click it, select Define Field⇨... form the pop-up menu. In the Define Field Object dialog box, click in the down arrow of the Special Field box to see the five field options. Click your choice and then click OK.

Treat it like just another field — move it, reformat it, do with it what you will. When you run the report, it displays whatever special value you selected.

One warning: don't use the Number of Pages field unless you're making a short report (less than 50 pages). Otherwise, you'll be sitting there all day and night while Paradox figures out how many pages there are and then prints each one. I've done it and it's not fun.

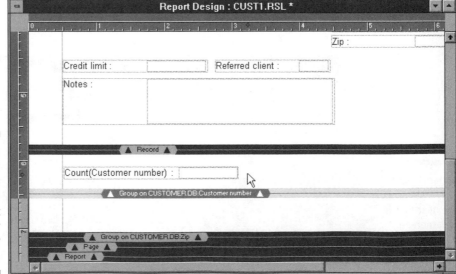

**Figure 22-3:** The finished field is safely in place but rather nerdily named.

There are plenty of things you can do with Calculated fields. They're popular for analyzing trends and doing simple math right in a report. For example, the report in Figure 22-4 uses calculated fields to show Available credit balance and the Average balance for the previous three months. The data for both calculations are in the table, but the answers themselves only exist in the report.

# Creating the Calculation

You'll be pleased to know that the hardest part of making a calculated field is giving it a name and lining it up with whatever else you have on your report. Have no fear, then, as you tackle these steps.

1. **Make a new field for the new calculation.**

   If you're not sure how to do this, refer to the section, "Adding a Stray Field," earlier in this chapter.

2. **Right-click the Calculated field-to-be.**

   As you expected, this opens the can of worms known casually as the Properties pop-up menu.

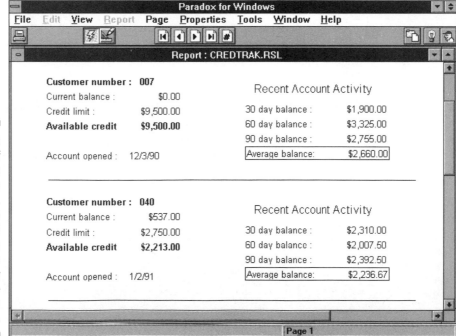

Figure 22-4:
Two of these fields aren't like the others. Available credit and Average Balance don't really exist— except in the report.

3. **Select Define Field⇨... from the menu.**

   The Define Field Object dialog box appears on your ever more cluttered screen.

4. **Tell Paradox this is a Calculated field by clicking the Calculated checkbox.**

5. **Using the pull-down table field list, the Copy Field, and your favorite mathematical operators, build your calculation.**

   Calculations look just like mathematical equations, except they have field names in place of the numbers. The calculation formula for the Average Balance field in Figure 22-4 looks like this:

   [CREDIT.Credit limit]-[CREDIT.Current balance].

   You don't have to type all that punctuation to make this stuff work. Instead, you use menus and buttons and let Paradox handle the techno-weenie stuff.

   *To insert a field into your calculation,* click the down arrow next to the table name and click the field you want. Click the Copy Field button to move the field name (and all its associated punctuation) into the Calculated field box. The field is automatically highlighted, so press the right-arrow key to unhighlight it before you do anything else.

   *To include math symbols,* type the symbol (+, -, *, /, or parenthesis) from the keyboard.

   All the normal rules of Paradox math apply to Calculated fields. If you need a quick brush-up on that, refer to Chapter 16.

   When your calculation is done, it should bear a resemblance to Figure 22-5.

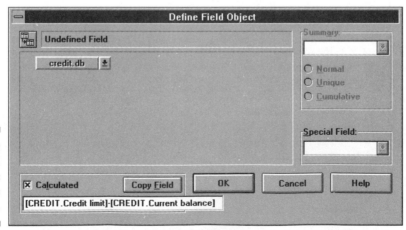

**Figure 22-5:**
A calculated field gets ready for its appearance.

6. **Click OK when it's a mathematical masterpiece.**

   When Paradox returns back to your report, it doesn't look like anything's different about the field. That's normal; Paradox doesn't know how to label Calculated fields so it just leaves them alone and waits for *you* to do something.

7. **If you're lining up the calculated field with other fields above it, double-click the data area of the field, and then click and drag it to wherever you want it.**

   Don't worry if it looks like you're dragging it out of the field box. When you let go of the mouse button, Paradox expands the box automatically.

8. **To change the boring and inappropriate LABEL to something else, double-click it and type the replacement.**

   This is just like using a word processor, so your arrow, Del, and Backspace keys are all there to help.

   Chapter 19 gives you the lowdown on fixing field names in the "Embellishing Your Report" section.

9. **Enhance the field with a new format, alignment, or what have you.**

   Again, all this stuff is in Chapter 19 for your cross-referencing pleasure.

If your calculated field doesn't line up with the other fields around it, double-click the field's data area, and then right-click to bring up the properties menu. Select Run Time and see if there's a check next to Fit Width. If there *is*, click Fit Width to remove the check. That little trick cost me so much hair I don't even want to talk about it.

# Chapter 23
# Recycling Your Work

● ● ● ● ● ● ● ● ● ● ● ● ● ● ● ● ● ● ● ● ● ● ● ● ● ● ● ● ● ● ● ● ● ● ● ●

### In This Chapter
▶ Filtering for a tighter view
▶ Same report, different table

● ● ● ● ● ● ● ● ● ● ● ● ● ● ● ● ● ● ● ● ● ● ● ● ● ● ● ● ● ● ● ● ● ● ● ●

*I*n these days of *reduce, reuse, recycle, or die in the attempt,* having two or three different reports for every table on your disk drive is a wasteful extravagance. Think of the megabytes you're wasting. Think long term — save some of it for your kids. (Today's games take a lot of space, you know.)

Paradox wants to save you time (and keep you environmentally correct), so it gives you several ways to reuse reports. They're explored in this chapter. Whether you need to see just a few of your records or use last year's data with this year's report, you're covered.

## Filtering for a Tighter View

Report filters let you limit a report to only the records you're interested in. They work just like table filters, so if you want to see everybody from Ohio, both customers who bought product #58827-9A (a stuffed, mauve armadillo), or all the payment records for last January, odds are you can do it without making any serious changes to your report.

Although filters are quite flexible, they're best for one-shot special uses. I don't recommend permanently building a filter into a report just because you might forget about it and end up with the wrong data. Then you'd be mad, your boss would be mad — heck, everybody would be mad.

When you work with filters, keep the following in mind:

   ✔ You can only put filters on regular table fields, not Calculated or Summary fields.

✔ If you simply *must* use a filter as a permanent feature of a report, make sure that you document how the report works so that someone can reproduce it years from now after your promotion.

✔ Paradox *doesn't* automatically save your filter. The only way to make the filter permanent is by manually saving the report.

Now that your appetite is whetted, here's how to make your own report filters.

1. **With the report in Design mode, right-click the field you're filtering.**

   This pops up the field properties menu. If you're using a tabular report (where the data comes out looking like the table that bore it), select the field you want to filter by double-clicking on it and then right-click on the field to bring up the field propertied menu. It's the same result as with the other report types, but with more steps to get there.

   Only actual table fields can have filters. Summary and Calculated fields can wish, hope, and beg, but Paradox won't let them have a filter. No way, no how, not today, not ever.

2. **Select Filter from the menu.**

   The field filter dialog box appears.

3. **Type in your filter.**

   Figure 23-1 shows a simple filter for the Credit limit field. The report will only show account information for customers who can charge more than $4,000 worth of goods.

   For help constructing a filter (or if you're bored and want to read something else), flip back to "Filtering Your Table for Cleaner Data" in Chapter 8.

4. **Click OK.**

   The filter is now loaded, cocked, and ready to fire.

 5. **To see how the filter worked, click the thundering View Data button on the ToolBar or press F8.**

   Hopefully, your report looks great and you're off and running.

 If things didn't work out *quite* that well, click the Design button on the ToolBar (or press F8) to go back to Design mode and try again.

To save the filter as a permanent part of the report, select File⇨Save from the menu. If the filter is a permanent feature, write down some notes (*lots* of notes) in case the report file ever self-destructs or something.

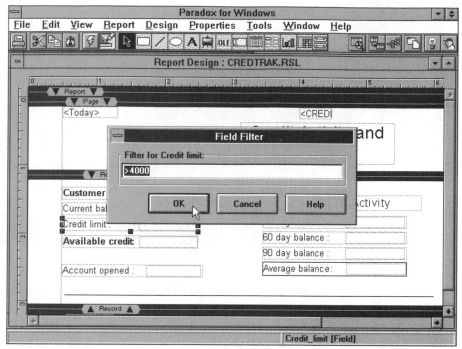

**Figure 23-1:**
A simple filter is far better than making a new report.

# *Same Report, Different Table*

Suppose that you have five tables with the same structure (annual invoice data or something like that). You create this incredible report for one of them; it's a masterpiece and the boss loves it. In fact, the boss loves it so much, he wants to see that marvelous report with the other table's data — all *four* of the other tables. Yikes! It took *forever* to build the first one. Making four more should take you until, oh, about next October. Well, job security *is* a nice thing ....

Don't faint yet — you don't have to recreate the same report for every table in the group. (Is that good news or what?) Tell Paradox to use your too-beautiful-for-words report, but fill it with data from *another* table. As long as the table structure is the same, Paradox doesn't care where the data comes from.

Well, it almost doesn't care. Paradox kinda chokes on the calculated fields in your report. Either rebuild the calculations from scratch or seek help from your local guru for other ways to fix them.

It's almost a one-step process, too. Here are the details (which aren't many).

**1. In the Project Viewer, right-click the report you want to use.**

This opens the faithful pop-up menu.

2. **Select View With from the menu.**

   The Select File dialog box pops into action.

   If you want to print the report instead of viewing it, select Print With from the menu.

   Don't ever tell it to print the *first* time you try mating a report with a different table. That's like crawling around on your knees *begging* to waste a ream or two of paper (plus a whole lot of your patience). View the newly created report first, *then* print it when you're satisfied with the results.

3. **Double-click the table you want to substitute into the report (Figure 23-2).**

   Paradox sets up the report and, barring any unexpected errors (such as Calculated field problems), displays it on-screen.

   If the report goes directly into Design mode, there's probably a Calculated field in your report. Either replace it with a new one or just trash it altogether. If your report is *filled* with them, get your guru's help — he may know a secret way to fix the problem.

4. **If you want to save the report so that it uses the *new* file all the time, click the Design button and then select either File⇨Save or Save As from the menu.**

   Use Save if you want to change the original report. Use Save As to make a *copy* of the report and leave the original intact.

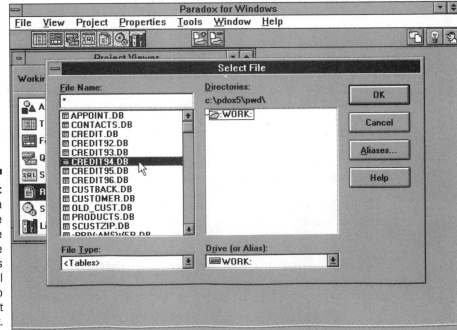

**Figure 23-2:**
Choosing a substitute table in the Select File dialog box is like, well, I'll get back to you about that.

## Using a query instead of a table

As part of Paradox's continued quest to amaze and utterly confound you with infinite options, I present you with this tidbit of technical twaddle: Instead of basing your report on a *table,* you can feed it from a *query.*

Yes—it's amazing but true. If your query includes all the fields in the table (or at least all that the report calls for), you can fill up the report *without* a table. This lets you ask questions that are too complicated for a simple filter to handle.

To do this bit of magic, create and save a query that provides the data you need, then start through the steps in "Same Report, Different Table."

When you're ready to double-click the table name Step 3, click in the down arrow in the File Type box instead. Select Queries from the pop-up list and watch the File Name area show you all the available queries. Double-click the query of your choice and you're done.

Now when you open the report, Paradox runs the query, then uses the Answer table to fill up the report.

# Part V
# Leftovers from the Fridge

## The 5th Wave
By Rich Tennant

"YEAH, I USED TO WORK ON REFRIGERATORS, WASHING MACHINES, STUFF LIKE THAT—HOW'D YOU GUESS?"

# In This Part...

*Pour, oh pour the pirate sherry;*
*Fill, oh fill the pirate glass;*
*And, to make us more than merry,*
*Let the pirate bumper pass.*

Act I, Gilbert and Sullivan's *The Pirates of Penzance*

There's a little bit of everything here — you know, the stuff that just didn't fit anywhere else. Forms, graphs, and philosophical ponderings about why anyone in their right mind would use multi-table databases abound in herein. Drink deep and enjoy.

# Chapter 24
# Form Is Everything

● ● ● ● ● ● ● ● ● ● ● ● ● ● ● ● ● ● ● ● ● ● ● ● ● ● ● ● ● ● ● ● ●

### In This Chapter
▶ Forming an opinion
▶ Making a quick (but plain) form
▶ Designing a better form
▶ Sprucing up an austere form
▶ Saving it when you're through
▶ Using your new form
▶ Tooling around in the Project Viewer

● ● ● ● ● ● ● ● ● ● ● ● ● ● ● ● ● ● ● ● ● ● ● ● ● ● ● ● ● ● ● ● ●

*W*atching Olympic gymnastics and figure skating often makes me think of Paradox forms. Before you get the idea I'm a green-skinned nerd wallowing in a vat of Jolt Cola (a fact I've worked *very* hard to disguise, I might add), let me say that the link is purely semantic. I see the athlete doing the aforementioned athletic thing, hear the commentator say something like "look at that form," and then KABOOM! — the artistic moment is shattered and I'm thinking of Paradox.

Well, since you're here too, let's talk Paradox for Windows forms. This chapter is one-stop shopping for all your on-screen form needs. It covers making a new form, tidying it up a bit (forms can *never* be too tidy), and doing other fun, form-like things. I did forms in one chapter because you probably won't use them as much as reports or the other things in the book. It's also because I was running out of space.

You may notice that this chapter bears an uncanny resemblance to Chapter 19, "A Simple Report Is Better than None." That's because it does. Creating a new report and making a form are *very* much alike. When you're familiar with one, you don't even break a sweat with the other. (I suppose that averages out the incredible amount of sweat you invested learning that first one.)

# Forming an Opinion

Forms are like reports, but different (ooh — that's *so* philosophical). The main difference between them is how they're used. Reports are mainly for *displaying* your data; forms are for *working* with it.

You generally don't print a form (although you can, if you want to). Instead, you use it on-screen to view, add, edit, and delete records from the table. The real strength of a Paradox for Windows form is its flexibility: It can include calculated fields, cross multiple pages, and look like the real, honest-to-goodness paper form you used to know and love (if that's what you want).

Designing a form is a lot like setting up a report. It's easier, though, because you don't have all those bands to contend with. Table data is in field objects, titles are in text boxes, all the objects have a properties menu when you right-click them — gosh, this *does* sound a lot like a report. The two are *so* much alike that after you get comfortable with one of them, using the other is no problem at all.

Forms are also the backbone of Paradox's programming power. Almost everything those programmer-types do in Paradox for Windows is done with forms. I just thought you'd like to know.

# Making a Quick (but Plain) Form

Depending on your frame of mind and what you're doing in Paradox, there are a couple of different ways to make a new form.

- ✔ If you're looking at a table right now, thinking to yourself "Hey, this table should have a form," the Quick Form button is probably for you.

- ✔ The less impulsive among you may prefer the menu or New Form button approach.

- ✔ For a lead-me-by-the-hand kind of interactive learning experience, check out the Creating a Standard Form section within the Queries, Forms, and Reports section of the Coaches.

## New forms from the Quick Form button

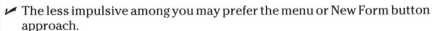

If you're viewing a table, kinda wandering aimlessly through it and wondering whether there's a better way to do this data stuff (or pondering why you're so hungry when you just ate an hour ago), you're just a mouse click away from a completed form. The answer to your longings is up there on the ToolBar; the steps that follow tell the rest of the tale.

1. **View your table on-screen.**

   You can't get around this — it's the only way to see the Quick Form button.

 2. **With your table in the workspace, click the Quick Form button.**

   A new form appears, displaying the current record. Was that easy or what?

   It's a *really* plain form, but you can fix that easily enough. Check out "Designing a Better Form" and "Sprucing Up an Austere Form" for all the details.

   When you're viewing data with a form, the ToolBar looks much like it does when you're viewing a table, doesn't it?

## New forms the old-fashioned way

From the Project Viewer (or if Paradox is running and you're just hanging out with nothing particular in the workspace), there's always the ToolBar (again) and the main menu.

Creating a form this way gives you some control over the field layout (and it makes an arguably prettier form).

1. **Either right-click the Form button or select File⇨New⇨Form from the menu.**

   Figure 24-1 shows the secret right-click ToolBar button menu in action. (Try saying *that* three times fast.)

   All this drama and suspense ends with the New Form dialog box innocently wandering out onto the screen.

**Figure 24-1:**
Right-clicking on the Form button brings up another hidden menu.

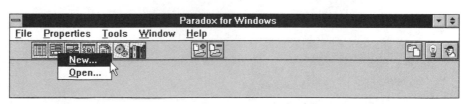

2. **Click the Data Model / Layout Diagram button in the New Form dialog box.**

   The Data Model dialog box takes center stage.

   The Form Expert is an interesting, timesaving option. Check out the sidebar for more information about it.

3. **In the File Name list, double-click the table for this form (just like Figure 24-2).**

   The table name appears in the big area on the right of the dialog box.

4. **Click OK to continue.**

   The Design Layout dialog box steps onto the screen and immediately begins hogging the limelight.

5. **The form fields are automatically laid out By Columns. If you don't like that, try clicking the By Rows radio button in the Field Layout area.**

   The sample area beneath the Show Layout button gives you a sample of what the form will look like with your chosen field layout.

   There are a great deal of interesting settings on this form, and I recommend leaving them all alone. They're nothing but trouble — trouble from the very start.

6. **Click OK to create the form.**

   Not a bad looking form, if I do say so myself. Granted, it's no work of art, but it's not disco, either.

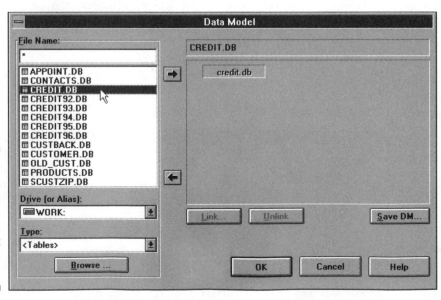

Figure 24-2:
Double-click
the file
name to
throw an
innocent
table out to
the form.

# *Designing a Better Form*

There are two ways to look at a report: in Design mode and in View mode.

Yes, you report hounds, they're exactly the same as Design and View mode when you're working with a report. They even have some of the same buttons on the ToolBar.

In *View mode,* you're interactively adding, changing, and generally mucking about with the data in the underlying table. The ToolBar looks much like it does when you're viewing a table, which is a little comforting. Many of your old friends are there, such as Locate, Filter, and the famous VCR buttons for scrolling through the records. Figure 24-3 shows the Credit table viewed through a simple form. You get here from Design mode by clicking the Thunder-  ing Thor Lightning Bolt button on the ToolBar.

*Design mode* is for changing the *form,* not the data. Here you add fields to the form, change the field formats, put in text titles, all kind of stuff like that. The ToolBar is different, and rulers appear along the sides of the form. Figure 24-4 shows the same form in Design mode. To flip into Design mode from View  mode, click the Design button on the ToolBar.

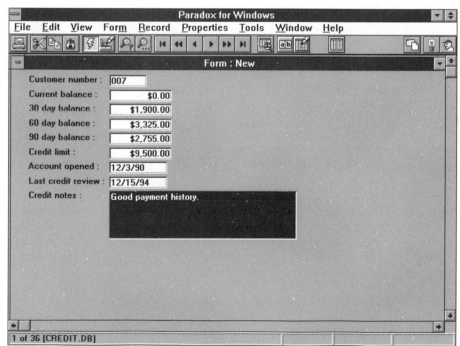

**Figure 24-3:**
A form in
View mode.

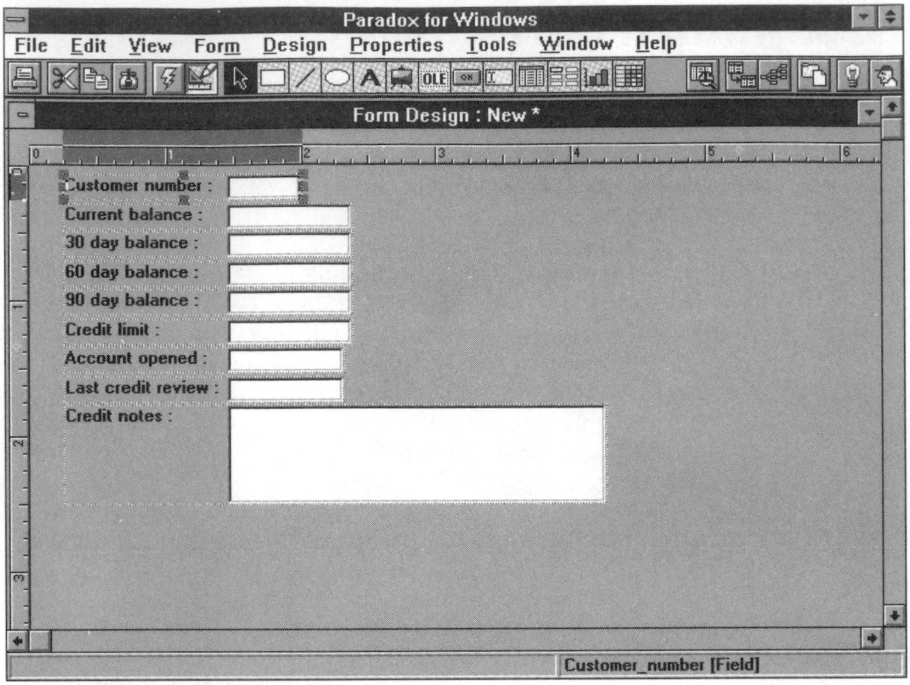

**Figure 24-4:**
The same
form in
Design
mode.

There isn't a whole lot to Design mode, as you can see in Figure 24-4. The
Customer number field is selected right now — that's why it's surrounded by
dark little boxes. The rulers along the sides of the form help you place things
precisely. They light up when you select a field or other object and show you its
exact position.

# Sprucing Up an Austere Form

Describing a basic form as *plain* is an understatement. Without making the form
feel bad, let's just say there are a lot of *opportunities for enhancement*. The
following sections outline the most common things you need to do with a form.
This isn't everything, but it's a really good start.

You make all these changes in Design mode, so the instructions assume that
you're already there.

## Getting a new style

All the number and time-related fields in a form can be formatted according to your whims. The precise options depend on the field you're using, but the steps to do it are the same everywhere.

1. **Right-click the field you're formatting.**

   The secret pop-up menu appears.

   You can format numeric, time-related, and logical fields, including the Number, Money, Short Integer, Date, Time, Timestamp, and Logical field types. Alpha fields can't be formatted.

2. **From the menu, select Format and then the type of formatting you're doing from the submenu.**

   Depending on the exact field type, the Format submenu may have only one option (like Number Format) or several.

   If there *isn't* a Format menu option, you can't format that field. Sorry, but that's life in the fast lane.

3. **Select the format of your dreams from the next menu.**

   Feel free to play with the various options — you can always change it if you pick one that's just horrible.

## Changing the alignment

The field's alignment governs how the data sits in the field. You have four choices: left, center, right, and justified.

Don't use justified — it looks stupid.

1. **Double-click the data area of the field you're changing.**

   When you're done, just the data side of the field, not the title, is selected (as shown in Figure 24-5).

2. **Right-click the highlighted data area.**

   Three guesses on what happens — you're right, the properties menu pops up. (You're getting good at this stuff. Don't go all nerdy on me, okay?)

3. **Select Alignment from the menu and then select your particular choice from the submenu.**

   Nothing really changes on the surface, so try viewing data with the form to make sure it's working like you thought it would. If it didn't, change it to something else.

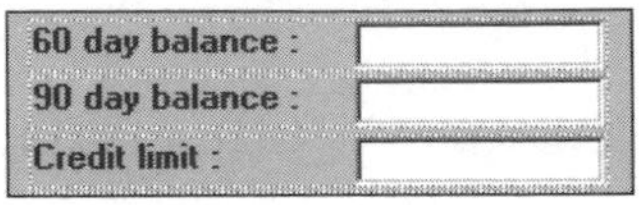

**Figure 24-5:**
The data area of the 90 day balance field is selected and ready for a swift right-click.

| 60 day balance : | |
| 90 day balance : | |
| Credit limit : | |

# Fixing the names

Sometimes, field names just aren't in any natural, human language. Most people enjoy using forms written in their native language, so Paradox lets you change any of those (ahem) peculiar field names to something a little more understandable.

I'm reasonably convinced that there are aliens in our midst simply because of field names like GI96RTY3QP. If you are, in fact, an alien, let this be a lesson: use better field names to avoid embarrassing discoveries (such as your true heritage).

Here's how to change a field name:

1. **Double-click the name part of the field.**

   If everything worked right, the field name is surrounded by a dotted border held up with several little square fence posts.

2. **Click it again.**

   Sometimes twice just isn't enough. The highlighting goes away and a little toothpick cursor appears.

3. **Change the field name to whatever you want.**

   At this point, it's just like working in a word processor. Use the Backspace, Del, and arrow keys to complete your edit.

Be careful when you're changing things. The changes are just about permanent the moment you make them. If you *seriously* hurt something, try selecting Edit⇨Undo from the main menu, but don't get your hopes up too high.

4. **When you're satisfied with the new name, click somewhere outside the field to save your work.**

## *Fiddling with the font*

You can choose any font you want for any text object on your screen. If you use a TrueType font, it can be any size, too. If you're not clear about TrueType fonts (or fonts in general), get a copy of *Windows For Dummies* from IDG Books Worldwide.

Here's how to change fonts:

1. **Select the object you want to change.**

Precisely how you do this depends on what you're changing.

To select a *whole field,* click once on the field, then Ctrl+right-click to open the properties menu. From here, skip ahead to Step 3.

To select *either the title or data part of a field*, double-click the part you're changing.

To select a *text area,* click it.

2. **Right-click the selected text thingie.**

If you're changing the *whole field,* remember to Ctrl+right-click instead.

3. **Select Font from the menu, then click the funny little button on top of the submenu.**

This brings up the Font dialog box, as depicted in Figure 24-6.

4. **Choose the appropriate font, size, and style from the options in the dialog box.**

Only use TrueType fonts. They're the ones with the *TT* graphic next to them in the font list.

5. **When you're done, click the button in the upper right corner of the dialog box to make your changes permanent.**

Don't panic when the cursor changes into a funny sand dollar-like apparition — it's supposed to do that.

**Figure 24-6:**
Make your prettiest picks from the full-featured Font dialog box

## Adding some color

All plain and no color makes for some pretty plain, uncolored forms. If you want to add a splash of excitement to your forms, try some color. Here's how:

1. **Right-click the field you want to color.**

   The infamous properties menu poofs into existence.

2. **Select Color from the menu, then click your choice from the super-cool pop-up palette.**

   The field immediately adopts your new color.

Don't go overboard with colors. The goal isn't to make an electronic crazy quilt data entry screen, but rather to highlight important stuff that you might miss otherwise.

## Using titles and other text

I think it's against the law in some states (and probably a violation of at least seven or eight different federal codes) to create a form without some instructions. Even electronic forms need notes and titles. Here's how to include them.

1. **Click the Text button on the ToolBar.**

   The button changes color to let you know it's *on*.

2. **Position the mouse pointer where you want the upper left corner of the text area. Click and drag the pointer to the lower right corner of the new text area. Release the mouse button when the area is the right size.**

   Figure 24-7 shows the mouse in the midst of the whole sordid maneuver.

   Don't be shocked that the cursor looks like a cross-hair with an A attached to its, rear.

3. **Type the text of your title, epistle, or missive in the box.**

   The text automatically wraps when it gets to the edge of the screen. Press Enter to start a new line.

4. **Click outside the text box when you're through.**

   If your box isn't the right size or shape, click outside of it and then click it. Put your mouse pointer over one of the dark gray fence posts and click and drag to resize the text area. The ones in the center of a side only move left or right; the fence posts in the corner let you move any direction.

   To adjust the alignment or change the font, refer to "Changing the Alignment" and "Fiddling with the Font" earlier in this chapter.

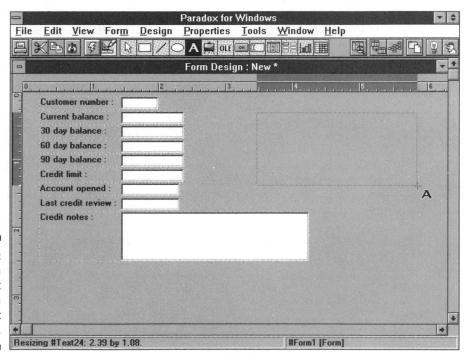

**Figure 24-7:** Making a new text area with the Text tool.

# Shuffling Fields around

Moving fields hither and thither is pretty easy. Really, it is — I wouldn't lie to you about something like this. Here's how you can do it:

1. **Click the field or other object you want to move.**

   The clicked-upon object is gratified with the attention and blushes in the form of a dotted gray border with little gray fence posts.

2. **Position your cursor near the center of the field, and then click and drag the field to the new location. Release the mouse button when you're there.**

If the whole thing goes *terribly* awry, just let go of the mouse button and drop the field somewhere, and then select Edit⇨Undo from the menu. If you've been living right (and you *know* you should be), the field pops back to its previous position.

## Including a calculated field

Forms can have calculated fields just like reports. In fact, the process to create a calculated field is *exactly* the same for both. Rather than bore you with simple repetition of all the instructions, see the Chapter 22 sections "Adding a Stray Field" and "Creating the Calculation."

Forms don't have bands, so just ignore that stuff.

# Saving It When You're Through

Unlike changing a table, Paradox *doesn't* automatically save your form. In fact, I have abused several walls over the years because of this very thing. To save *your* wall from similar head-shaped dents, remember to save your forms. Here's how:

1. **If you're not already there, get into Design mode.**

   You have to be in Design mode to save the form — there are no two ways about this one.

2. **Select File⇨Save from the menu.**

   If this is a new form, the Save File As dialog box appears and anxiously waits for you type a name into the New File Name box. When it's there, click OK to save your form.

   If you were just making a few changes to an old form, Paradox saves the changes with no further ado.

   If you changed an old form and want to save your changes to a *new* file (leaving the old one untouched), select File⇨Save As from the menu. This tells Paradox to create a new file and let the old one rest unmolested.

# Using Your New Form

As you might expect, Paradox has a couple of different ways to call your forms up for use.

The direct way is through the Project Viewer. Click the Forms icon and then double-click the name of the form you want to use. As always, change the Working Directory if you need to.

Find out all the details of the Project Viewer and the all-powerful Working Directory in Chapter 3, "Places for Your Stuff." Also see the next section in this chapter, "Tooling Around in the Project Viewer" for more about the form management utilities it has to offer you.

The indirect way to open a form is through the menu or the main ToolBar. On the menu, select File⇨Open⇨Form. In the Open Document dialog box, double-click the name of the form you want. You can change the Working Directory here, as well.

If you want to open the form in Design mode instead of View mode, click the Design radio button in the Open Mode area of the dialog box before you double-click the file name.

Instead of going through the menu, you can use the Form button on the main ToolBar. Click it to see the Open Document dialog box and then continue as if nothing special happened.

# Tooling Around in the Project Viewer

In the spirit of fairness, justice, and saleable functionality, Paradox includes several tools for the use (and abuse) of your forms. They're all briefly explained in the list that follows. None of the tools are particularly wild, but they collectively contribute to the paradigm-shattering experience that *is* Paradox for Windows.

For access to these tools, click the Forms icon in the Project Viewer and then right-click the particular form in question. The properties menu immediately pops up, ready to do thy bidding (within the boundaries of programming and good taste, of course).

*Saleable functionality* means *it does stuff that makes people spend money to buy it.* Saleable functionality is at the heart of every piece of commercial software.

| | |
|---|---|
| <u>V</u>iew Data | Opens the form in View mode. |
| De<u>s</u>ign | Opens the form in Design mode. |
| View <u>W</u>ith | Opens the form but lets you look at a *different* table than the one the form usually works with. Seek help from your guru before messing with this. |
| <u>C</u>opy | Brings up the Copy dialog box so you can make a duplicate of your form. The original is unchanged. |
| <u>R</u>ename | Brings up the Rename dialog box and lets you change the name of your form. |
| <u>D</u>elete | Frantically asks whether you *really* want to erase the report for ever and ever. Click <u>Y</u>es to send the little guy into digital oblivion. |

## Getting some Expert advice

Unlike the Creating a Standard Form Coach, the Form Expert doesn't *teach* you how things work; it asks you some questions and then builds the form for you.

The whole Expert process is pretty self-explanatory, so I don't think you'll have any problems with it. It even turns out some okay-looking forms (which you can change with the Form Designer should you feel the need).

I recommend using the Expert as a tool to learn about more complicated kinds of forms. Let the Expert do the hard part, then take its product into the Form Designer and figure out what makes it tick — or just embellish it with a couple of well-placed flourishes and take credit for the whole thing.

# Chapter 25

# Lines, Bars, and Yummy Data Pies

• • • • • • • • • • • • • • • • • • • • • • • • • • • • • • • • • • • •

• • • • • • • • • • • • • • • • • • • • • • • • • • • • • • • • • • • •

*E*verywhere in the world today, things are getting graphic. Graphic violence, graphic protests, graphic speedometers, and graphic interfaces are part of everyday life. Brace yourself, because there's a new menace on the horizon: *graphic data.*

Okay, so graphs aren't *really* a menace to society, but that sure did give the chapter a sensationalist start, didn't it? Back in Reality (a place I usually just visit), graphs are a popular tool to figure what the heck your data is trying to say. Seeing a trend is *much* easier if you're looking at a line wandering across the page rather than three pages of tightly spaced numbers.

Paradox gives you plenty of graphing options, but this chapter focuses on the graphs you really need, graph terms, and how to make a Quick Graph.

## *Getting Graphic*

All told, Paradox offers 17 different graphs for your visual presentation pleasure. These include both normal two-dimensional (2D) and *Wow!* three-dimensional (3D) versions of all the popular business graphs, plus some more specialized things like the X-Y chart. Before you go into graphic possibility overload, let me quickly say that you don't really need most of these charts. They're just marketing fluff.

To do real-world work, all you need is the three classic charts everybody knows and loves: bar, line, and pie. Add *combination* to that list because sometimes it takes a line *and* a bar to really get the point across.

Your charts shouldn't even be 3D; just use simple, flat, 2D charts that say what they have to say and leave the audience wowing to their message. Figures 25-1 and 25-2 illuminate the point. Each chart displays the *same* data. Which one looks *primo wow cool?* Which one actually tells you something? I rest my case.

Table 25-1 gives you some quick ideas for using bar, line, pie , and combination charts. Don't just take my word for it — try different charts with your own data. Sometimes using the wrong chart leads to interesting discoveries as you see your data in a new way.

| Table 25-1 | Chart Types |
|---|---|
| Bar | Great for displaying a lot of figures over time or drawing comparisons. Bars are nice because almost everyone knows how to read one. |
| Line | Marvelous for trends or anything else that happens over time. They're lines — what more can you say? |
| Pie | Good for seeing what makes up a set of data — *one* set. It *doesn't* do comparisons. Like bar charts, pies are easy to read and interpret. |
| Combination | Although it's not really a specific *type,* Paradox lets you mix bar and line elements in the same graph. This is very powerful when you're combining trends and straight numbers (like monthly sales and the percentage each month represents of the annual total). Figure 25-2 is a bar/line combination. |

Here are some things to keep in mind:

- ✔ Regardless of what you're using graphs for, stick to the simple ones that let your message shine. That means 2D charts — period.

- ✔ Seriously, there's a backlash against 3D charts in business. Although they look great (sometimes *truly* breathtaking), they just don't *communicate* like their old-fashioned 2D counterparts. Don't get carried away by the *Wow!* factor of a 3D chart.

- ✔ Is there *ever* a time for 3D charts? Yes, I guess. The only time I recommend using a 3D chart is if your data doesn't really say *anything* and you want to obscure that fact from the audience. 3D charts are unbeatable for that, as Figure 25-1 shows.

Before setting out to create your own graphs, take a glance at Figure 25-3 for a refresher of the graph lingo you learned (and appropriately forgot) back in school. This is just enough terminology to get you through Paradox's gauntlet of pop-up menus, pull-down lists, and sundry dialog boxes.

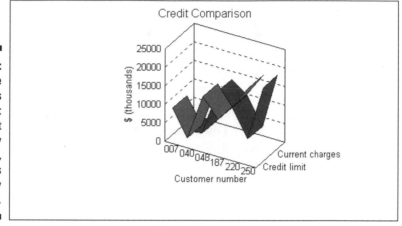

**Figure 25-1:**
The politician's dream chart: it doesn't say anything, but looks absolutely great.

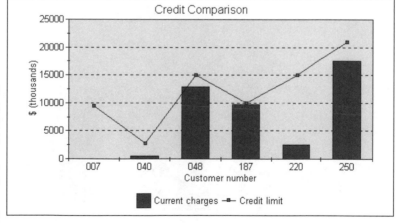

**Figure 25-2:**
A plain chart that has a message and delivers it.

One final thing: graphs in Paradox can't live alone — they're electronic parasites and have to live on either a form or report. Quick Graphs are automatically born on a form; graphs in a report are an entirely different matter. See "Graphs in reports" later in the chapter for the bad news about them.

# Building Really Quick Graphs

Borland calls this the *Quick Graph* option because it's quick and it makes a graph (they're sharp people, those programmers). In keeping with that spirit, I'll make this fast.

   **1. When you're viewing the table you want to graph, click the Quick Graph button or press Shift+F7 on the keyboard (see Figure 25-4).**

The Define Graph dialog box appears, looking a little formal for my taste.

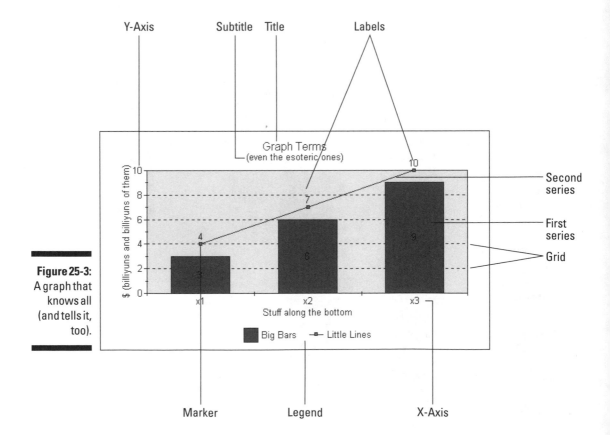

**Figure 25-3:** A graph that knows all (and tells it, too).

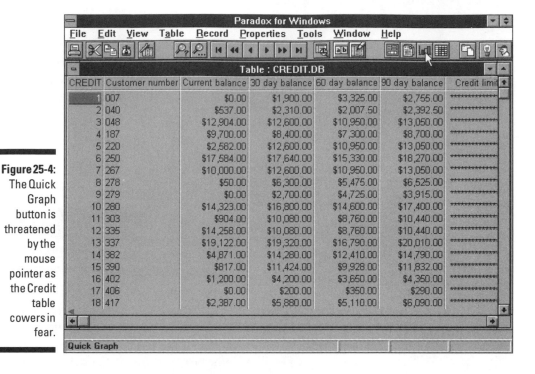

Figure 25-4:
The Quick
Graph
button is
threatened
by the
mouse
pointer as
the Credit
table
cowers in
fear.

Menu mavens can select Tools⇨Quick Graph from the main menu if they simply *must* do it that way.

2. **Click the down arrow next to the table name, then select the field that goes along the bottom of your graph (the *X-Axis value*).**

When you click it, the field name appears in the X-Axis box on the right side of the dialog box, as shown in Figure 25-5.

If you click the wrong field by accident (or deliberately, just to be that way), fix it by clicking the right field. Paradox automatically replaces the old one with the new.

The X-Axis value is usually something like a Customer number, date, or Product ID. Often, it's the table's key field.

3. **Click the Y-Value radio button.**

X is set, so it's time for Y.

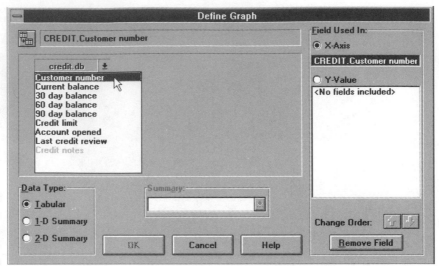

**Figure 25-5:**
Picking the
X-Axis field.

**4. Click the down arrow next to the table name again. This time, pick all the fields you want to show as lines, bars, or whatever you want.**

Choose the field names in the order you want them graphed. As you click, the field names appear in the Y-Value box, as shown in figure Figure 25-6.

Here are some things to keep in mind:

- Bar and line charts can display several different data series, but a pie chart can only use one.

- If you choose one out of order, just click it in the Y-Value list and then use the Up and Down arrow buttons in the bottom right corner of the dialog box to put it in the right spot.

- To remove a field from the Y-Value list, click it and then click Remove Field.

- The specific order everything's in may or may not be a big deal. Odds are it *won't,* so don't get all hung up about it.

Don't pack your graph too full of data. Usually one to four data series are fine, but you're on shaky ground if you go beyond that.

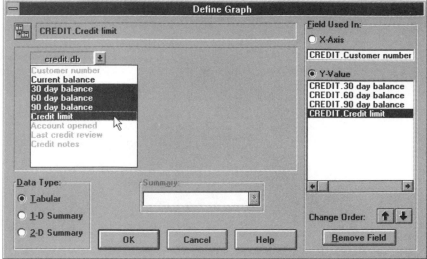

**Figure 25-6:**
Doing the
same for the
Y-Axis
fields.

5. **Click OK when you're done.**

   Your new graph appears, looking as beautiful as Figure 25-7.

   If you are suddenly overwhelmed by sick dread (or just don't want to make a graph anymore), click Cancel instead.

6. **To save your graph, click the Design button, then select File⇨Save from the menu. Type in a name for the form your graph is on, then click OK to save it.**

   Your new Quick Graph lives on a form — a form that contains _nothing_ but the graph. If you want to spruce up the form with some text or something like that, you can — heck, it's _your_ form. The important thing to remember is that you're _not saving a graph;_ you're _saving a form that contains a graph._

## Graphs in reports

Paradox has the interesting capability to use graphs right in Reports. You can do some pretty spiffy tricks with this feature, but it's not meant for mere mortals like you and me.

Although Borland made this version of Paradox _by far_ the easiest Paradox of them all, there are still places where simplicity and ease of use are foreign. Sad to say, this is one of them.

If you're brave enough to try for the knowledge and risk your hairline in the attempt, corner a guru and prepare to comb your cranial tufts for the last time.

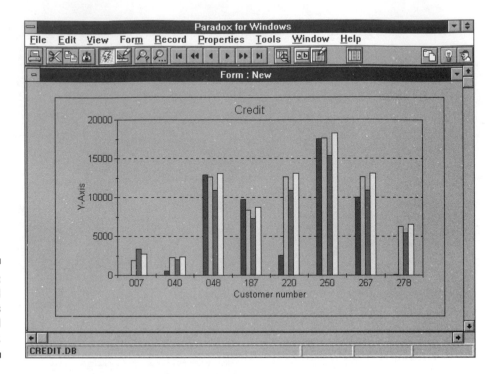

**Figure 25-7:**
The finished
graph — it's
a sight, all
right.

# Prettying It Up a Bit

Like most things that Paradox for Windows makes by itself, Quick Graphs aren't the most beautiful things in the world to behold. In fact, from a simple charm and elegance point of view, they're rather, well, *challenged*.

You, however, can turn these graphs into digital Cinderellas with some gratuitous right-clicking. Below are the most common things you need to change in a graph. All the settings are available by inspecting (with the good ol' right mouse button) the graph in Design mode.

## Before you begin

Before you can do *any* of these fun and amazing things to your graph, you have to be in Design mode. With that done, select the graph by clicking anywhere (yes, *anywhere*) on it. That's it — you're cleared for takeoff.

## *Putting titles here and there*

There are titles all over the graph: at the top, on the X and Y axis, even in the legend. Many of them are real yawners, which is why this is the first thing in the section. Here's how to make your own titillating titles:

1. **Put the pointer right on top of the title you want to change and right-click.**

   The pointer turns into a small up-arrow when you put it on the title. That's Paradox's way to say *you're here.* When you right-click, the properties menu for that title pops up.

2. **Select Title⇨Text from the menu.**

3. **Type your new title text into the Enter Title dialog box. Click OK when you're done.**

   If you change your mind and don't want to make a new title, click Cancel.

   To remove a title you created, go back through Step 1 and select Title⇨Use Default from the pop-up menu.

## *Coloring inside the bar*

Paradox picks its own colors for the bars, but you can substitute your own in a couple of clicks.

1. **Put the pointer on top of the bar you want to change and right-click.**

   The mouse pointer changes to an up-arrow, and then the properties menu pops up.

2. **Select Color from the menu.**

   An impressive little color chart pops colorfully into view.

3. **Click the color of your choice.**

   The bar changes color immediately.

   Don't get carried away. The goal is to communicate, not induce a psychedelic stupor.

# Turning bars into lines (and vice versa)

If you want one data series to stand out or otherwise massively contrast with the others, change it into a different display type.

You're making a combination chart — one that combines lines and bars together.

1. **Put the pointer on top of the line or bar you want to recast and right-click.**

   First the mouse pointer changes to an up-arrow, then Paradox hears the right-click and the properties menu pops up.

2. **Select Type Override from the menu, then select either 2D bar or 2D line as the alternate display type.**

   The sample graph shows what the new setting looks like.

   If you're mixing bars and lines, the lines should be the *last* series on the graph. Otherwise, Paradox ends up hiding part of the lines behind the bars.

   If the field you want to display with a line happens to be the *first* series instead of the *last*, right-click on the graph itself, select Define Graph, and then use the Change Order buttons to move your field to the bottom of the Y-Value fields list. Change the last series (the bar furthest to the left in the group) into a line.

# Playing with the line markers

By default, Paradox for Windows uses square markers the size of Luxembourg on your line charts. This is something you're gonna want to change.

1. **Put the pointer on one of the massive markers and right-click.**

   You're in the right position when the mouse pointer changes to the little up-arrow. Shortly thereafter, the properties menu appears.

2. **To change the marker's size, select Marker⇨Size from the pop-up menu. Click on the size you want.**

   Six weight is good for all-line charts. Ten weight helps a line stand out when it's alone in a combination graph, fending for itself among a bunch of bars.

3. **To change the marker's shape, select Marker⇨Style from the pop-up menu, and then click on your choice from the massive submenu.**

   There are many options, so feel free to play around and be creative.

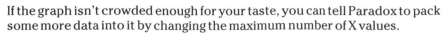

## Showing more stuff

If the graph isn't crowded enough for your taste, you can tell Paradox to pack some more data into it by changing the maximum number of X values.

1. **Move the mouse pointer to the left of the graph title. When it becomes a regular pointer shape (*not* the little up-arrow), right-click.**

   This brings up the properties menu for the *graph itself*.

2. **Select Max x-values, then click on the number you want to include.**

   If the number you want is greater than eight, click the ... and type your *own* number into the dialog box that pops up.

   You won't see any change on-screen until you click the View Data button or press F8.

## Customizing the look

You have lots of choices for what appears in your graph. Specifically, you can have a title, legend, grid lines, axes, and data labels — or *not* have them if you want them off. All these are set in the Options menu. Here's how it's done:

1. **Move the mouse pointer away to the side of the graph title. After it changes from the increasingly annoying little up-arrow into a plain, common pointer, go ahead and right-click.**

   The graph's properties menu appears.

2. **Select Options, then click on the specific one you want to turn on or off.**

   A check mark next to the option means it's on; nothing there means it's off.

## Moving the legend

The legend can be in one of two different places: along the bottom of the graph or on the right side. Here's how to move it:

1. **Right-click one of the words in the legend.**

   This opens the legend's properties box.

2. **Select Legend Pos, and then Right or Bottom, depending on your preference.**

   The legend quickly and without complaining moves to the other position.

You have to have a legend before you can move it. See "Customizing the Look" for help turning it on in the first place.

## *Framing the graph*

Like any other object in a form's universe, you can put a nice frame around your graph.

1. **Move the mouse pointer away to the side of the graph title. When it becomes a regular pointer shape (*not* the little up-arrow), right-click.**

   This brings up the properties menu for the graph.

2. **Select Frame⇨Style, and then click the frame style that piques your visual interest.**

# Chapter 26

# Deliberately Using Two (or More) Tables

· · · · · · · · · · · · · · · · · · · · · · · · · · · · · · · · · · · · · · · · · · · · ·

### In This Chapter

▶ Single and loving it

▶ Relationships aren't so bad, either

▶ Doing the Data Model Hop

· · · · · · · · · · · · · · · · · · · · · · · · · · · · · · · · · · · · · · · · · · · · ·

*L*ike it or not, sometimes you just *have* to use two Paradox tables. After all (say the nerds), Paradox *is* a relational database program. You're missing out on the real *power* of Paradox. Yeah — and the best way to use your computer is with DOS commands.

If you get the urge to try making forms and reports with two tables, this chapter can help you survive the trauma. It gives you more information about the differences between using one table and having your head drilled — um, using *two* or more tables. There's also a section about the Data Model, which is Paradox's electronic answer to a blind date for your tables.

If you start getting a headache while reading this, close the book and think about lying on a sandy beach near a glittering lagoon. Close your eyes and feel the ocean breeze caress your hair. Breathe deeply — smell the sweet, clean air. Wave to the big white ship as it leaves the dock. Then pretend it's the one you're supposed to be on and think of all the ways you can to get aboard now that it's 12 miles from shore. There — isn't that relaxing?

# Single and Loving It

Most people in this crazy electronic world use single tables to do stuff. It's the original database model. It's still the simplest model to understand: think "phone book" and you have it clearly in mind. If you ever created a shopping list, phone list, or almost anything else that ended in the word *list,* odds are it was an example of the flat file way of doing things.

The technical name for a single table database is a *flat file,* because, well, there's technical reason that nobody really cares about anyway. By the way, there is no *bumpy file* format, at least not in database software.

In a flat file, everything is in a single table. It's one-stop shopping for all your data. Each line contains all the fields you need, so there's nowhere else to look — ever. It's great for most simple projects. In fact, most everything you'll ever do with a database can be done with a flat file.

# Relationships Aren't So Bad, Either

A relational database is just a bunch of tables that work together. Usually, each table has a unique key field that keeps all the records in order. Each table contains different data. In fact, that's the key concept of a relational database: as much as possible, data is stored in one place only — it's not repeated anywhere.

The classic example of a relational database is a retail store. You, the customer, have an Account Number. Your personal information (address, credit limit, phone number, and so on) are filed in a Customer table under your Account Number. That's why Customer Service departments always ask for your account number before asking your name (which never fails to make me angry).

When you buy something, the purchase gets an Invoice Number. The time, date, sales clerk number, and method of payment all get squirreled away in the Invoice table, organized by the Invoice Number.

Each item you buy has a Line Number on the invoice. All the relevant information about your purchases (item number, quantity, price, and discount) is recorded in the LineItem table. This table might be organized by both invoice number and line item number, seeing as though theoretically no two sales could have the same invoice number, but one invoice number might have a lot of line items (especially if I'm doing the shopping).

Together, the Customer, Invoice, and LineItem tables are a relational database. Here are some tips to keep in mind:

- ✔ When in doubt, start with a flat file. If you realize later that it's just not working, you can easily convert it to a relational system.

- ✔ Yes, it *does* sound cumbersome and complicated. Unfortunately, it is.

- ✔ Take heart — it's nowhere *near* as cumbersome and complicated as it would be trying to do the same thing with a single table. (It gives me chills just thinking about it.)

The *linking fields* keep this whole ethereal thing together. They connect the different tables, relating them to each other. In the retail monstrosity above, the Customer links to Invoice by Customer number; the Invoice table links to LineItem by Invoice number. There's no direct link between Customer and LineItem *except* via the Invoice table.

Now do you understand why it's harder to design these systems than use them? To *use* a bunch of related tables, all you need to know is how they're linked together. To *design* them, you practically need a doctoral degree.

# *Doing the Data Model Hop*

To use related tables in either reports or forms, you explain the whole sordid relationship with the Data Model dialog box. You get the same easy-to-use dialog box regardless of what you're ultimately building.

Before using the Data Model dialog, you need to know how the relational tables in question fit together. Usually, the link is a single field (like Customer number, Invoice number, or their ilk). In rarer circumstances, it takes *two* (or more) fields to make the link.

- ✔ If you're not sure how to join the tables together, seek help from someone who is sure. The link *must* be correct or nothing else you do is going to work right.

- ✔ Joining tables in a query is a completely different process. It's covered in glorious detail way back in Chapter 17.

- ✔ Unless you're very comfortable with the particular related tables and Paradox itself, I don't recommend trying to make multiple table forms and reports. Get your guru to help if you absolutely must do this.

---

# The almost, but not quite, relational database

According to the purists, there is no such thing as a truly relational database program. Not even Paradox for Windows, in all its glory, is truly relational. The key word in that thought is truly. Allow me to explain.

To be a truly relational database, a program must pass a series of 12 tests called the "relational model." This thing that data dreams are made of was developed over 20 years ago by a man with way too much time on his hands. His rules define a system so frustratingly complex and austere that any program which earns the truly *relational* moniker would be promptly laughed off the market.

Back here in the Real World, Paradox for Windows is considered a relational database. It follows the important parts of the relational model. The parts it blows off are, frankly, not that important to people with work to do.

---

Here's how to join your tables in digital matrimony for forms and reports with the helpful services of the Data Model dialog box:

1. **Start creating your form or report.**

   For forms, right-click the Form button on the ToolBar or select File⇨New⇨Form from the menu.

   For reports, right-click the ToolBar's Report button or select File⇨New⇨Report from the menu.

2. **When the New Whichever-it-is dialog box pops up, click the Data Model/Layout Diagram button.**

   Finally, the Data Model dialog box appears. Whew.

   The button you want is the big one at the bottom of the heap.

3. **In the File Name list, double-click on the names of each table you want to include.**

   When you click, the names hop over into the big open area on the right of the dialog box. Figure 26-1 shows two tables awaiting the linking moment.

4. **Put the mouse pointer on top of the table you're linking from, and then click and drag to the table you're linking to. Release the mouse button when it's on top of the other table.**

   When you do the click and drag, a line follows your mouse pointer from one table to the other, as shown in Figure 26-2. The mouse pointer changes, too, but that's no big deal. It should change back shortly.

When you let go of the mouse button, the Define Link dialog box disappears. And the mouse pointer changes back. (See, I told you it would.)

**5. If the tables are well designed, the Define Link dialog box is already filled out (see Figure 26-3). In that case, click OK.**

When the Define Link dialog box goes away, don't be startled to see an arrow connecting the table names back in the Data Model dialog box. That means the link is established and they're officially dating.

Now, what if the dialog box *isn't* all filled out? Well, your link is in peril. Paradox couldn't figure out how to link the tables on its own, so it wants your help. Unfortunately, there's little that normal humans can do in such instances. Sigh loudly and with feeling, click Cancel, and then haul out the goodie bag to feed the soon-to-be-visiting guru.

*Well designed* means that the linking field in each table has the *exact* same name, field type, and size.

**6. Click OK again and continue creating the whichever-it-is.**

The Data Model dialog goes away (finally). You're left to continue creating the form or report. Good luck.

For more help with a form, see Chapter 24. If you're making a report, see Part 3 in its entirety.

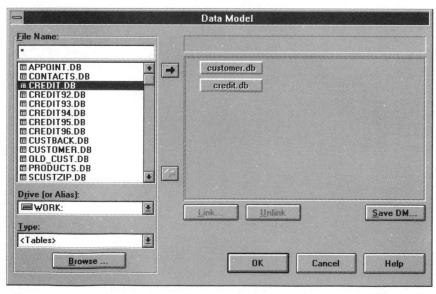

**Figure 26-1:**
The Customer and Credit tables are ready and waiting to be linked.

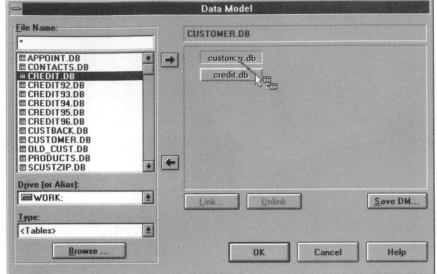

**Figure 26-2:**
It's not much of a first date, but at least the relationship got started somehow.

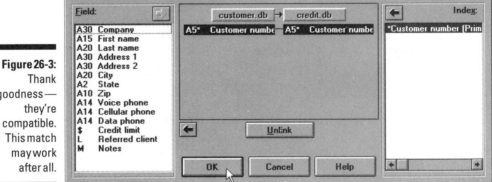

**Figure 26-3:**
Thank goodness— they're compatible. This match may work after all.

# Part VI
## The Part of Tens

"DO YOU WANT ME TO CALL THE COMPANY AND HAVE THEM SEND ANOTHER REVIEW COPY OF THEIR SPREADSHEET SOFTWARE SYSTEM, OR DO YOU KNOW WHAT YOU'RE GOING TO WRITE?"

# In This Part...

*Though counting in the usual way,*
*Years twenty-one I've been alive,*
*Yet reckoning by my natal day,*
*I am a little boy of five!*

Act II, Gilbert and Sullivan's *The Pirates of Penzance*

Miscarriages of arithmetic aside, this wouldn't be much of a *Dummies* book if it didn't close with the ever-anticipated Part of Tens. Worry no more — you're here! Welcome to five of the best Tens you ever saw in your life.

# Chapter 27
# Ten Remedies for What Ails You

. . . . . . . . . . . . . . . . . . . . . . . . . . . . . . . . . . . . . . .

## In This Chapter
▶ When in doubt, press F1
▶ Press Esc to make it go away
▶ Cancel if you aren't sure
▶ Keep backups
▶ Buy a foam rubber ball bat
▶ Fixing KEYVIOL and PROBLEMS tables
▶ Get some coaching
▶ Seek advice from the Experts
▶ Unchoosing something on a list
▶ Take a TUtility and call your guru in the morning

. . . . . . . . . . . . . . . . . . . . . . . . . . . . . . . . . . . . . . .

**S**ometimes, using Paradox is like working up a good sweat and then walking into a room full of mosquitoes. It seems like everything's out to get you. This chapter is the quick remedy stick to soothe your little bites and scratches.

## When in Doubt, Press F1

This is the 90s version of *when in doubt, ask for help.* These days, once you're past that magic three months of free support, there *isn't* anybody to ask — at least not cheaply. But there's always the on-line help system, ready and waiting to dump a lot of fascinating information on your shoes and run away giggling. It's great for memory-jogging once you know how to do stuff, but don't ask it to *teach* you how things work. Look to the Coaches and books (like this one!) for that level of help.

## Press Esc to Make It Go Away

If you try some things while your brain is in Hawaii and return to find yourself goodness knows where in Paradox, the Esc key is a quick way to get found pronto. Pressing Esc once or twice rescues you from errant menu choices, misclicked ToolBar buttons, and even the Help system. If you're in too deep for the Esc key to help, check out the next section for some heavy-duty assistance.

## Cancel If You Aren't Sure

Almost every dialog box has a Cancel button. As you're teetering at the edge of some hideous electronic abyss, put your mouse back on solid ground with a quick Cancel. You'll be glad you did.

## Keep Backups

Okay, maybe I harped on this too much, but it *really* is important. Regardless of the problem, crisis, or peculiar data anomaly, a good backup is almost certain salvation. If you don't know how to get started, ask your guru or local computer store. It's not expensive — particularly when you consider how much your data is worth to what you do.

## Buy a Foam Rubber Ball Bat

In the business, these are known as ASRDs, or Analog Stress Release Devices. Look for them under the more generic name *toy baseball bat* at the local toy store. Get a nice soft one so you don't damage the computer when you pretend to beat the *$&(#$^! out of it during periods of intense stress. In periods of dire stress, you can always beat your head on the wall (although it's not very good for the wall).

## Fixing KEYVIOL and PROBLEMS Tables

When Paradox gives you a KEYVIOL or PROBLEMS table, it's telling you that what you just tried didn't work like you intended. Don't ignore them — if you do, you risk losing the data in them (which is not a positive thing).

KEYVIOL tables contain records with key field values that are the same as other records *already* in whatever table your using. Compare the records to the table, find out why the keys are already there, and either fix or delete the records in KEYVIOL. See Chapter 11 for more information about this.

The PROBLEMS table usually crops up if you restructure a table and change a field's type (convert something from Alpha to Number, for example). Any records that can't make the switch are shoved into PROBLEMS for your personal attention. Look at the records and figure out why Paradox couldn't convert them into the new type, and then correct what you can and Add them back into your table. See Chapter 11 for help with both table restructuring and the Add command.

# Get Some Coaching

Paradox's new Coaches give you one-on-one (or *you against the computer*) explanations and walk-throughs for many of the most common things you do with Paradox. The main focus is on tables: designing and building them, entering and changing data, and all the other fun things you can do *with* and *to* them. There's also help with general Paradox stuff like queries, forms, and reports. They're always available — just click the little Coach fellow on the far right end of the ToolBar.

# Seek Advice from the Experts

Unlike Coaches, Paradox's Experts actually do work *for* you. They interview you for things like the tables you're using and what exactly you want to do, and then they do it and present you with the finished product (but, thank goodness, no bill). They're hiding under the light bulb (as in *gosh, these Experts are a bright idea)* button on the ToolBar, right next to the Coaches.

# Unchoosing Something on a List

I can't tell you how many times every day I *mis-mouse* something (that's where you know what you want to click on but the mouse pointer doesn't quite get in the right place, so you end up with the thing right next to it). Well, I guess I *could* tell you, but then you'd start laughing and probably drop the book on your foot, and the last thing I need is some liability lawsuit on my hands, so I'm not gonna tell you. Hmpf.

Anyway, if *you* suffer the same mousing malady that afflicts me, don't get all upset because it's easy to unchoose things in Paradox for Windows. If you clicked something in a menu to highlight it, just click something else (like what you *intended* to hit in the first place). If you double-clicked a field or file into another list (like in the Data Model or when you're choosing fields for a sort), look for a Remove or left arrow button and try that. Sometimes just double-clicking the item in its new home makes it feel unloved enough to go back home. And if worse comes to worst, look for one of those famous Cancel buttons and let it safely self-destruct whatever you accidentally created.

## Take a TUtility and Call Your Guru in the Morning

The bad news is that tables sometimes get corrupted. The good news is that it's not always fatal. Paradox for Windows comes with a DOS program called TUtility (so you won't make any cocktail party gaffes, you should know it's pronounced *tee-utility*, not *too-tility*). This is your table repair emergency room.

Well, it's actually your guru's table repair emergency room. All you need to know is that you have it if you need it and Someone Who Knows should help you use it. Don't try to salvage a corrupted table on your own — you might accidentally turn a repairable table into digital goulash. When your data is at stake, don't try things just to see if you can do it yourself. Having an adventuresome spirit is exactly what you need with Paradox, but this isn't the place to have it.

# Excel For Dummies, 2nd Edition

**Cheat Sheet**

## Shortcut Keys in Excel 5.0

| Windows keys | Mac keys | What it does |
|---|---|---|
| Ctrl+A | ⌘+A | Selects all |
| Ctrl+B | ⌘+B | Turns bold on and off |
| Ctrl+C | ⌘+C | Copies the selection |
| Ctrl+D | ⌘+D | Fills down |
| Ctrl+I | ⌘+I | Turns italics on and off |
| Ctrl+N | ⌘+N | Creates new workbook |
| Ctrl+O | ⌘+O | Opens workbook |
| Ctrl+P | ⌘+P | Prints |
| Ctrl+R | ⌘+R | Fills right |
| Ctrl+S | ⌘+S | Saves |
|  | ⌘+T | Changes cell reference |
| Ctrl+U | ⌘+U | Turns underline on and off |
| Ctrl+V | ⌘+V | Pastes |
| Ctrl+X | ⌘+X | Cuts the selection |
| Ctrl+Z | ⌘+Z | Undoes last action |

Copyright © 1994 IDG Books Worldwide.
All rights reserved.

Cheat Sheet $2.95 value. Item 050-0

For more information about IDG Books, call
1-800-762-2974 or 415-312-0600

*. . . For Dummies: #1 Computer Book Series for Beginners*

## Excel 5.0 Function Key Template — ©1994 IDG Books Worldwide

| | F1 | F2 | F3 | F4 | F5 | F6 | F7 | F8 | F9 | F10 | F11 | F12 |
|---|---|---|---|---|---|---|---|---|---|---|---|---|
| **Ctrl+Shift** | | | Create name | | | Previous window | | | | | | Print |
| **Ctrl** | | Info window | Define name | Close window | Restore window | Next window | Move | Size | Minimize workbook | Maximize workbook | Excel 4.0 Macro sheet | Open |
| **Shift** | Contextual Help | Note | Function Wizard | | | Previous pane | | Add | Calculate worksheet | Shortcut menu | Insert worksheet | Save |
| **Alone** | Help | Formula bar | Paste name | Repeat or absolute | Go To | Next pane | Spelling | Extend | Calculate workbook | Menu bar | Insert chart sheet | Save as |

# Excel For Dummies, 2nd Edition

**Cheat Sheet**

FOR DUMMIES™

COMPUTER BOOK SERIES FROM IDG

## More Cool Shortcut Keys in Excel 5.0

| Shortcut keys* | What it does |
| --- | --- |
| Ctrl+; (semicolon) | Enters the date |
| Ctrl+: (colon) | Enters time |
| Ctrl+5 | Applies or removes strikeover |
| Ctrl+9 | Hide rows |
| Ctrl+Shift+( | Unhide rows |
| Ctrl+0 (zero) | Hides columns |
| Ctrl+Shift+) | Unhides columns |
| Ctrl+Shift+~ | General number format |
| Ctrl+Shift+$ | Currency number format |
| Ctrl+Shift+% | Percentage number format |
| Ctrl+Shift+# | Date format with day, month, and year |
| Ctrl+Shift+@ | Hour, minute, and A.M. or P.M. |
| Ctrl+Shift+! | Comma number format |
| Ctrl+Shift+& | Outline border |
| Ctrl+Shift+_ | Remove all borders |

*Ctrl key on PCs; Control key on Macs

## Excel 5.0 Function Key Template — ©1994 IDG Books Worldwide

| | Home | End | PgUp | PgDn | ← | → | ↑ | ↓ |
| --- | --- | --- | --- | --- | --- | --- | --- | --- |
| **Ctrl+Shift** | Select to top of wks. | Select to last active cell* | | | Select to left edge of range | Select to right edge of range | Select to top edge of range | Select to btm. edge of range |
| **Ctrl** | Top of worksheet | Last active cell | Previous worksheet | Next worksheet | Move to left edge of range | Move to right edge of range | Move to top edge of range | Move to btm. edge of range |
| **Shift** | Select to beg. of row | Select to active cell* | Select up one screen | Select down one screen | Select one cell left | Select one cell right | Select one cell up | Select one cell down |
| **Alone** | Beg. of row | End mode | Screen up | Screen down | Move one cell left | Move one cell right | Move one cell up | Move one cell down |

*with Scroll Lock

IDG BOOKS

Copyright © 1994 IDG Books Worldwide.
All rights reserved.
Cheat Sheet $2.95 value. Item 050-0
For more information about IDG Books, call
1-800-762-2974 or 415-312-0600

*. . . For Dummies: #1 Computer Book Series for Beginners*

# Chapter 28
# Ten Terms to Say You've Heard

*A* minefield just wouldn't be the same without the mines. Likewise, computing wouldn't be the experience it is without its body of ever-changing names and acronyms. Here are the latest selections from the Database Special Interest subsection of The Cryptic Term of the Month Club.

## Client/Server

If you put 50 serious computer degenerates in a room together and shout "How about that Client/Server thing?" you'll quickly have a full-scale riot on your hands. You see, nobody really agrees on what it is, how it works, or what it does, but everyone who's anyone wants to be counted among those who are already doing it. Kinda reminds you of high school, doesn't it?

In its simplest form, Client/Server is a fancy way to use at least two computers to handle large databases. One machine, the Server, is the keeper of the data. The Client (the other machine) requests data from the Server and processes it in one way or another. This way, two big, expensive machines work together to accomplish what you and I do on one little, inexpensive machine.

So what's the big deal? Search me. It's supposed to change our lives forever, but darned if I can see how.

# Normalized Form

As with all things in life, there are rules governing how to set up a database. Normalized form is nothing but a series of rules explaining how to organize your tables for maximum adherence to the aforementioned series of rules, with little regard for how easy or hard it will be to do something useful with the newly-normalized database. The main thing you gain from following the rules is the chance to say "I just reached the fifth normal form and boy are my tables tired." If you're that hard up for party conversation, then normalizing is for you.

Most of what you and I do with databases can be accomplished without getting mired in stuff like this. If one of your computer fixated friends asks, tell her you planned to do it, but decided to wait for a Client/Server solution instead. That'll teach her.

# Referential Integrity

This is a fancy form of table lookup, something that almost any database program can do. Because it's a hot new feature of Paradox for Windows, lots of people are talking about it. To look in on lookups, look at Chapter 31. Meditate on what you find there and then consider the fact that referential integrity is infinitely more complicated. Please don't try it at home — leave it to the trained professionals.

# Relational Database

You'll be pleased to know that Paradox for Windows is a relational database program. That's why you can tie two or more tables together and end up with something that doesn't look like week-old goulash. For the practical side of relational databases, see Chapters 17 and 26.

# SQL

Here's another term that was condemned to nerd-dom and escaped into mainstream computer conversation. SQL is an acronym for Structured Query Language. It's a powerful and cryptic tool for asking questions of databases larger than some Third World countries.

The first thing you must know about SQL is how to pronounce it: "sequel." This alone will indelibly mark you as One Who May Know Something. Beyond that, be aware that you may actually run across this at work because many companies use SQL on their central computer systems. Take heart, though: if worse comes to worst, Paradox for Windows can communicate with SQL-based systems. That way, you can use a powerful and cryptic program explained by this wonderful and funny book, instead of being stuck with a powerful and cryptic tool supported by an odd and tiresome programmer. The choice is yours.

# IDAPI

This is Borland's attempt at cornering the market on database standards. It stands for Independent Database Application Programming Interface and it's just one of many contenders in a crowded field. Unless something earth-shattering happens in the industry, that's all you'll ever have to know about it. Consider yourself lucky.

# OOP

Here's one I never thought you and I would have to deal with face to face: object-oriented programming. OOP is a kind of programming that's particularly adapted to mouse, menu, and button-based environments like Windows.

Traditional programs are like college lectures: the professor (the program, in this example) drones on from point to point while the students (the computer's resources and data) try to stay awake and not do anything too stupid. There's a specific start, end, and a great deal of linear points in the middle.

OOP programs resemble a cross between ballet and a commodities trading pit. There's a good degree of organization and a feeling that we're collectively getting somewhere in a beautiful, flowing manner. The behind-the-scenes details involve a lot of shouting, waving, scurrying about, and sheer amazement that *anything* gets done at all.

Paradox for Windows has its own OOP-based language, ObjectPAL, for your use and frustration. For more information about it, steel yourself and turn to Chapter 31.

## DDE & OLE

These terms come from Windows. Dynamic Data Exchange and Object Linking and Embedding are the two ways programs within Windows can actively share data. Paradox for Windows supports both of these standards — it's a good citizen of the Amazing Environment of Windows. For lots more information about using and abusing these capabilities, see *Windows For Dummies* from IDG Books Worldwide.

## CBS

This started out as a radio network known as the Columbia Broadcasting System. Given the general state of television today, it arguably should have stayed that way.

Among many noteworthy achievements, CBS broadcast the famous 1938 *War of the Worlds* radio drama, staged by Orson Welles and the Mercury Theatre on the Air. Despite the minor *faux pas* of pretending to blow up the planet and having the entire country believe it, CBS managed to become a major player in news and entertainment programming on both radio and television.

The nicest thing about CBS is that it has nothing whatsoever to do with Paradox for Windows.

# The 5th Wave     By Rich Tennant

©RKHTENNANT

"TSK, TSK—ANOTHER FINE EMPLOYEE FALLS VICTIM TO
THE SHREDDER OBJECT."

# Chapter 29
# Ten Tips That Save Your Sanity

● ● ● ● ● ● ● ● ● ● ● ● ● ● ● ● ● ● ● ● ● ● ● ● ● ● ● ● ● ● ● ● ● ● ● ● ● ●

## In This Chapter

▶ Make backups

▶ Think

▶ Take your time

▶ Back up your environment

▶ Use paper and pencil first

▶ Do backups regularly

▶ Aliases make your life easier

▶ Try a new icon

▶ Keep your stuff organized

▶ Good backups help you win the lottery

● ● ● ● ● ● ● ● ● ● ● ● ● ● ● ● ● ● ● ● ● ● ● ● ● ● ● ● ● ● ● ● ● ● ● ● ● ●

Sanity, I've found, is a fairly good thing to have. There are certainly sound arguments about how much sanity is enough and what to do if you find that your sanity is out of date, but, as a general truism, having sanity is better than being sanity-challenged.

Working with complicated programs like Paradox for Windows doesn't usually enhance one's sanity; it often has the opposite effect. I know that my personal mental welfare is scarred, traumatized, and sometimes dresses up in a small polka-dot dragon costume because of the cumulative effects of the many software packages I've dealt with over the years.

This chapter is devoted to making sure your sanity (or what's left of it) doesn't have to endure these same hardships. It contains general tips for dealing with both computers and life, plus some specific Paradox for Windows techniques designed to protect your precious mental resources.

# *Make Backups*

There's nothing like starting off with the top dog, the mother-in-law of all computer truisms, the one that wags its finger at you and says "I won't say I told you so because you know I did." Yes, I'm a True Believer in keeping good backups. That doesn't always mean I always do it, but it does mean I feel *very* guilty if I don't and something bad happens.

Start cheap, simple, and easy: save copies of your tables on good-quality floppy disks and put the disks somewhere safe (that means *not* in your desk drawer). Every now and then, get the disks out and copy your tables again. Then put the disks back and continue with your previously scheduled life.

At least now you're started — and that's a load off my mind.

# *Think*

What would a computer book be that didn't take a moment to pay homage to IBM founder Thomas J. Watson, Sr., and his timeless, monosyllabic advice? Well, it would probably be written by someone fixated on Apple computers, for one thing. I'm not, so here goes.

Despite the fact that it dates from a period when slide rules and slick hair were the norm, the simple advice embodied in "Think" is timeless. The next time you're challenged to do something *right now,* resist the urge and *think* first. Is there a second plan of action that's better than the obvious one? Are you solving the problem or treating a mere symptom? Is there a better way? Sit on your hands and let your brain exercise for a while. Who knows where it will lead? One place might be Chapter 5 for further insight on the problem solution thing.

Remember: thinking adds value to almost anything you do. Try it.

# *Take Your Time*

A rushed solution is a problem in drag. By the time I'm through fiddling with this, shoring up that, and tying the whole mess together with strapping tape, I could have done it the *right* way and been finished. Believe me — I've tried it both ways and the hurried answer rarely works the first, second, or fourth time.

I'm not recommending that you blow off deadlines in the name of perfection. I *am* telling you that the 1-10-100 rule is alive and well and waiting to ambush your quick-and-dirty databases. For review, the rule says it takes 1 time period to fix a problem now, 10 periods to fix it later, and 100 periods to find a new job after the slap-dash solution you rushed into production fails completely and becomes a problem in and of itself.

Take the time to think about the problem and think about a solution. Then think up another solution and see if that leads you to a third. Refer to Chapter 5 to refine the solution and Chapter 6 to turn it into a Paradox for Windows table. Most of all, make the best of the time you have. You'll usually find you have more than you thought.

# Back Up Your Environment

I'm not talking about your tables, documents, spreadsheets, and high-score records here — I beat that into the ground a couple of sections ago. I mean the whole environment you've created: your colors, custom icons, workspace arrangement, hotkeys to cover up the games when your boss wanders by. I'm talking about *important* stuff here.

How long did you spend getting everything set *just so?* How long would it take to *rebuild from scratch?* Sure, you can reload all your software from the master disks (don't worry — the disks are around here somewhere). All you need is about an hour to install plus another hour or two per program to customize but then you're right back to work. Multiply that by the number of programs you use and ... ouch! You're running up some real time here.

To get serious about backups, consider a tape backup system. They're available in many capacities and price ranges. I'm sure there's something that perfectly matches your needs. Gird up your tolerance for pain and do that first backup. The first one isn't quick, easy, or painless. Nothing is, the *first* time. But once you've started doing it, you'll be on much safer ground. If your business relies on your computer, your business relies on your backups.

# Use Paper and Pencil First

Yet another ditty from Chapter 5, but it bears repeating because it flies in the face of common computer wisdom. When you're creating a database, designing a spreadsheet, or doing nearly anything else requiring a computer, collect your thoughts on paper first. It doesn't have to be a formal outline or anything — just a collection of relevant ideas to get the compu-process going.

I usually brainstorm and list my thoughts. Then I reorganize them a couple of times until they make sense even to me. If I'm setting up a Paradox for Windows table or two, I write down the field names, sizes, and brief descriptions of why I think I need them. Not only does this help keep me organized, it acts as documentation of my thought process (such as it is).

One note for aspiring nerds out there: if you have a psychological need to be high-tech at all times, think of (and describe) this step as an "analog linear enigma analysis."

# Do Backups Regularly

The first backup isn't what changes your life. It's the second, third, fourth, and two hundred seventy sixth backups that make the difference. Regular backups are the key to the whole process. The receivable data from January isn't going to help your October billing very much ....

Regular backups are like regular exercise: the more you do it, the easier it becomes. Your local computer guru can help design a plan that ensures you back up enough without overdoing. Once the plan is in place, work it consistently. Then laugh in the face of disaster — you're backed up!

# Aliases Make Your Life Easier

Aliases, those funky Paradox for Windows pointers to your disk directories, are a real boon to people who are either on a network or that have a complex directory structure. Either way, creating a few aliases makes finding and using your tables quite a bit easier. They insulate you from the seedy DOS underside of Windows, the arcane directory paths, and all the other things that Windows users pretend don't exist in their graphical world.

Take a sanity break and check out Chapter 10 for the alias *modus operandi.*

# Try a New Icon

This is a just-for-fun kind of thing, but it relieves some stress and that counts toward saving your sanity.

Back in the Windows Program Manager, you can change the dull yellow check mark Paradox for Windows icon to something *really* interesting — and it doesn't cost a dime.

Click once (not twice or you end up in Paradox) on the Paradox for Windows icon and then select File⇨Properties from the menu (or press Alt+Enter to get the same effect). In the Program Item Properties dialog box, click the Change Icon button.

The Change Icon dialog box shows you all the built-in icons at your disposal. Scroll right in the list to find my three favorites: the Pair 'O *Ducks,* Pair 'O *Docks,* and the Japanese-art tidal wave (inspired by the code name of the first Paradox for Windows, *Tsunami).* Double-click the new icon of your liking, and then click OK to save the change. Now Paradox has a new look, one that hopefully puts you in a little more playful mood than the old one did.

# Keep Your Stuff Organized

The advent of super-size hard drives and big networks means you and I have to organize more carefully than ever before. When you have 10 square feet of space, almost any organization is more bother than help. Those same habits applied to a 25-story building cause severe problems.

Take the time to create useful directories and aliases for your Paradox for Windows tables. Heck, do the same thing for your other programs, too. Chapter 10 will give you a few words of wisdom, as will *DOS For Dummies* and *Windows For Dummies* from IDG Books Worldwide.

# Good Backups Help You Win The Lottery

OK, they probably won't, but they're worth ten times their weight in lottery tickets when you need them. Try it and see for yourself.

# Chapter 30

## Ten Things to Never Ever Do

- - - - - - - - - - - - - - - - - - - - - - - - - - - - - - - - - - - - - - - - - -

### In This Chapter

▶ Never erase files you don't recognize

▶ Never erase the IDAPI subdirectory

▶ Never use DOS or the File Manager to move, copy, or erase tables

▶ Never turn off your PC while Paradox is running

▶ Never turn off your PC while Windows is running

▶ Never keep original tables on floppy disks

▶ Never run with scissors

▶ Never make a brand new field the table's key

▶ Never ignore KEYVIOL and PROBLEMS tables

▶ Never believe everything you read

- - - - - - - - - - - - - - - - - - - - - - - - - - - - - - - - - - - - - - - - - -

*W*hen I was a kid, it seemed like *all* the rules began with *don't* or *never*. There weren't that many positive rules, like "always have ice cream after dinner." Now that I'm a parent myself, I understand why that is.

In keeping with the spirit of the whole rules thing, here are 10 rules covering what you should never, ever do. Never forget them!

## Never Erase Files You Don't Recognize

This isn't just a Paradox rule; it goes for everything on your computer. Despite the fact that you bought software called Paradox, C In *EddyVision*, or SumoSound for Windows, it's not just one big file any more. Today's software is the collaborative effort of literally hundreds of files, many of which have clever names such as BEVTMGR.DLL and SQLPCENT.FDL (which sounds like it's going to crawl off and do something utterly disgusting in the corner).

Just because it looks weird doesn't mean it's not absolutely vital to making your software work. Don't erase stuff that isn't familiar simply on the grounds that you *never used that anyway*. You're getting down on your knees and begging for program trouble. Really, you are.

If you're getting low on disk space, try *uninstalling* programs you don't use anymore. Check the program's manual for instructions or corner your guru with a batch of fresh brownies for some personal help.

## Never Erase the IDAPI Subdirectory

This is a specific corollary to the "Never Erase Files You Don't Recognize" topic. The IDAPI subdirectory lives outside your regular Paradox directory, so you're more likely to see it, think "I never created anything like *that*," and promptly trash it before Paradox even knows what happened. Treat it like a wasp nest: leave it alone and Paradox won't hurt your data.

## Never Use DOS or the File Manager to Move, Copy, or Erase Tables

Even your tables aren't just one file anymore. They're a committee of the data file, index file, secondary index file, memo data, and anything else that freeloads along for the ride. If you move all the .DB files (the actual data in your tables) to a new place *without* the rest of the herd, Paradox would have a conniption.

When you're ready to reorganize things on the disk, be sure that you have a good backup before starting. With that done, it's okay to move entire directories with the File Manager or DOS commands, but only use Paradox to shuffle individual files around. Otherwise, you risk some *massive* table problems.

## Never Turn Off Your PC While Paradox Is Running

This is the *ultimate* no-no for Paradox. It barely edges out trashing the IDAPI subdirectory for Most Heinous Paradox-Related Crime. The occasional accident that shuts down your computer (dog bites the power cord, toddler pulls out the power cord, earthquake removes the local substation from the face of the Earth) will still happen, but never get in the routine of just turning everything off for the night.

When you select File⇨Exit from the menu, Paradox goes through some shut-down gyrations to protect your data and leave itself notes for next time. If you just turn the machine off, Paradox is unceremoniously terminated without so much as a *gosh today was fun.* Most of the time, Paradox handles this successfully, but there's no point in stressing the software's good nature.

Take the extra 15 seconds to quit Paradox and Windows before shutting everything down. It's worth it.

# Never Turn Off Your PC While Windows Is Running

On a more general note, don't turn off your computer if Windows is running, either. Reach for the power switch only when you see the **C:\>** prompt waving from the screen. Then, and only then, is it safe to shut everything down.

# Never Keep Original Tables on Floppy Disks

If you don't use floppy disks at all, just skip this one entirely — I don't want to give you any bad ideas. If you're using floppies for one reason or another, only use them for *backup* copies of your data. Never keep your original tables on them.

Floppies have a habit of expiring after a certain period of time. They often die without any warning — yesterday (or worse, a few minutes ago) it worked fine; now all you see is `Disk error attempting to read A:`

The best way to avoid this problem is to use floppies as the computer deities intended you to use them: for backups. Keep your original tables on the hard drive or the network (if you're on that kind of system).

# Never Run with Scissors

If someone needs scissors *that* badly, just overnight them a pair and let somebody else take care of the safety issues.

# Never Make a Brand New Field the Table's Key

Here's one for people fixing up old tables. If you're restructuring some poor, antiquated table that doesn't have anything approximating a good key field, don't make a new field and *immediately* bless it as the key. If you do, when the dust settles, your table will contain exactly one record and the rest of them will be in the KEYVIOL table prominently displayed for your enjoyment.

Here's what happened: Paradox successfully added the new field to your table. Because it is a new field, it doesn't have any data in it yet; it's blank. As Paradox was busy checking for perfect hospital corners on all the records, it noticed that many records (all the records, in fact) had the *same* key value — and something *had* to be done. Paradox promptly stuffed all the incorrect records into a KEYVIOL table and patted itself on the head for a job well done.

To prevent this little problem, go through two rounds of restructuring. The first time, add the new field, but don't make it the key yet. Fill the field with your new key values — make sure that every record has a value in this field and that none of the values are duplicated (if they are, you'll just end up with a KEYVIOL table, so it's no big deal). With the soon-to-be key field full of soon-to-be keys, restructure the table again and turn on the field's key marker. Paradox finds all those marvelously individual and unique keys values and life is good with your world.

# Never Ignore KEYVIOL and PROBLEMS Tables

Please, oh *please* don't ever just ignore a KEYVIOL or PROBLEMS table. When Paradox creates one of these, it's telling you there is a problem and giving you the opportunity to fix it. If you blow off the tables, you're blowing off whatever data is in there. Once you get over the shock of seeing them when you were expecting everything to proceed smoothly, collect yourself enough to figure out what went wrong.

# Never Believe Everything You Read

This classic advice is a bit of a paradox, which is why I included it in a book that's entirely *about* Paradox. I mean, if you're not supposed to believe everything you read, how can you be sure you're even supposed to believe *that?* (After all, you did just *read* it.) Is it any different than someone saying "Don't believe everything you hear"?

Please put your thoughts into an essay of not less than 5,278 or more than 5,279 words. Print three copies, tear them into tiny little pieces, then shout "it just doesn't matter!" as you throw them into the air.

Don't you wish *all* philosophy was this easy?

# Chapter 31
# Ten Features You Might Someday Use

*A*s an author, I use my word processor all day, every day. That's no Earth-shattering news. What might surprise you is that I only use about 30% of its features — maybe less than that, really. Sometimes, I wander into a menu by accident and find some feature that changes my entire day (for better or worse, depending on the day I'm having).

It's the same way when you're working with Paradox. Often, you learn enough to get started and stay at that level until someone shows you a neat trick or a manual falls off the shelf and you accidentally flip to an interesting page while you're putting it back. Think of this chapter as a planned accident that introduces you to a few interesting things you can explore in your copious free time (whenever *that* is).

The things in this chapter aren't covered in this book. Sorry, but I had to draw the line somewhere. For more about this stuff, check out IDG's other Paradox books or, if you simply have no other recourse, you can always try the manuals.

# The Sample Files

The samples are a group of tables and an ObjectPAL application created by Borland to show off what Paradox for Windows can do in a perfect world. This is stuff you can fold, spindle, and mutate while you're learning new features. Even if you completely destroy the whole directory, just whip out those Paradox master disks and reinstall the little buggers from scratch.

Apart from being interesting reading once you're through the day's junk mail, the sample files show you the *proper* way to think through and create multi-table databases. The accompanying storyline isn't "Gone with the Wind," but it *is* marginally entertaining.

The Paradox for Windows *Getting Started* manual includes an entire chapter explaining (allegedly) how the tables came to be. The *User's Guide* employs a more clinical approach, giving a brief discussion of each table's contents, followed by a full, graphical dissection of its structure. If you feel nauseated during this autopsy, compose yourself in the hallway before continuing. (You don't want to ruin your keyboard.)

# ObjectPAL

This is only for the dedicated techno-weenie-wannabe's out there. ObjectPAL is Paradox's programming language. If you hear someone call it a *macro language,* they're mistaken. Object PAL is an honest-to-goodness *programming* language, with all the complexity and bizarre nuances that accompany such power.

If I accidentally piqued your curiosity (really, I didn't mean to), look in the *Guide to ObjectPAL* for the mind-numbing details.

# Custom Forms That Do Cool Stuff

Remember those innocent Paradox forms in Chapter 24? They have a secret double identity. When combined with ObjectPAL, they become *Super Forms!,* capable of almost any esoteric task.

Unfortunately, you have to know ObjectPAL to make this fun stuff happen. (Sigh.) It's *always* something, isn't it?

For now (and the foreseeable future), keep this knowledge in the back of your mind. If you ever get to the point that you need Paradox to do something *really* wild, talk to your guru about it. Perhaps she can whip up a *Super Form!* that meets your needs.

(Yes, you have to use the italics *and* the exclamation point when you describe a *Super Form!* It's just one of those things.)

# (Relatively) Easy Mailing Labels

Here's a feature that's vitally important to a few people and a real yawner to everyone else: making mailing labels. Because the audience is so terribly skewed on this, I'll keep the explanation short.

Yes, Paradox for Windows can do mailing labels. No, it isn't too hard, primarily because there's an Expert to do it *for* you. Click the light bulb button on the ToolBar, and then click Mailing Labels to experience this yourself, provided you even care to at all.

# Form and Report Style Sheets

Once you develop a particular group of settings for your reports (field font, color, and such), wouldn't it be great if new reports included those settings already made? Then instead of fiddling with the settings, you could get right down to the business of making that new form or report. Oh, to experience such joy here on Earth.

Paradox for Windows now includes a feature called *style sheets* that does this very thing (please, control yourself). It remembers how you like the fields, text, and everything in between. When you create a form or report, you casually mention to Paradox that you want to use this particular style sheet. *Poof!* and everything's set the way you want.

There isn't a whole lot of documentation about this feature, though. Look in the *User's Guide* index under the heading *style sheets* to find what little there is.

# Graphics Fields

Yet another new, super-sexy feature of Paradox for Windows, graphics fields let you incorporate — are you ready? — graphics files directly into your tables. You can store pictures in several different graphics formats, including bitmap (BMP), Postscript (EPS), PC Paintbrush (PCX), tagged image file (TIF), graphical interchange format (GIF), and anything pasted from the Windows Clipboard (which really *is* just about anything).

Imagine a table containing the company catalog, complete with product pictures customers could view directly on screen. Or, if you scan pictures or line art for desktop publishing work, you could create your own clipart database. What about an international order entry screen that automatically displays a customer's national flag when you enter their customer number? Hey, if you added a BLOB field with a digitized version of their national anthem, it could play in the background while you're taking their order! (STOP!!! Down, boy! Get back in the cage. Sorry, folks — the nerd in me got away for a moment. Don't worry, everything's under control. Let me adjust the tape on my glasses and we'll be rolling again.)

The Paradox for Windows *User's Guide* provides several brief, but informative discussions about graphics fields and their various uses. Beyond that, pick up a package of color clipart at the local computer store and see what you can make Paradox for Windows do.

# Secondary Indexes

When you put a key field in a table, Paradox creates an index on the data in that field. It's a lot like the index in this book — to find a particular record, Paradox looks up its key in the index and then goes directly to the record in the table. That's why it's so fast to query or locate with the key field.

Not *every* query involves the key field, though. If you find yourself querying the daylights out of some other field in your table (like zip code or something), you can build a *secondary index* on that field. It works just like the key field's primary index and speeds up your queries *significantly*. You can have as many secondary indexes as you want, too. Don't go hog wild, though, because they do take up disk space.

The *User's Guide* has all the details you need to start using secondary indexes in your tables. Go forth and speed (but not on the highway, okay?).

# *Password Protection*

Security is a big buzzword in these days of crackers, hackers, and phreaks. Paradox is sensitive to the need for secrecy and provides you with a surprisingly useful password feature.

One table can have several different passwords, each with different levels of access. You can limit both what the password holder can do (add, delete, or edit records) and which fields he has access to. The password is only good for that particular table, so you need to go through the process again for all the other tables you want to protect.

Before going gung-ho on the password front, discuss your security needs with the local guru. Get her input on the best ways to protect your data. Remember that passwords are only *one* kind of protection — and even they have limits. Check the *User's Guide* for the details, but make sure nobody's looking over your shoulder when you do it (eeek!).

# *"Like" Queries*

This is the ultimate "I'm not sure what I'm looking for" kind of query. The *Like* query operator lets you find things that may or may not exactly match your example. If you're looking for a record on someone named Smith but you know they use an alternate spelling of their name, you can tell Paradox to look for records that are *like* Smith. That yields records for *Smith, Smythe,* and anything else that's close enough.

*Like* queries aren't something you want (or need) to use every day, simply because they're inexact — you never know quite what they'll bring home from the store. Use them to find records that seem to be hiding from you, but limit it to just that. The few times I used *like,* I was disappointed in the results, but perhaps it will work better for you.

As with just about everything *else* in this section, the *User's Guide* contains the secrets of this vaguely interesting operator.

# *Lookup Tables*

A lookup table builds some (dare I say it?) intelligence into your database. It tells Paradox for Windows to only let you enter something in a field if it matches an entry in a master table (the "lookup table"). If it doesn't match perfectly, Paradox verbally abuses you and demands immediate attention to resolve this dire crisis.

Here's how this lookup stuff works in the real world. Assume for a moment that I'm not very good with the Post Office's two-letter state abbreviations — I tend to either make up my own or enter the right code for the wrong state (this is, in fact, true). To compensate for my mental "feature," I created a table containing all the commonly accepted state abbreviations.

When I need a "state" field in a table, I tell Paradox for Windows to check the abbreviations I enter against the ones in my state abbreviations table (it's the lookup table again). If I try to make up a new abbreviation, it won't match anything in the lookup table and Paradox for Windows tells me to try again (it's not particularly subtle — it won't let you leave the field until it's happy). Thus, the abbreviation is ultimately correct, even if it's the wrong state.

This is a simple lookup example. Notice that Paradox for Windows didn't stop me from putting in the *wrong* abbreviation — it merely made sure that what I entered was valid. However, it wouldn't be hard to fix that problem with a slightly more advanced technique: if my lookup table had all the US zip codes and their associated states, I could type in the zip code and tell Paradox for Windows to provide the correct state *by itself.* It could even fill in the city, too. What a deal!

# Appendix

# Installing Paradox for Windows

● ● ● ● ● ● ● ● ● ● ● ● ● ● ● ● ● ● ● ● ● ● ● ● ● ● ● ● ● ● ● ● ● ● ● ● ● ● ● ● ● ● ● ● ● ● ● ● ●

*W*ithout getting on too big a soapbox, I really think Borland is an industry leader in installation programs. Their stuff is easy to use, somewhat entertaining, and gets the job done with a minimum of technical hassle. With that stirring recommendation, here's how to install the new software you just lugged home.

I recommend accepting *all* the default values that Paradox offers you. This is my general approach to software installation, not something I specifically believe about Paradox. It's easier to fix any problems later on if your guru doesn't have to guess where the software is. Please, unless you have some driving reason to do otherwise, just accept what Paradox suggests and extend your creativity in other areas.

1. **Carefully and thoroughly shred the plastic wrap around your software box.**

   Open up everything and marvel at how little of the stuff they included will ever see the light of day again.

   If you shred the plastic *just right,* you can get almost all of it off and *still* not be able to open the box.

2. **Search frantically through the stuff until you find the diskettes. Remove them from their wrapping and stack them in numerical order on your desk.**

3. **Take Disk 1 from the top of the stack and put it into your computer's floppy disk drive.**

   If you knock the other disks askew, take a moment and straighten up the stack. Neatness counts, particularly in software installation.

4. **With Windows running and the Program Manager on-screen, select File⇨Run. In the Run dialog box, type** A:\INSTALL **and then press Enter.**

   Nothing appears to happen for a moment, but keep the faith. As long as Windows doesn't come back saying that it can't find A:\INSTALL, everything should work.

If Windows *does* complain that it can't find the installation program, make sure you spelled the command A:\INSTALL correctly. If you did, take out the diskette and make sure you put in the right one. If that's okay too, something's wrong with your software. (Rats!) Take it back to the computer store and demand the immediate execution of the clerk who sold it to you. Be satisfied if they offer to exchange the one you have for one that works.

If your floppy disk drive is B:, type **B:\INSTALL** instead.

5. **When the Paradox for Windows Installation dialog appears, click Continue to get on with the installation.**

If you're *really* hard pressed for disk space, click the Custom radio button to reduce the amount of space Paradox takes on your hard disk.

6. **Carefully type your name into the Name field. Press Tab to go down to the Company field, and then type your company name. Click Continue when everything looks hunky-dory.**

7. **Click Continue again to accept the default location for your new copy of Paradox for Windows.**

Don't change the subdirectory name unless you have a serious reason for doing it.

If Paradox warns you that it found an existing copy of Paradox in that subdirectory, click Overwrite. If you don't think you have Paradox on your computer, click Change Directory, and then click Cancel to abort the installation. Grab your guru and find out what's going on.

8. **If you selected the Custom installation option, click in the Connections Application checkbox and the Workgroup Desktop checkbox to turn those off. If you're *really* short on disk space, also click in the Samples and Examples checkboxes to turn them off as well. Click Continue when you're done.**

If you chose to do the full installation (basically, if you clicked Continue and not molested any of the installation controls), skip this step.

9. **Click Install when Paradox gives you one last chance to abort the whole process.**

The screen clears and suddenly you're presented with the Borland installation dashboard, complete with the famous *percent complete* speedometer.

10. **Keep an eye on the screen and insert a new disk when it demands one.**

Figure A-1 shows the first of these demands. This process continues for some time.

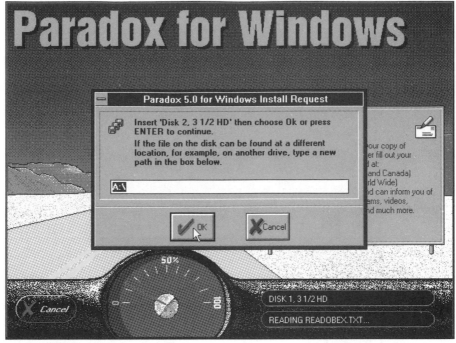

**Figure A-1:**
Paradox
demands
more food.
For your
own sake,
give it what
it wants.

Be sure you use the disks in the right order.

If the Installation program asks repeatedly for the same disk and that's the one you're putting in, um, it looks like you have a bad disk. Wander back to the computer store and patiently throttle someone until you get a replacement.

Any miscellaneous messages about not being able to read a file also mean you have a dead diskette. Now, off to the store with you!

Don't forget to read the billboards that flash by. That's the most entertaining part of the whole process.

11. **Once you get past Disk 7, Paradox informs you that it's busy configuring. Wait patiently (pensive foot tapping is okay). When Paradox asks if it should create a Program Manager group for you, click ⊆ontinue.**

The screen briefly flips back to the Program Manager while Paradox sets up the program group.

12. **Click §kip to avoid being bludgeoned with the Read Me file.**

13. **Click OK and you're through!**

Take the last disk out of the computer and stack it neatly with the others. Put them all away somewhere safe in case there's a flood in your office.

14. **Select File⇨Exit Windows from the Program Manager menu to quit Windows. When you're back at DOS, start Windows again by typing** WIN **and pressing Enter.**

This reloads all the Windows configuration files so they're updated with the information Paradox just wrote into them.

That's it—you're done. Check out Chapter 1 to get going with your new copy of Paradox for Windows.

"APPARENTLY MOST STUDIES INDICATE THAT WHAT PEOPLE REALLY WANT ISN'T MORE POWER OR INCREASED APPLICATIONS, BUT JUST REALLY NEAT TAIL FINS."

# Index

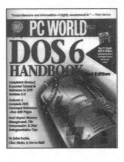

# IDG BOOKS

# Order Form

**Order Center: (800) 762-2974** (8 a.m.-5 p.m., PST, weekdays) or (415) 312-0650

**For Fastest Service:** Photocopy This Order Form and FAX it to: (415) 358-1260

| Quantity | ISBN | Title | Price | Total |
|----------|------|-------|-------|-------|
|          |      |       |       |       |
|          |      |       |       |       |
|          |      |       |       |       |
|          |      |       |       |       |
|          |      |       |       |       |
|          |      |       |       |       |
|          |      |       |       |       |
|          |      |       |       |       |
|          |      |       |       |       |
|          |      |       |       |       |
|          |      |       |       |       |
|          |      |       |       |       |

## Shipping & Handling Charges

| Subtotal | U.S. | Canada & International | International Air Mail |
|----------|------|-----------------------|------------------------|
| Up to $20.00 | Add $3.00 | Add $4.00 | Add $10.00 |
| $20.01-40.00 | $4.00 | $5.00 | $20.00 |
| $40.01-60.00 | $5.00 | $6.00 | $25.00 |
| $60.01-80.00 | $6.00 | $8.00 | $35.00 |
| Over $80.00 | $7.00 | $10.00 | $50.00 |

In U.S. and Canada, shipping is UPS ground or equivalent.
For Rush shipping call (800) 762-2974.

Subtotal _____

CA residents add
applicable sales tax _____

IN and MA residents add
5% sales tax _____

IL residents add
6.25% sales tax _____

RI residents add
7% sales tax _____

Shipping _____

Total _____

## Ship to:

Name _____

Company _____

Address _____

City/State/Zip_____

Daytime Phone _____

**Payment:** ❑ Check to IDG Books (US Funds Only)　❑ Visa　❑ Mastercard　❑ American Express

Card# _____ Exp._____ Signature_____

Please send this order form to: IDG Books, 155 Bovet Road, Suite 310, San Mateo, CA 94402.

Allow up to 3 weeks for delivery. Thank you!

# IDG BOOKS WORLDWIDE REGISTRATION CARD

**Title of this book:** **PARADOX 5 FOR WINDOWS FOR DUMMIES**

**My overall rating of this book:** ❑ Very good [1]  ❑ Good [2]  ❑ Satisfactory [3]  ❑ Fair [4]  ❑ Poor [5]

**How I first heard about this book:**

❑ Found in bookstore; name: [6]

❑ Advertisement: [8]

❑ Word of mouth; heard about book from friend, co-worker, etc.: [10]

❑ Book review: [7]

❑ Catalog: [9]

❑ Other: [11]

**What I liked most about this book:**

**What I would change, add, delete, etc., in future editions of this book:**

**Other comments:**

**Number of computer books I purchase in a year:** ❑ 1 [12]  ❑ 2-5 [13]  ❑ 6-10 [14]  ❑ More than 10 [15]

**I would characterize my computer skills as:** ❑ Beginner [16] ❑ Intermediate [17] ❑ Advanced [18] ❑ Professional [19]

**I use** ❑ DOS [20]  ❑ Windows [21]  ❑ OS/2 [22]  ❑ Unix [23]  ❑ Macintosh [24]  ❑ Other: [25]_____
(please specify)

**I would be interested in new books on the following subjects:**
(please check all that apply, and use the spaces provided to identify specific software)

❑ Word processing: [26]

❑ Data bases: [28]

❑ File Utilities: [30]

❑ Networking: [32]

❑ Other: [34]

❑ Spreadsheets: [27]

❑ Desktop publishing: [29]

❑ Money management: [31]

❑ Programming languages: [33]

**I use a PC at** (please check all that apply): ❑ home [35]  ❑ work [36]  ❑ school [37]  ❑ other: [38] _____

**The disks I prefer to use are** ❑ 5.25 [39]  ❑ 3.5 [40]  ❑ other: [41]_____

**I have a CD ROM:** ❑ yes [42]  ❑ no [43]

**I plan to buy or upgrade computer hardware this year:** ❑ yes [44]  ❑ no [45]

**I plan to buy or upgrade computer software this year:** ❑ yes [46]  ❑ no [47]

Name: _____ Business title: [48] _____ Type of Business: [49]

Address (❑ home [50] ❑ work [51]/Company name: _____ )

Street/Suite# _____

City [52]/State [53]/Zipcode [54]: _____ Country [55]

❑ **I liked this book!** You may quote me by name in future
IDG Books Worldwide promotional materials.

My daytime phone number is _____

**IDG BOOKS**

THE WORLD OF
COMPUTER
KNOWLEDGE

# ❑ YES!

Please keep me informed about IDG's World of Computer Knowledge.
Send me the latest IDG Books catalog.